Making Waves

MUSIC AND PERFORMING ARTS OF ASIA AND THE PACIFIC

SERIES EDITOR: FREDERICK LAU

Javaphilia: American Love Affairs with Javanese Music and Dance
HENRY SPILLER

Hearing the Future: The Music and Magic of the Sanguma Band
DENIS CROWDY

Vamping the Stage: Female Voices of Asian Modernities
EDITED BY ANDREW N. WEINTRAUB AND BART BARENDREGT

Broken Voices: Postcolonial Entanglements and the Preservation of Korea's Central Folksong Traditions
ROALD MALIANGKAY

Making Waves

TRAVELING MUSICS IN HAWAI'I, ASIA, AND THE PACIFIC

Edited by
FREDERICK LAU and CHRISTINE R. YANO

University of Hawai'i Press
Honolulu

This publication was supported by a contribution from
the Music Department, University of Hawai'i at Mānoa.

Paperback edition 2021

Printed in the United States of America

26 25 24 23 22 21 6 5 4 3 2 1

Library of Congress Cataloging-in-Publication Data

Names: Lau, Frederick, editor. | Yano, Christine Reiko, editor.
Title: Making waves : traveling musics in Hawai'i, Asia, and the Pacific / edited by Frederick Lau and Christine R. Yano.
Other titles: Making waves (Honolulu, Hawaii) | Music and performing arts of Asia and the Pacific.
Description: Honolulu : University of Hawai'i Press, [2018] | Series: Music and performing arts of Asia and the Pacific series | Includes bibliographical references and index.
Identifiers: LCCN 2017030700 | ISBN 9780824873769 (cloth alk. paper)
Subjects: LCSH: Dissemination of music. | Music and transnationalism—Asia. | Music and transnationalism—Hawaii.
Classification: LCC ML3917.A78 M35 2018 | DDC 780.9—dc23
LC record available at https://lccn.loc.gov/2017030700

ISBN 978-0-8248-9255-5 (paperback)

University of Hawai'i Press books are printed on acid-free paper and meet the guidelines for permanence and durability of the Council on Library Resources.

Cover photo: *Sandy Gem,* by Zak Noyle

CONTENTS

ACKNOWLEDGMENTS

A PROJECT like this is only made possible through incurring a string of debts. The editors first of all thank Masako Ikeda of University of Hawai'i Press, who provided special fast-track shepherding from beginning to end. Masako recognized the worthiness of this collection, trusted that all the authors would understand the process and deadlines, successfully interfaced with the editorial board of the press, and provided encouragement and guidance throughout. A big *mahalo*.

The editors are also personally grateful to all the authors involved. This book has had a remarkably quick turnaround from inception to finish, in no small part due to the cooperative hustle of the authors making deadlines and responding to sometimes last-minute requests—in short, helping make this Ric Trimillos project happen. We presented Ric with a book proposal at his seventy-fifth birthday party; the gift of this volume was made possible through the dedication of friends and colleagues contained therein.

Thank you to the University of Hawai'i Department of Music for their contribution of a publication subvention to help defray costs. Ric's career in that department (as graduate student and professor) and his shaping of the field of ethnomusicology find recognition in this kind of funding. The contribution may not have made this a better book, but it at least will make it a more affordable one. And a special thanks to the editors of *Japanese Studies* and the Taylor & Francis Group (www.tandfonline.com) for allowing reprint of a modified version of Christine R. Yano's chapter, published in 2015 as "Plucking Paradise: Hawaiian 'Ukulele Performance in Japan," *Japanese Studies* 35, no. 3: 317–330.

Making Waves

Sounding Waves—Introduction

Christine R. Yano and Frederick Lau

MUSICAL sounds are some of the most mobile and malleable of human elements, crossing national, cultural, and regional boundaries at warp speed in the twentieth and twenty-first centuries. Whole songs or even bits of songs travel long distances via musicians, CDs (and earlier, cassettes), satellite broadcasting, digital downloads, and streaming. They become part of global human flows, enabled through ideologies and technologies of circulation, shaped by the infrastructures of movement. And in the process they become transformed —warped, bent, tweaked, twanged, electrified, digitized, ornamented, indigenized, performed on makeshift instruments. Traveling musics may be interpreted as mis-heard, mis-read, mis-sung, mis-remembered. This is not to suggest a single "correct" way to hear, read, sing, and remember. But it is to suggest that the idea of correctness in the name of authenticity may suffuse these processes of traveling and the hegemonies that litter that path. It also suggests the ways in which traveling musics lead multiple lives of hearing, reading, singing, and remembering, as well as the unintentional consequences of the practices of contact. They may act as basis for innovative renderings in new hands, so that the "mis-" processes identified above take on varying degrees of creative intentionality. At the same time, in new contexts traveling musics may take on new meanings, suggesting nostalgized sounds of home, and thus become emblematized and codified. They become badges of identity. In new contexts, these sounds incite, seduce, and sometimes repulse. They may be music overheard by eager ears or music barely heard over the cacophony of competing sonic backdrops. Some arrive on distant shores folded into the baggage of colonialism or missionization, flaunting prestige or salvation like a banner of entitlement. Others arrive as stowaways, sung in subterfuge as whispered sounds of illicit engagement, resistance, and sometimes salve. Songs can soothe and motivate as the sound of the familiar amid arduously traveled lives.

As musics in motion become intimate parts of human encounters often thousands of miles from their original settings, they inevitably undergo transformations in meaning and context. Traveling musics undergo change even as they effect change in new settings. Listeners take heed, their ears primed by sociopolitical conditions, and that heed may result in new creations and selective borrowings—a melodic turn, a rhythmic pattern, a vocal quality, an instrumental timbre. These borrowed elements become the basis for newly reconfigured sonic expressions and creativity. In some cases this kind of borrowing may symbolize or even encourage cross-cultural understanding; in others the impetus may simply arise from an attraction to novelty as a fresh sound, an aural prompt. By tracking how music travels, we are also interested in identifying the agencies, dynamics, circumstances, and processes that make each journey possible. There is always a backstory behind each movement. Together we demonstrate that any piece of music or an instrument can become resources that enable social actors to construct, shape, and imagine appropriate meanings for the context. In other words, music is at once a sign vehicle pregnant with significance and symbolism as a possible agent for creative impulses and marking boundaries.

This volume of essays by veteran ethnomusicologists examines traveling musics in Asia and the Pacific as integral to sociopolitical practices of mobility. We look at musics—songs, makers, groupings, performance practices, instruments, audiences, aurality, aesthetics, and images—as they traverse oceans, continents, and islands. In the process of landing in new homes, music interacts with older established cultural environments, sometimes in unexpected ways and with surprising results. We see these traveling musics in Asia and the Pacific as "making waves"—that is, not only riding flows of globalism and migration, but also instigating ripples of change and generating new possibilities. We ask, what is the nature of those waves? What are the infrastructural elements that constitute the wave itself? What are some of the effects of music landing on, transported to, or appropriated from distant shores, and what kinds of responsibilities lie in the process? And furthermore, how does the Asia-Pacific context itself shape and get shaped by these musical waves and their effects? How might we reconfigure our practices and reflections upon listening by refocusing from the solidity of land masses to the fluidity of ocean environments? What might be gained in the process by accepting the indeterminacy of waves—the rogue wave amid a generally perceived orderly backdrop? The goal of this volume is to position music as at once ritual and entertainment, esoteric and exoteric, product and very much process, sources of tradition and creativity, local and very much global, within the cultural geopolitics of Asia and the Pacific. In doing so, we situate music at the very core of global human endeavors.

On Moving: Conditions of Displacement

In the 2000s, mobility serves as a keyword that captures the sense of displacement and instability in a rapidly changing world (Creswell 2006; Urry 2007). Mobility is more than a signpost; it is a framing device that embraces the shifting grounds of the contemporary world. The very movement of populations, goods, and ideas—sometimes at dizzying speeds—provides pause to consider what effects this may have upon the human condition at both individual and group levels. Arjun Appadurai focuses on goods in arguing that we have to consider not just the "thing" (that is, goods of exchange, including music) but its circulation (here, traveling musics) to understand contemporary interaction and its meaning: "We have to follow the things themselves, for their meanings are inscribed in their forms, their uses, their trajectories. It is only through the analysis of these trajectories that we can interpret the human transactions and calculations that enliven things...It is the things-in-motion [here, songs, instruments, sonic aesthetics and concepts] that illuminate their human and social context" (1986, 5). *Making Waves* focuses on music as a thing-in-motion, connecting not only people but their very ideas of who they might be, framed as part of sonic identities, and even part of an "audible empire" (Radano and Olaniyan 2016).

James Clifford's seminal volume, *Routes: Travel and Translation in the Late Twentieth Century*, demonstrates ways in which contemporary cultures must be seen in transit, whether literally in airport lounges or other thoroughfares, or within internalized modes of circulation (1997). Even twenty years after its publication Clifford's work is relevant: "The new paradigms begin with historical contact, with entanglement at intersecting regional, national, and transnational levels. Contact approaches presuppose not sociocultural wholes subsequently brought into relationship, but rather systems already constituted relationally, entering new relations through historical processes of displacement" (ibid., 7). In suggesting contact and displacement as the beginning points of inquiry, Clifford emphasizes the intertwining of "routes and roots" of pathways of mobility that have become fundamental to identity. The attention to mobility also shifts our conventional view of spaces as having the power to divide rather than the ability to unite, a point that Greg Dening forcefully argues in his approach to oceans as uniting and defining Austronesian cultures (1989; cf. Gilroy 1995). *Making Waves* makes mobility and identities—routes and roots united by oceanic flows—an assumption of contemporary life and music-making, arguing that the inherent rootedness of roots may be expressed and asserted sonically. These become inherent to the aesthetics of sounding waves, built upon ongoing admixtures wrought in mobility.

Ana Maria Ochoa Gautier and others note ways in which music carries particular affinities for mobility: "One of the central properties of songs is their capacity to incorporate great mobility. Songs are easily transduced (inscribed from one medium to another and back), translated (in the specific sense of changing the language of the song), transported (taken from one place to another through different media), adapted (malleably changing form as when a song sung by a single singer is taken up by a whole audience), arranged (transformed musically without losing their identifiable shape), and transferred from one person or group of people to another" (Ochoa Gautier 2014, 80). The practices that Ochoa Gautier inscribes—songs transduced, translated, transported, adapted, arranged, and transferred—point to the flexibility of music that makes the encounter not only possible, but generative, and even desirable. Music can make smooth inroads where other forms of interaction may stumble.

Music may not only create inroads, but the road may in part create it. Particular musical instruments may be known explicitly for their portability—the harmonica, jaw harp, mbira. As discussed by Christine Yano in her chapter, the Hawaiian-Portuguese ʻukulele, too, travels easily and lightly, its mobility resting in its physical and aesthetic portability, as well as its ease in playing. Whole genres may be built upon assumptions of movement, traveling embedded into its own grooves of sound. David Novak analyzes Japanoise as music only understood in circulation as it travels between Japan and North America: "In these rapid fluctuations—from place to place, impulse to impulse, person to person, moment to moment—Noise became a wave" (Novak 2013, 7). This is not the ripple-in-the-pond encounter of sound systems, but rather a tidal wave of sound, energy, and feedback that can be defined only through movement.

Mobility as Creative Agent versus Conservative Force

Circulation may have contradictory effects, as traveling musics can function as both a creative agent and a conservative force. In his chapter, David Harnish provides two contrasting island views from Indonesia: the heavily touristic and Hindu island of Bali compared with the far more isolated island of Lombok (located east of Bali), subject to Muslim religious intervention and deliberate, conservative artistic restraint. Bali is admittedly exceptional within Indonesia, but Harnish is careful to point out ways in which traveling musics are embedded and recontextualized in both islands with varying results. Harnish takes a macro view of the creative possibilities in traveling musics. Deborah Wong, by contrast, takes a micro view in her chapter, examining one composition by Los Angeles–born Hawaiʻi resident and third-generation Japanese American *taiko* (drum) master Kenny Endo. Endo's inspiration comes from the multicultural environment of Hawaiʻi, borrowing thus from the Hawaiian tradition of *pahu* drumming in conversation with Endo's own expertise in *taiko*. The result, "Yume no Pahu" (Dream of the Pahu Drum), written in 1992 and performed since then by Endo in a number of different arrangements and settings, enfolds travel within itself, including the two languages of its title. Here the travel may not take place at great distances, but attempts to broach unrelated drumming cultures through innovative new compositions by a creative individual.

One of the framing devices of traveling musics rests in the idea of cosmopolitanism. Martin Stokes reminds us that in spite of its "messy and compromised" nature (not the least of which he lists as distinctions between sacred/secular, elite/popular, male/female, heteronormative/queer, white/black), cosmopolitanism "restores human agencies and creativities to the scene of analysis, and allows us to think of music as an active process in the making of 'worlds'" (2008, 8, 18). What Stokes refers to is nothing less than the process of music "making waves." In recognition of the many constituent parts that may be glossed by the term, Stokes proposes differentiating "competing cosmopolitanisms" that emphasize the partial, overlapping, and hegemonic factors; these include elite cosmopolitanism, vernacular cosmopolitanism, regional cosmopolitanism, and diasporic cosmopolitanism (ibid., 10–16). Each of these adheres to a locally defined prestige system that gives force and agency to their framing. Performing traveling musics thus enacts its own kind of cosmopolitanism with an inherent mix of mobility and status. Steven Feld, for example, discusses the music scene surrounding African musicians of jazz (an African American–originated genre), many of whom have performed in the United States with mixed reaction; in Feld's words, they perform their own kind of "jazz cosmopolitanism" (2012a).

In some cases, an instrument invested with the sonic and natural ecology of place and in the hands of an educator who sets out to transform the traditional way of musical learning undergoes transformations through traveling notions of musical modernity. In his chapter, Henry Spiller walks us through this scenario for the Sundanese *angklung* (bamboo frame rattle), which spans changed framings from symbol of indigenous sound to the adoption of an expanded repertoire that includes what some might consider the most innocuous Western pop, in the name of an updating. That updating performs its own cosmopolitanism—not situated anywhere near the edge in global terms, but firmly ensconced in the middle of "easy listening" (by Western definition) reverie. That dream celebrates the newly repurposed *angklung* for its confident mix and borrowings, its own "diachronic modernity." Might we call this wave an Edelweiss moment of transport, from one dream to another?

In other cases, the traveling instrument adopts layers of meanings (and sonic results) along its route. Yano here discusses the 'ukulele as a traveling symbol of "paradise" as it travels to Japan by way of Hawai'i-inspired novelty music from America's Tin Pan Alley. Whereas in Hawai'i the 'ukulele may have been an instrument that spanned social boundaries, in Japan, following the prestige system of importations from the West, the ʻukulele became a symbol of elite status. To play the ʻukulele was to be a cosmopolitan, on a par with the modernism of the West, producing sounds that originated in exotic far-off lands (Portugal, Hawaiʻi, America). The sounds of paradise exemplified by the ʻukulele thus became the sounds of cultural appropriation, American style. Here, as elsewhere, it is the social and political circuits that are important for understanding the meanings given mobility.

Traveling musics ride the coattails of powerful institutions. One of these throughout Asia and the Pacific is the Christian church, with its practices of choral singing. In her chapter, Kati Szego examines some of the repercussions by which historic Christian-based choral singing becomes a template for twentieth-century group music in Hawaiʻi. This practice extends broadly and popularly, including men's occupation-based performance ensembles. The two case studies of singing policemen and dancing firemen combine the traveling aesthetic and practices of Western choral groups within masculine frames of civic protection. Outside observers may react in wonder at the enthusiasm that surrounds and pervades these groups. However, within the context of touristic Hawaiʻi, with its ready audiences an assumption of public life, it should come perhaps as no surprise that policemen should sing and that firemen should dance. These performances display the power of the template and the naturalization of the stage.

Another powerful institution is that of Western art music. R. Anderson Sutton's chapter on the avant-garde in Korea demonstrates that musical waves may have sonic dimensions, but at times even more profound are the aesthetic ideals and assumptions that they carry, particularly as these tap into such a heavily laden prestige system as Western art music. For these musical cosmopolitans in Korea, aesthetic inspiration comes not from happenstance or casual listening, but through rigorous training in both Western and Korean musics. The resulting mixed bag challenges categories (e.g., free versus experimental versus fusion versus "new" versus avant-garde), defies expectations, and expands our sonic repertories, specifically through the enactment of traveling and its implicit backdrop of the soundstage of mobility.

The stage can act as a public display of private subjectivities or aestheticisms, or at least their assertion. In the case of traveling musics, those assertions may rest in the prestige of the labels, as Sutton shows. To be modern, to be cosmopolitan: these are powerful claims anywhere, but perhaps especially so in the margins of global power. Notably, these can also be resistant claims. That cosmopolitanism and this modernity may be construed regionally (see Stokes's notion of "competing cosmopolitanisms"), sometimes as an alternative to the hegemony of popular culture from the West and as an assertion of an Asian-based shared or borrowed identity.

In his chapter, Andrew Weintraub provides an example of intra-Asian traveling musics in his study of Indian film music in Indonesia. With a fairly long and favorably received history, these Indian songs became the basis of a new hybrid genre, the wildly popular *dangdut*, entangling borrowings and rootedness. Weintraub speaks to the deep imbrication of travel as part of the admixture island music that is part of Indonesia's daily life. Mobility is part of the constitutive ostinato of a certain shared sonic language, particularly in the commercial world of pop, whether it occurs in Los Angeles, Tokyo, Seoul, Mumbai, or Jakarta. This is not to assert that all pop music worldwide sounds alike, but it is to suggest the possibility of an aesthetics of global commercialism, industrially produced, mass consumed. These are some of the shared tracks of traveling music.

At times the shared sonic language is created in the iconicity of one song. Frederick Lau's chapter follows the East China folksong "Molihua" as it travels from regional villages to urban centers to garner the attention of eighteenth-century British travelers and eventually Italian composer Giacomo Puccini (1858–1924), who enshrined it in his opera *Turandot* (completed by Franco Alfano in 1926), which catapulted the song (internationally known as "Jasmine") to global and continuing national fame. With each shift in context, the song gains different meanings and significance. What Lau describes is part of the power laid to imagination, resignification, and the snaking pathways of some traveling musics—whether songs, instruments, or genres.

In his chapter, Ricardo D. Trimillos provides an example of another iconic song, particularly in the hands of an iconic singer. That singer—Israel Kamakawiwoʻole ("Iz"; 1959–1997), Hawaiian icon of the ethnic and cultural revitalization movement of the 1970s and beyond known as the Hawaiian Renaissance—has become a folk hero in Hawaiʻi, known as much for his smooth vocalizations (including falsetto), ʻukulele playing, and huge body as for his political stance in support of Hawaiian sovereignty. His 1990 cover recording of the Harold Arlen popular ballad "Over the Rainbow," originally sung by child star Judy Garland (1922–1969) in the classic 1939 movie *The Wizard of Oz*, has had a viral presence globally. Here are icons built upon icons: Judy Garland, *The Wizard of Oz*, "Over the Rainbow," and now Iz (voice, ʻukulele, body). Simply put, icons travel with each new rendition, and with sometimes surprising results.

Mobile Listening

The mobility of musics makes mobile practices of listening all the more critical, as we listen to music as not merely a sound event but as a sounding process whose influences may run far, wide, and deep. Ana Maria Ochoa Gautier positions listening—aurality—at the center of notions of language, music, sound, and politics (2014). She takes aurality as central to the politics of identity: "I am particularly interested in what the endurance of . . . local expressive cultures, especially in a 'globalized' world and one increasingly marked by the condition of displacement, is supposed to invoke, provoke, and incarnate for different peoples and the different formulations of what they are supposed to acoustically embody and be" (ibid., 5). Radano and Olaniyan echo this sentiment, positioning "music as a means of comprehending empire as an audible formation, whose very audibility draws the listener into a vast network of language, supralinguistic sensory fields, regimes of knowledge, and new modes of subjectivity" (2016, 13). What is key here is the notion that aurality and audibility define who one is through sound, especially in the midst of competing sounds juxtaposed as practices of mobility. Steven Feld reminds us that traveling musics provide an imperative for mobile listening, creating a need for "acoustemology": "Listening to histories of listening is my way to shift attention to acoustemology, to sound as a way of knowing . . . worlds, and particularly to the presence of intervocality, to intersubjective vocal copresence, to the everyday immediacy and power of stories" (2012a, 7).

Sound as a way of knowing vocal practices informs more than music, of course, including within its realm other genres of utterances that are important for our consideration. Thus, Niko Besnier's study of gossip as a form of the everyday production of power on Nukulaelae Atoll in Tuvalu (Central Pacific) suggests ways that ethnomusicologists may share with sociolinguists a concern for public–private verbal exchanges "in a broad context of power relations, commodity circulations, and historical processes" (Besnier 2009, 3). Besnier's point here is that without a consideration of these contextual elements, gossip lacks the kind of social traction in its analysis. So, too, any study of music in motion must likewise take into account similar contextual elements—power, circulation, history—that give traveling musics their social force. Clearly voice-in-music conveys more than semantic or even aesthetic meanings, but the very underpinnings of its sociopolitical moorings (Utz and Lau 2013). These moorings capture the ear as part of the mobile practices of listening.

Unintentional Design: Indeterminacy of the Encounter

Capturing the ear is one thing, but what exactly is heard? And what kinds of interpretations may be given with what results? One element of traveling musics that is important to note is the place of unintentional design—of what may be understood as part of hegemonic practices as misinterpretations, mishearings, miscuings, or in another cooptational sense as reinterpretations, rehearings, recuings. These and other elements within new contexts may have significant sonic repercussions. In fact, acknowledging the lack of intention or design in some traveling musics only proves our humility in accepting some of the limits of agentive practices. Doubtless, the unintentionality of the result may be a source of creativity as well as consternation. How do we interpret "mistakes"? (See Trimillos's chapter on a Hawaiian singer misremembering lyrics.) How do we adjust our aural landscape to re-listen for the creative possibilities inherent in the act of movement? How do we reposition these many "mis-" practices not for what is lost, but for what might be gained, especially as resignified elements in a new context? This is how a "mis-X" becomes a newly configured "re-X."

Anna Tsing's writing on matsutake—a prized mushroom gathered in the wild in places such as the forests of Oregon and crossing the Pacific for gourmet Japanese consumption—is useful here. What ties mushrooms and musics together is what Tsing calls "unintentional design, that is, the overlapping, world-making activities of many agents" (2015, 132). In mushrooms, as sometimes in music, what makes for enhanced propagation is not well-tended and plowed fields—the planning and plowing inherent vehicles of modernity—but "disturbance": "a change in environmental conditions that causes a pronounced change in an ecosystem . . . Disturbance opens the terrain for transformative encounters, making new landscape assemblages possible." (ibid., 160). In short, disturbance, by its very precarity, refigures possibilities.

Tsing asks, "How do transnational conjunctures make forests?" tracing connections that move in and out of nations, regions, and local landscapes, through "unexpected convergences and moments of uncanny coordination" (ibid., 206). Likewise, we may ask a parallel question concerning traveling musics: how do transnational sonic conjunctures make bodies of music, tracing threads of sound that move in and out of nations, regions, and local soundscapes, including the unexpected points and contexts of contact? It is the indeterminacy of the encounter—even taking into account infrastructures of history—that is significant here, keeping us mindful of the intertwined routes of precarity, serendipity, fragility, and resilience. It is exactly in the rereading of misses into opportunities that hold forth the possibility of transforming ripples of traveling musics into unexpected waves. Tsing uses assemblages as her foci of analysis because of their multifaceted processual nature: "If we are interested in livability, impermanence, and emergence, we should be watching the action of landscape assemblages. Assemblages coalesce, change, and dissolve: this is the story" (ibid., 158). To take assemblages and transnational conjunctures to the field of traveling musics suggests an approach that embraces the indeterminacy of wildly moving parts. Here might lie the sonic shipwreck landing on distant shores, whose contents may instigate new possibilities of musical expression.

Cultural Appropriation, Repatriation, and the Inevitable Politics of Traveling Musics

Part of the indeterminacy of the traveling encounter rests in the decontextualization that may be a part of the mobile act. The bad politics of mobility rests in regarding music as a purely sonic phenomenon, rather than a sociocultural and political project. By taking a song/instrument/genre out of context, the music traveler robs this artistic expression of its humanity. This is part of the "art for art's sake" argument that depoliticizes mobile acts of music in the name of "pure sound." For example, when Paul Simon pleads artistic innocence regarding his use of South African musicians and sound genres in the making of his 1986 hit album *Graceland*, he does so while claiming ignorance of the apartheid-related boycott as well as the sociopolitical implications of his appropriation, saying, "We didn't have anything to do with color, race—it was purely music" (quoted in Sanneh 2016, 65; see Meintjes 1990). On the contrary, this volume argues that music is never quite "pure," but always embedded within sociopolitical forces that shape the wave. Those same forces also shape the individual musicians who might find inspiration in traveling musics.

Just as traveling musics inspire, they also incur debts. In some cases, musics travel without agency but are taken—some might say, stolen—from native voices, instruments, and contexts. First World archives are filled with the bounty and booty of Third World recordings; sadly this, too, is part of the ethnomusicology historical record, shared with other colonial projects of scholarship. These kinds of traveling musics may have been "discovered" and "preserved" or even "promoted," but in the process slip out of the hands of those who dream them. This process calls into question culturally embedded concepts of ownership, sovereignty, and copyright. It calls into question the role of the archive and those who would "travel" musics into them.

Histories, gladly, are not writ in stone. And a number of ethnomusicologists have embarked upon the task of sound repatriation. For example, the Center for Ethnomusicology at Columbia University has committed to repatriating to their source communities the extensive holdings of the Laura Boulton Collection of Traditional and Liturgical Music, consisting of field recordings of folk and traditional musics made by collector Laura Boulton, from the 1930s through the 1960s (Fox 2013). The Center joins a wave of archives and museums who are engaged in similar projects. The efforts for sound repatriation pave the way for these and other musics to travel "home," which in many cases is a good and ethical thing. But the processes and issues are not as simply laid as that. Each step of the way is paved with fraught issues of ownership, rights, communities, pasts, and collective representations. Although the end result may be a positive uplift for source communities—however identified and defined—these results take the establishment of new relationships and carefully tended pathways to effect that seemingly simple "return." In other words, simply retracing tracks of travel is impossible because of changed times, circumstances, and personnel. As Sylvia Nannyonga-Tamusuza and Andrew N. Weintraub explain in their article "The Audible Future: Reimagining the Role of Sound Archives and Sound Repatriation in Uganda": "Repatriation is more than a unidirectional act of giving back. Repatriation projects are context-sensitive and must be tailored to community-defined needs and circumstances. Successful projects build sustained future cooperation between repositories and communities" (2012, 225). What their cautionary reminds us is the critical human dimension of traveling musics and the continual need to listen to—that is, to be mindful of—the various stakeholders involved in the journey.

Listening to Hawai'i-Asia-Pacific: An Ocean-Based Ethnomusicology of Waves

This volume of musical case studies is purposefully situated in an ocean (Pacific) and the islands within (particularly Hawai'i), even if anchored by surrounding land masses (particularly those of Asia). And in doing so, this volume argues for the generative possibilities laid in the essential fluidity and connectivity of oceans. Here we echo the insights of Karin Amimoto Ingersoll, calling for a "seascape epistemology," "an approach to knowing presumed on a knowledge of the sea, which tells one how to move through it, how to approach life and knowing through the movements of the world" (2016, 5). If oceans are central to a Pacific-based regional conceptualization of music cultures, then certain elements become less significant (e.g., structures, stability, fixity), while others gain analytic priority (e.g., movement, circulation, flows). Islands and other landmasses undoubtedly situate the terrain in which some (although not all) of the music-making occurs, but these are less important than the oceans that surround them and the vessels that traverse them, inspiring researchers to address the dynamic processes that go into music's making. Those dynamic processes rest in the hands of culture bearers and brokers, itinerant music-makers, whether people, institutions, technologies, or mediated images that carry powerful traveling messages. Here are both the vessels and their cargo. The point, however, lies in the inseparability of vessels and cargo, of means and content—in parallel with the ways in which routes and roots intertwine.

In suggesting analytic possibilities of ocean-based ethnomusicology, we reposition music in culture as elements always in flux, always in processes of becoming. An ocean-based ethnomusicology gives us pause to listen to music in different ways—as shifting structures that instantiate a particular time and place. Those instantiations embody the fleetingness of form—catching the here, the now, the heard—even as form draws upon powerful large-scale structures. The momentary form enacts a snapshot (or better yet, a screen shot), a needle drop that is not insignificant for its quick passing. Just as any waves occur in constant flux—building, taking shape, cresting, receding, always in processes of going somewhere else, as well as returning—so, too, do music cultures amid an ocean-based framing both captivate and elude us. We may even yearn to apprehend it, but are humbled by the impossibility, whether observed from afar or involved from within—riding it, floating above, diving below, or tumbling through its forces. The wave captures an inevitability that supersedes its observers. The musical wave may be said to embrace the collective, even while slipping through the observer's grasp. Oceanographers may quantify waves, measuring volume, speed, length, crests, angles, energies, frequencies; ethnomusicologists in this volume attempt to qualify and characterize their force. How to capture a (musical) wave? Only by assuming the wisdom and integrity of its flow.

To push the heuristic metaphor a bit further, let us consider the sonic implications of the ocean wave. Waves lap, crash, roar, sound, and resound. They can be heard at a distance as a general din, as well as up close. Note Steven Feld's audio installation recorded in and around Anomabo Beach in Ghana, mixing eight separate tracks of ocean waves in its different manifestations, whether at water's edge, in the middle of the ocean, or amid rocks (Feld 2012a, 152–153; also a related DVD, *Where Water Touches Land* [2012b]). The sound of waves can be meditative, a hypnotic presence in their regularity, as well as fearsome in a crashing roar. They can both lull and terrify. Waves awe by their presence, nature quite obviously taking the upper hand. Their endlessness, reaching perpetual shores over and over again, gives them the capacity to weather jagged rocks, grind coral into fine sand, etch whole shorelines with shapes of their design. In effect, they do their work through both incremental efforts and more dramatic onslaughts. Their sonic embodiment rests in the conditions that surround them, but their presence is continual, multiple, and overlapping in what seems to be an orderly progression. They infill space by their presence—a backdrop of near-white noise. In the shallows their sounds incorporate the materials beneath them—sand, coral, rocks. They travel, sometimes great distances and with destructive force as the result of tectonic shifts thousands of miles away. And when they do—as a tidal wave (more accurately, a series of large-scale waves)—they can be most notable in their initial absence, draining the sands of their liquid presence, leaving fish to fend for themselves, before returning in an escalating series of tidal force. That absence serves as a lure for bystanders, many of whom converge on the novelty of stranded fish and exposed shorelines. But that lure proves the seductive demise of common sense, a folly that dismisses caution and results in untold destruction. Waves meet up, coming and going, front to back, at angles to the shore, clashing in their convergence. And each encounter produces the logic of its own force, whether joining energies or causing a backwash of renewal. Pebbles tossed in a pond may produce concentric ripples—the instigator distinct and separate from the effect. But waves produce nothing but further waves and counterwaves, each of which may travel great distances and with great effects. The eddies within a wave caused by an obstacle (a rock, a protruding object, a buoy) form patterns of interaction, creating new structures of sound. The metaphor here may be overworked—although we contend that everything written in this paragraph could find a musical analogy—but its utility lies in considering musical waves as dynamic forces of encounter that, like ocean waves, travel, transport, transform, and transfix. Ocean waves, like their sonic counterparts, constitute the surface expression of currents that run deeply and broadly.

Proposing a Pacific-based, ocean-focused ethnomusicology of waves must be framed within its relative marginality in global terms. It is exactly because many of these music cultures exist outside dominant power structures—not First World, but Third World—that this repositioning can take place. Far less invested in grand traditions of global music power and their attendant investment in stability, these traveling musics suggest that the ephemerality of ocean-based cultures has something to contribute to thinking through sonic organization and aesthetics. Traveling musics (here, Pacific) challenge musical canons to suggest the centrality of circulation, not as a by-product of human interaction but as part of the core of music-making. Thus music-making does not exist in a vacuum. In fact, an ocean-focused ethnomusicology assumes the exact opposite—flows of influence, amid power structures that might create a ready ear to listen or particular circumstances to play.

This volume positions itself in conversation with "Native Pacific Cultural Studies," a millennial initiative inspired by the intellectual leadership of Pacific Islanders such as Epeli Hauʻofa. In his landmark essay "Our Sea of Islands," Hauʻofa draws attention to an ocean-based, regional fluidity that emphasizes mobility and interconnectedness, rather than a Western-based modernism that conceptualizes the Pacific as a congery of scattered, isolated islands (1993, 7). Hauʻofa's call to action inspired a key symposium, "Native Pacific Cultural Studies on the Edge," held in February 2000 at the University of California, Santa Cruz, sponsored by the university's Center for Cultural Studies with funding from a University of California Pacific Rim Research Grant, resulting in a special edition of *The Contemporary Pacific* edited by Vicente M. Diaz and J. Kehaulani Kauanui. In their introduction, Diaz and Kauanui emphasize the dynamic oceanic focus: "The Pacific is on the move, unleashing forces along its edges (especially) that have the twin powers to destroy and to create... [Those forces include] colonialism, patriarchy, militarism, Christianity, nationhood, development, tourism, literacy, athletics, other forceful modes of modernity, and for us especially, scholarship" (2001, 316). In the wake of such powerful forces—including scholarship itself that may be implicated in many of the rest—a call to Native Pacific Cultural Studies serves as an intervention upon the existing postcolonial conditions. Among the interventions is conceptualization of the Pacific itself—not as empty, marginal space ("aqua nullius," empty seas), but centrally defining an ocean-focused region (Roher 2016, 32). As Elizabeth DeLoughrey asserts: "The Rim's construction of the Pacific Basin as aqua nullius or empty ocean is founded on a remarkable spatial collapse of the world's largest geographic region to bring the powerful northern economies into a neighborly alliance" (2007, 98). That neighborly alliance places the Pacific as at "empire's edge," a convergence of various First World colonial empires that have laid claim to it (Davis 2015, 11). The goals of Native Pacific Cultural Studies include dismantling the empire by triangulating Native studies, Pacific studies, and Cultural Studies (Diaz and Kauanui 2001, 315).

This volume does not claim complete overlap with Native Pacific Cultural Studies, for the primary reason that it does not include enough of the indigenous voice in scholarship. However, what it does share with Native Pacific Cultural Studies is the placement of the literal and figurative ocean at the center of the intellectual map, refiguring the lens of conceptualization. The overlapping currents between *Making Waves* and Native Pacific Cultural Studies include "the primacy of place (landed and oceanic)...; the historical 'rooted and routedness' of Pacific peoples...; a strain over debates regarding 'authenticity'; and an emphasis on inclusivity and fluidity in identity formations" (Roher 2016, 34). In asserting the primacy of these elements and the geographies of their concerns, *Making Waves* suggests ways by which ethnomusicology may extend its repertoire of analytical tools, reconfiguring ways of listening to critically include waves of oceanic expression and sociality.

The Wave Maker

This volume is inspired by the long and illustrious career of the ethnomusicologist in our midst, Professor Emeritus Ricardo D. Trimillos—"Ric." This is explicitly not a festschrift, even though Ric retired in 2011 and celebrated his seventy-fifth birthday in 2016—both events noteworthy and cause for festivities. Rather, this collection of essays centers upon Ric's template of sound, movement, and connectivity—that is, music in motion, connecting moving points, producing supple ripples of effect, and inciting yet further motions to come. In fact, that template may be considered a kind of "home" for these various contributors, each of whom has found inspiration in the restless intellectualism with which Ric has embraced musics of many cultures. Indeed, finding a "home" in wave making is what this volume is about. Steven Feld's eloquent evocation of this destabilized centering provides fitting expression, as the authors of *Making Waves* have found through Ric's inspiration "new ways to know home to be multiple, transportable, detoured, a recycling figure washing in from the waves" (Feld 2012a, 243). We wash in constantly upon Ric's moveable shores.

Ric's contributions to the field of ethnomusicology are multifaceted: as a scholar and performer of a variety of Asian musics; as a consultant for the governments of Hong Kong, the Philippines, Malaysia, Poland, and the former Soviet Union, for UNESCO, and for the Smithsonian Institution and the National Endowment for the Arts; as council member and vice president for the Society for Ethnomusicology; as chair of the International Initiatives for the College Music Society; and as editor of the journal *Asian Music* since 2009. These kinds of achievements may be readily found in his curriculum vitae.

But equally valuable and inspiring aspects about Ric's career lie beyond the page. These aspects rest in the social realm—sometimes relentlessly so. Ric's social legacy lies in his recognition of and commitment to the value of interpersonal relations. He recognizes that music-making may, in some instances, be a solo endeavor, but more often than not is the product of social relations—musician to musician, musician to composer, musician to audience, audience to musician, musician to management—that create music as community. These are collaborative relationships created by grooves of interaction that inevitably shape waves of sound. The list goes on and on through the infrastructures that mark social pathways of listening, playing, replaying, singing, tuning, strumming, plucking, mimicking, blending, echoing, riffing, inventing. Ric the musician and audience member is a part of this resounding infrastructure particularly by way of his personal involvement in performance: piano; organ; cello; Japanese koto and *gagaku* (ancient court music); Filipino *rondalla* (string band), *kulintangan* (gong-chime), and *sarsuwela* (vernacular operetta); and Javanese gamelan (orchestra). Many of these genres rest in ensemble performance, of which Ric has been a vital part. But even within ensembles, those in the Japanese kabuki offstage music group or the Filipino *rondalla* at the University of Hawaiʻi know well that this is not simply about practicing and performing. Rather, the music-making goes hand in hand with the socializing, before, during, and after official performance.

It is the shared after-performance energy and fatigue that forges long-term relationships. Japanese performances often end with the offstage expression "*Otsukaresama deshita*" (We are together exhausted), which recognizes the shared exertion and satisfaction of performance. This is not a high-five moment, but a quiet expression of understated pleasure in recognition of mutual effort. The pleasure lies in the aesthetic result, but even more so in the social bonds of people pulling together. Clearly, the sound product reflects the ongoing social process: a well-nurtured relationship paves the way for a smoothly flowing performance, built upon the metaphoric coordination of breaths, heartbeats, muscular contractions and releases, as well as the countless pre-performance details of tinkering large and small. That relationship is built not only in rehearsal halls and dressing rooms, but also in cafes, bars, and lounges, and if you're lucky, on Ric's *lanai* (veranda).

Some of these same mechanisms of sociability enhance research on music as well. Ethnomusicology in particular rests upon the social embeddedness of the music-in-culture project, and Ric has long been a leader of researchers who pay heed to this very sociability. Ric has led and taught by example of the need for anyone who studies music in culture to be part of the social interaction that makes up that culture. The importance of sociability among ethnomusicologists attends not only to the subjects of research but also to the collegiality among researchers. Ethnomusicologists form communities with each other through their interactions, sometimes collaborating in academic panels or edited volumes. In this, then, Ric has provided a fond rallying cry of ethnomusicologists who have been inspired by his ideas, his mentorship, and his work-as-play ethic. Some of the fruits of that inspiration may be found in this volume.

Ric's blurring of work and play inspires us. By now his three-day New Year's celebrations at his condominium on the edge of Waikīkī have become legendary. Begun far more modestly in 1971 and expanded upon yearly, these multi-part celebrations speak to Ric's committed sociability. (The New Year's party also speaks to the contagion of that commitment: Ric confesses that he has missed two of these parties when he has had to be out of town; however, others around him have upheld the tradition as usual at his condominium for forty-four years, as of 2016. Ric has attended forty-two of these.) The points to be made here are multiple. Yes, parties are fun, and Ric's particularly so. But it's the party as tactic that works so well. Parties are opportunities for networking in the best sense of the word—of creating a working (and playing) web of acquaintances whose relationships may be forged and extended in the process. These parties become curated events, less about music-making or its study and more about the social relationships that accrue through leaders like Ric. Students learn to socialize with scholars, scholars learn of the current crop of students, each wave of guests representing different pathways through Ric's life. At these parties, Ric, the ringmaster, may be the only one who knows everyone there at least initially. But by dint of personality and considerable appetite for interaction, the central eddy of Ric soon comes to be shared. Undeniably, no one can exactly emulate Ric's lifestyle. But many have used his largesse and hospitality as a template for forging and maintaining a wide swath of relationships that find equal warmth for a senior scholar (some in their eighties or nineties) as for a ten-year-old.

These parties and this approach to people are important for ethnomusicology and for the impetus behind *Making Waves*. In drawing upon Ric's inspiration we celebrate the very human endeavor by which every contribution becomes a stone thrown into a pond of concentric and overlapping ripples. Our thoughts converge in places and diverge in others, and the results of that shifting meeting ground, that lapping and overlapping, may not be known. And yet, this is exactly what makes the waves so very vital. They are not only reflective but also generative of new ideas in yet uncharted waters. The widening ripples float unpredictably and endlessly to points that surprise us.

This is why the authors of this volume look to Ric. He has been magnanimous through the waves he has generated. These waves demonstrate the way by which scholarship and sociality combine to produce a critical mix—call it the "Ric Canoe," if you will. That mix may be characterized by the Hawaiian word *kuleana* (rights and responsibilities). Ric's life and career embody the *kuleana* he enacts for those around him, the big people and the little ones, intermixed at parties, collaborating in performance, sharing the table at conferences, holding the attention of policy makers. At the very least, these chapters can attempt to cast some waves his way, intersecting, crossing paths, and creating new ripples, even as his chapter floats among them. If the metaphor that guides this volume lies in the intersecting waves that result from a confluence of factors—liquid and solid alike—then let these chapters serve as many waves cast, their ripples flowing with great warmth to shores yet unknown. Leading the way, the Ric Canoe moves with ease and grace in multiple directions at once. Here the shores may be of less importance than the canoe in motion and the waves upon which it both rides and generates.

References

Appadurai, Arjun. 1986. "Introduction: Commodities and the Politics of Value." In *The Social Life of Things: Commodities in Cultural Perspective*, ed. Arjun Appadurai, pp. 3–63. Cambridge: Cambridge University Press.

Besnier, Niko. 2009. *Gossip and the Everyday Production of Politics*. Honolulu: University of Hawai'i Press.

Clifford, James. 1997. *Routes: Travel and Translation in the Late Twentieth Century*. Cambridge, MA: Harvard University Press.

Cresswell, Tim. 2006. *On the Move; Mobility in the Modern Western World*. New York: Routledge.

Davis, Sasha. 2015. *The Empires' Edge: Militarization, Resistance, and Transcending Hegemony in the Pacific.* Athens, GA: University of Georgia Press.
DeLoughrey, Elizabeth M. 2007. *Routes and Roots: Navigating Caribbean and Pacific Island Literatures.* Honolulu: University of Hawaiʻi Press.
Dening, Greg. 1989. "History 'in' the Pacific." *The Contemporary Pacific* 1, no. 1–2: 134–139.
Diaz, Vicente M., and J. Kehaulani Kauanui. 2001. "Native Pacific Cultural Studies on the Edge." *The Contemporary Pacific* 13, no. 2: 315–341.
Feld, Steven. 2012a. *Jazz Cosmopolitanism in Accra: Five Musical Years in Ghana.* Durham, NC: Duke University Press.
———. 2012b. *Where Water Touches the Land.* DVD. https://vimeo.com/50123356. Accessed September 30, 2016.
Fox, Aaron. 2013. "Repatriation as Re-animation through Reciprocity." In *The Cambridge History of World Music: Vol. 1 (North America),* ed. Philip V. Bohlman, pp. 522–554. Cambridge: Cambridge University Press.
Gilroy, Paul. 1995. *The Black Atlantic: Modernity and Double Consciousness.* Cambridge, MA: Harvard University Press.
Hauʻofa, Epeli. 1993. "Our Sea of Islands." In *A New Oceania: Rediscovering Our Sea of Islands,* ed. Epeli Hauʻofa, Eric Waddell, and Vijay Naidu, pp. 2–16. Suva: School of Social and Economic Development, University of the South Pacific in association with Beake House.
Ingersoll, Karin Amimoto. 2016. *Waves of Knowing: A Seascape Epistemology.* Durham, NC: Duke University Press.
Meintjes, Louise. 1990. "Paul Simon's Graceland, South Africa, and the Mediation of Musical Meaning." *Ethnomusicology* 34, no. 1: 37–73.
Nannyonga-Tamusuza, Sylvia, and Andrew N. Weintraub. 2012. "The Audible Future: Reimagining the Role of Sound Archives and Sound Repatriation in Uganda." *Ethnomusicology* 56, no. 2: 206–223.
Novak, David. 2013. *Japanoise: Music at the Edge of Circulation.* Durham, NC: Duke University Press.
Ochoa Gautier, Ana Maria. 2014. *Aurality: Listening and Knowledge in Nineteenth-Century Colombia.* Durham, NC: Duke University Press.
Radano, Ronald, and Tejumola Olaniyan, eds. 2016. *Audible Empire: Music, Global Politics, and Critique.* Durham, NC: Duke University Press.
Roher, Judy. 2016. *Staking Claim: Settler Colonialism and Racialization in Hawaiʻi.* Tucson: University of Arizona Press.
Sanneh, Kelefa. 2016. "Cool Papa: Paul Simon's Afterlives." *New Yorker,* May 9: 62–65.
Stokes, Martin. 2008. "On Musical Cosmopolitanism." *Macalester International* 21, no. 8: 3–26.
Tsing, Anna. 2015. *The Mushroom at the End of the World: On the Possibility of Life in Capitalist Ruin.* Princeton, NJ: Princeton University Press.
Urry, John. 2007. *Mobilities.* Cambridge, UK: Polity Press.
Utz, Christian, and Frederick Lau, eds. 2013. *Vocal Music and Contemporary Identities: Unlimited Voices in East Asia and the West.* New York: Routledge.

CHAPTER 1

From the Rice Harvest to "Bohemian Rhapsody"

DIACHRONIC MODERNITY IN *ANGKLUNG* PERFORMANCE

Henry Spiller

PERHAPS no musical instrument is more evocative of the West Javanese countryside than the bamboo frame rattle called *angklung*. Its invention long ago was likely inspired by the sound of indigenous bamboo stalks rustling in the breeze. The musical style associated with it, in which musicians (each of whom is responsible for only a single note) collaborate to produce ostinatos and melodies, embodies the egalitarian cooperation so essential for the agriculture that sustained Sundanese people in West Java for centuries. The *angklung* music that was performed for rice harvest ceremonies symbolically resounded the relationships between individuals, human groups, and the landscapes that nurtured them.

As modernity took hold in colonial Java, the sound of *angklung* came to index premodern, "backward" rural values. In the early twentieth century, however, Indonesian nationalists reimagined these bamboo sounds to index a connection to a distinctly Sundanese modern identity rooted in those rural values. This essay follows the *angklung* as it travels from the West Javanese countryside and is transformed for modern urban contexts. The kind of *angklung* ensemble now popular in Indonesian schools and universities, promoted by several private organizations, and which has even been designated an item of intangible heritage by UNESCO (2010), are elaborations of the innovations of one Sundanese music educator, Daeng Soetigna (1908–1984), who was active from the 1930s until his death. Current incarnations of *angklung* ensembles feature large numbers of performers, each of whom controls two to four *angklung* rattles to produce elaborate arrangements of international hits, such as Strauss's "Blue Danube Waltz," Queen's "Bohemian Rhapsody," and Rodgers and Hammerstein's "Edelweiss," along with light classics and well-known Indonesian songs (see fig. 1.1). This

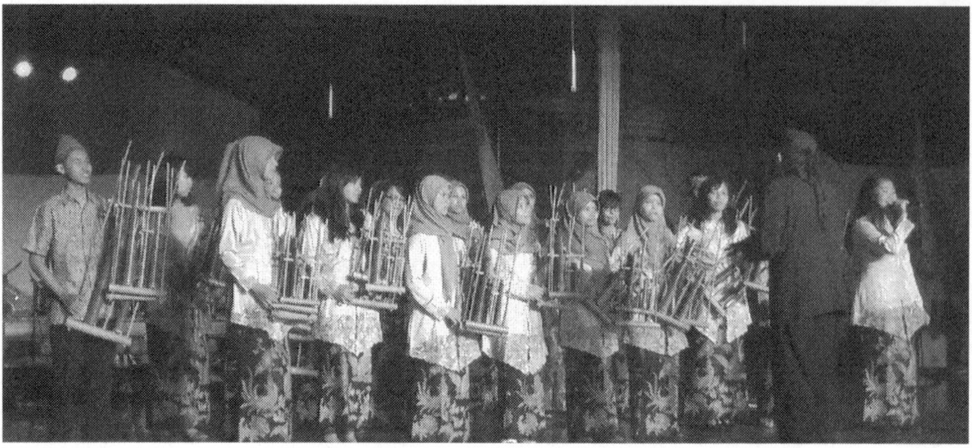

Figure 1.1 A diatonic *angklung* group performs at Taman Budaya in Bandung, Indonesia (August 24, 2013). Each performer controls two to four *angklung*. Photo: Henry Spiller.

chapter traces this transformation by examining the aesthetic and social ideals of modern *angklung* ensembles and delving into *angklung* arrangements and performances to understand how this repertory confirms and confronts both traditional Sundanese values and modern cosmopolitan ideals. *Angklung*'s persistent appeal to Sundanese citizens has much to tell us about the relationship of humans to the places in which they live, the social structures that sustain them, and the strategies they concoct to remain grounded in a changing world.

Bamboo and *Angklung*

It is difficult to overstate the significance of bamboo for the Sundanese people who make up the dominant population of West Java. From the moment their umbilical cords are cut with bamboo knives until their eventual burial in plaited bamboo shrouds, Sundanese individuals live in bamboo houses, eat bamboo shoots, and use myriad bamboo implements for a host of other purposes (Aprianti 2007). Bamboo is inherently musical—it makes musical sounds even without human intervention, when the wind whistles through it, or when its individual stalks rustle against each other. Human pleasure in these sounds, and in the harnessing of them for musical pursuits, provides a profound conceptual connection between the physical environment and cultural meanings inscribed by humans. Music made with bamboo is a sensual manifestation of the relationship between Sundanese people and their environment.

There is an old custom of placing tall bamboo poles, with slits made in tops of the bamboo, in the rice fields; the wind makes the bamboo whistle to entertain the spirit of the rice (Wilken 1912, 40; see also http://www.windmusik.com/html/bamborgl.htm).

Such aeolian bamboo whistles likely provided the inspiration for *suling*, the bamboo whistle flute that is emblematic of Sundanese music. The invention of the first bamboo rattles, *angklung*, similarly, was likely inspired by the observation of the musical qualities of bamboo shaking in the wind.

An *angklung* consists of two or three bamboo tubes, each of which is closed by a node at one end. The node ends are mounted in notches in a frame (made of rattan and bamboo) in such a way that the tubes have a limited range of motion. One end of the bamboo tube is open and can be tuned to particular pitch (see Zainal et al. 2009). When a player shakes the frame, each of the tubes hits the frame to produce a pitched tone. The slots are designed in such a way that a skilled player can keep the tubes constantly concussing to produce a tremolo, which creates the illusion of a note sustained with tremolo. The tubes in a single *angklung* typically are tuned in octaves, so that the instrument appears to sound a single pitch with a rich profile of overtones.

For generations, *angklung* were associated with small-scale dry-rice (*ladang*) and wet-rice (*sawah*) agriculture (Masunah et al. 2003, 3–4), for which residents of small rice-growing communities needed to carefully coordinate their efforts to achieve a successful harvest. This spirit of cooperation is modeled by the *angklung* music that was an integral part of harvest festivals. Consider, for example, the piece "Kacang Buncis," one of the three or four tunes associated with an *angklung* tradition known as *angklung buncis* from Ujungberung (see Baier 1985). Its well-known melody, which provides a template for endless song verses, is the result of four coordinated one-pitch ostinatos, each occupying a sixteen-beat phrase. In figure 1.2, the pitches are numbered 1, 2, 3, and 4 in the leftmost column (from high to low, approximately, 1=A, 2=G, 3=E, 4=D).

beat/ pitch	*1*	*2*	*3*	*4*	*5*	*6*	*7*	*8*	*9*	*10*	*11*	*12*	*13*	*14*	*15*	*16*
1	x				x				x				x			
2	•	•	•	x		x	x	~		x		•	•	•	•	•
3			x								x					
4		x		•	•	•	•	•	•	•	•	x		x	x	~

Figure 1.2 *Angklung* parts for "Kacang Buncis" from the *angklung buncis* repertory (as taught to me by Undang Sumarna; see also Baier 1985, 14).

The pitch 1 player shakes every four beats. The pitch 3 player shakes every eight beats. The pitch 2 and pitch 4 players each perform a more complicated pattern that occupies eight beats, and then remain silent for eight beats (the "~" symbol represents a tremolo, while the "." symbol represents a silent beat (i.e., a rest). The careful offsetting and coordination of these simple ostinatos produces a catchy tune. I should note that *angklung* tuned to a fifth pitch plays every other beat, providing a driving offbeat to the whole texture. The other *angklung buncis* pieces work similarly, with simple ostinatos creating rich musical textures (see Baier 1985; Masunah et al. 2003).

Short, one-note ostinatos, carefully coordinated to interlock, create an audible analog to the agricultural endeavors they celebrate in that the individual tasks/parts are relatively simple and repetitive, but their cooperative execution yields a result that is more valuable than the sum of its parts. *Angklung* ensembles' cooperative approach to music-making celebrated the social nature of small-scale village agriculture, and bamboo's close association with the landscape reinforced the connections that Sundanese farmers forged between community, agriculture, and the environment.

Bamboo has direct ties to the pre-Islamic Sundanese, pre-Hindu/Buddhist rice goddess Nyi Pohaci. According to legend, when Nyi Pohaci, whose origins straddle the heavens and the underworld, was interred in the earth, she became the source of all sorts of useful plants, including rice and bamboo (Sumardjo 2005). The bamboo from which *angklung* are made are thus a part of Nyi Pohaci herself, and *angklung* music awakens the sleeping goddess, who personifies the earth's latent fertility and ensures her cooperation in growing a bountiful crop (Masunah et al. 2003, 10).

Music is not the only way that bamboo has been associated with the Sundanese value of cooperation. On a recent trip to Bandung, I noticed that large-scale bamboo monuments had been installed in several traffic circles—rings of gigantic bamboo logs, with one end of each log arranged in a large circle, and the other ends leaned against one another far above the ground. I learned that these were called *api unggun*, and that they had been erected to commemorate the sixtieth anniversary of the 1955 Asian-African Conference held in Bandung. Literally, they represent a structure for building a fire. Figuratively, however, this structure is well known among Sundanese as a representation of the power of cooperation: by "working together" (leaning against one another), the bamboo logs are able to nourish and sustain a fire. Sundanese youth are sometimes encouraged to build (and burn) such structures as a team-building exercise.

Likewise, *angklung*'s association with Sundanese values of cooperation is not limited to musical style. The presence of several bamboo tubes on each *angklung* suggests the social nature of humans because a single *angklung* is made up of several components that complete one another (Tryana 2011). Furthermore, the presence of tubes of various sizes is thought by some to represent the obligation of more powerful individuals (the larger tubes) to stand with and protect the less powerful (smaller tubes).

Presumably, in the distant past, each rice-growing village and region in West Java had its own unique *angklung* traditions and repertories. There are reports that nineteenth-century Dutch colonial officials repressed *angklung* music because they believed it could incite rebellious or violent feelings among rural Sundanese (Sumarsono and Pirous 2007, xxvii; Caturwati 2013). A 2011 blog post (http://pasmandas-sman12plg.blogspot.com/2011/02/angklung.html) about *angklung* relates a story told by Baduy (insular Sundanese groups who maintain separation from the outside world, also called Kanekes), which suggests that *angklung* ensembles were associated with the armed forces of the medieval Sundanese Pajajaran kingdom. Several sources cite early twentieth-century Dutch journalists who claimed that "*angklung* is military music" (e.g., the blog post mentioned above cites an author with the initials G.J.N. in *Indië*, no. 21, August 22, 1917, p. 330: "de angkloeng is militaire Muziek") and that "it is proven that this music incites the people; they hear in it the sounds of war" *(Dat deze muziek indruk op de bevolking maakt, is bewezen. Zij beluisteren in de klanken krijgsmuziek)*, attributed to an anonymous author in *Wolanda Hindia* vol. 12, no. 6 [1939]) (Caturwati 2013; Sumarsono and Pirous 2007, xxvii; Wiramihardja 2007).

With changes in West Java's agricultural patterns over the past centuries, first with wet-rice agriculture under Javanese influence, then with Dutch *cultuurstelsel*, irrigation projects, and management systems, and most recently with the promotion of "green revolution" high-yielding varieties of rice in the 1960s (Bolman 2006, 16–21), only a few rural *angklung* traditions have survived into the present day. Some remote communities of Baduy/Kanekes still perform *angklung* music for harvest rituals (see Wessing 1977; Zanten 1995; Ekadjati 1995, 100–101; Atmadibrata, Danumiharja, and Sunarya 2006, 4–6; Masunah et al. 2003, 25–27), as do residents of the self-consciously traditional *kasepuhan* ("adhering to the old") communities centered around the village of Ciptagelar near Sukabumi (Keen 2015; Masunah et al. 2003, 30–41). Several other communities have maintained purely folkloric versions of their *angklung* traditions. *Angklung buncis*, from the village of Cipurut (east of Bandung), for example, has not been performed for agricultural ceremonies since the 1940s, but has been taught, learned, and performed as a form of entertainment continuously since then (Masunah et al. 2003, 63). The situation is similar with *angklung gubrag* from Cipining (near Bogor), *angklung badeng* from the village of Sanding (near Garut), *angklung bungko* from the village Bungko (near Cirebon), and *angklung badud* from areas around Ciamis (Masunah et al. 2003; Hermawan et al. 2012).

For the most part, these rural, agrarian *angklung* traditions index premodern Sundanese culture. Traditional *angklung* holdovers in the late twentieth century were the result of self-conscious and deliberate resistance to modernization (Baduy and *kasepuhan*) or calculated recontextualizations of rural traditions in the service of local identities and economies (e.g., *angklung buncis*). In urban areas, around the turn of the century, *angklung* were associated with beggars—at least until *angklung* took a decidedly modern turn in the 1930s, pioneered by Daeng Soetigna (1908–1984), whose life and career situate him as perhaps the very model of a modern Sundanese citizen.

Daeng Soetigna and Sundanese modernity

During the Dutch colonial period, upwardly mobile Indonesians embraced a monolithic European modernity. From this modern twentieth-century European point of view, Asia was a timeless, backward place, outside of history, whose residents were "people without history," as Eric R. Wolf famously described them ([1982] 2010, 18)—living representatives of the premodern, backward past, who looked to their colonizers' homeland in Europe as the point of origin for history (Benite 2011, 643). According to the ethnomusicologist Philip Yampolsky (writing about early twentieth-century Indonesian radio), "the essential procedure for making an Indonesian . . . music modern was to fuse it, in one way or another, with Western popular music" (2013, 234). Yampolsky argues that what made music modern in the first part of the twentieth century in Java might involve changes to instrumentation, or repertory, or forms and genres, but not necessarily all of those things (ibid., 230–232). In the case of modern *angklung* ensembles, it is not only the traditional instrument that provides a base for such a fusion; the raw material itself—bamboo—obliquely indexes a Sundanese past. Bamboo is readily available, easily worked, and entrenched in the oldest strata of the region's human history. This local history is masked, however, by the imposition of an almost entirely different set of musical values.

Daeng Soetigna was born in Garut to a mother from an aristocratic Sundanese family and a father from the emerging *santana* class—a modern innovation in Sundanese society, endorsed by the Dutch colonial administration, in which individuals of nonaristocratic birth could aspire to positions of responsibility and a middle-class lifestyle through education and hard work (Lubis 1998, 68–69). From his mother, Daeng became familiar with the cultivated arts of the Sundanese aristocracy, including gamelan, poetry, and crafts (Sumarsono and Pirous 2007, 11). By virtue of his father's *santana* status, Daeng was allowed to attend the Dutch-language Hollands-Inlands School (HIS) in Garut (but not the Europeesche Lagere School [EPS], which admitted only the children of aristocrats; ibid. 2007, 59). Later he attended the upper-level school for teachers (Kweekschool [KS]) in Bandung, then started his teaching career at the Schakelschool (a middle school for commoners that taught some Dutch language skills) in Cianjur (ibid. 2007, 89). After moving to Kuningan to take a position teaching at the local HIS, he broadened his personal interests to include scouting and music. He taught his students and his scouts a variety of international songs, and learned to accompany them on violin (ibid., 103).

When a beggar appeared on his doorstep one day playing an *angklung* and singing, Daeng was intrigued. Although he had encountered *angklung* before, at the home of one of his HIS teachers in Garut (ibid., 31), this time he became captivated by the instrument's sound, and he convinced the beggar to sell the instrument to him (ibid., 101). Daeng sought out an old *angklung* maker, Djaja, who agreed to teach him to make the instruments and how to tune them—once Daeng convinced him that he wasn't planning to teach Sundanese children how to beg (ibid., 106–107).

By 1938, Daeng had completed a set of *angklung* tuned to the European system. His first sets reflected his limited knowledge of Western music. He based the set on the range of his violin: approximately two-and-a-half octaves of chromatic pitches—thirty *angklung*, which he numbered from 1 to 30—with the lowest pitch of G below middle C (i.e., g3). He tried the *angklung* first with his scout troop, mostly as a team-building exercise; they played *kroncong* melodies and foxtrots with simple harmonies (ibid., 210). In these earliest experiments in *angklung* education, Daeng wrote notation on a poster-sized piece of paper that he hung on a wall where all the participants could see it (ibid., 114)—a practice that characterizes diatonic *angklung* performance into the present day, although a digital projection of a PDF file often replaces the handwritten poster. Daeng's groups made a splash at various scouting rallies. According to a later account in a Dutch newspaper, a scout campfire without *angklung* music was soon unthinkable—"Spoedig daarna was een padvinderskampvuur zonder angkloeng-group voor zijn troep ondenkbaar" (Haas 1964, 5).

A Dutch scout leader, who also was a teacher, suggested that the new *angklung* might be useful in the classroom (Sumarsono and Pirous 2007, 211). It occurred to Daeng that *angklung* could help overcome several problems he was encountering teaching music to children. For one thing, some of the children were disinclined to sing; playing an *angklung* was likely to be less uncomfortable for shy students. For another, his efforts to teach children to play guitar, harmonica, and mandolin were stymied by the difficulty of basic technique and the expense of acquiring the instruments; *angklung* could be produced inexpensively from local materials and were easy to play (ibid., 103).

Daeng became the head of the school when the Dutch were ejected from

Java and the Japanese occupation began. He continued to conduct a student *angklung* group, which added some Japanese songs to its repertory and played for Japanese events (ibid., 124). Although the Japanese occupiers scrubbed the school curriculum of Dutch influences, they approved of *angklung* because of the instrument's "Asian" roots and its use of bamboo—a material valued by the Japanese (ibid., xxvii). Daeng also earned attention and praise of important leaders of West Java's modernization movement, who appreciated both the sheer creativity of Daeng's instruments as well as the adaption of this symbol of Sundanese tradition with a modern educational context (ibid., 117).

His *angklung* activities continued, too, after the Japanese occupation ended and Indonesia declared its independence in 1945—including an invitation from Soekarno to make a risky trip through war-torn territory to perform in Jakarta in 1946—and throughout the revolution until the Netherlands withdrew in 1949. For a time, the Dutch controlled Kuningan and closed the school, but they established sometimes cordial relations with Daeng. Soldiers visited his home to play music, and the Dutch even invited Daeng and his troupe to present a performance in Bandung. At the same time, however, Daeng surreptitiously allowed revolutionaries to use his home as a meeting place, and Dutch soldiers once rained a volley of shots at the house, leaving a bullet lodged in one of the chairs, and eventually took over the house for lodging Dutch troops (ibid., 136–137).

After the war, Daeng moved to Bandung (the capital of West Java) and continued his advocacy of *angklung*. He sought out European music teachers to guide him in the basics of standard-practice harmony and voice leading. Daeng, along with some of his former students, now teachers themselves, set up *angklung* ensembles in several Bandung schools. Daeng also founded an ensemble that included the best students from each school, which performed for a variety of local governmental events as well as at President Soekarno's palace in Jakarta. As the 1950s and 1960s wore on, Daeng's group appeared at events of international importance, including the Asian-African Conference in Bandung in 1955, the 1959 Consultative Committee Meeting of the Colombo Plan in Yogyakarta, and the 1962 Asian Games in Jakarta (ibid., 140–142). Daeng also facilitated *angklung* performances at the New York World's Fair in 1964 (ibid., 175).

Daeng eventually realized that lower pitches were necessary for satisfying multipart arrangements, so he added a pitch 0 (f#3) as well as an additional bass octave (g2–f3) around 1958 (Winitasasmita and Budiaman 1978, 24). So many people were already accustomed to the 0–30 numbering system, however, that the new bass notes had to be accounted for separately, and were named after their pitches rather than given numbers (Sumarsono and Pirous 2007, 201–202). Travels abroad and consultations with music experts in Australia and the United States precipitated other innovations, including a set of "accompaniment" *angklung*, each of which had three or four tubes that were tuned to a three- or four-note chord rather than to a single pitch (Sumarsono and Pirous 2007, 203; Wiramihardja 2011, 25–28).

Angklung and Modernity

It is not easy for anybody brought up in a postmodern world, in which the juxtaposition of conflicting worldviews and contradictory aesthetic forms is commonplace, even banal, to appreciate the audacity of Daeng's *angklung* innovations. Traditional *angklung* music was fundamentally different from European-influenced music: it did not focus on tunes the way European music did, and the one-pitch instruments were optimized for ostinatos, not for producing intricate, fast-paced melodies (Sumarsono and Pirous 2007, 113). *Angklung*'s association in rural areas with premodern rice agriculture and in urban areas with poverty and beggars essentially precluded its inclusion in any legitimately upper-class Sundanese music, let alone modern musical expressions.

Nor can we appreciate the predicament of someone such as Daeng, who was enticed with all the promises of modernity—economic comfort, global awareness, and political equality—but at the same time was excluded from complete access to many of these benefits because of his background as a colonial subject. Iwan Meulia Pirous (Daeng's grandson) perceptively summarizes Daeng's dilemma, which was shared by all upwardly mobile Sundanese citizens under Dutch colonial rule: "one's identity as a Sundanese person could never be enough to make one a genuine modern subject, but at the same time the idea of becoming like the Dutch was absurd" *(identitas sebagai orang Sunda tidak akan cukup untuk membuatnya menjadi subjek manusia modern yang bersinar, sementara menjadi seperti Belanda pun merupakan hal terlalu absurd)* (ibid., xxvi).

It was precisely Daeng's position between traditional Sundanese culture and global modernity that eased the way for his development of diatonic *angklung*. His family's upward mobility engendered his own commitment to education, while his mixed-class parentage exposed him to both Sundanese and European values. Daeng's serendipitous encounter with an *angklung*-playing beggar, around the same time he was teaching children to play in mandolin ensembles, may have precipitated the insight: he likely noticed that although the sounds are quite different, the technique of both instruments is characterized by tremolo.

Daeng's Legacy: Diatonic *Angklung* in Bandung and Beyond

Two interrelated "streams" of diatonic *angklung* emerged in the 1960s: *angklung* ensembles as a mode for music education in schools, and *angklung* ensembles that present polished performances for both local and foreign audiences. In 1968, the Indonesian Ministry of Education released Decree No. 082/1968, declaring *angklung* a national tool for music education and legitimizing its role in the nation's public schools (Wiramihardja 2007), and most schools have access to sets of *angklung* for children's use. Quite a few schools sponsor *angklung* ensembles as an extracurricular activity as well. Daeng summarized *angklung*'s efficacy for public education with his "five *Ms*": *mudah* (easy), *murah* (inexpensive), *menarik* (interesting), *mendidik* (educational), and *massal* (suitable for large groups) (Sumarsono and Pirous 2007, 276–277; Wiramihardja 2011, 10–11).

Part of the educational (*mendidik*) benefits of *angklung* was the embodiment of Sundanese values, even while applying these approaches in novel ways to Western music. Western-trained musicians learn to carefully keep separate the individual melodic "voices" that comprise Western homophonic and polyphonic textures. In music theory classes, Western students spend an inordinate amount of time studying Bach chorales, in which each of the four voices remains independent because Bach avoided having two voices move in parallel fifths or octaves (which tended to make the two voices sound as one) or crossing voices (which created confusion about which voice was which). In contrast, those creating *angklung* ensemble arrangements willfully ignore the separation of voices. Each performer in a diatonic *angklung* ensemble holds one to four individual *angklung*, the pitches of which are from different ranges. While *angklung* ensemble notation is organized into separate voices (see fig. 1.3), each player is responsible for shaking his or her assigned *angklung* regardless of which "voice" it belongs to at any given time. It is entirely possible for a single player to shake the same *angklung* two times in rapid succession, first for one voice and then for another.

In figure 1.3, player 3 shakes her *angklung* continuously in one measure, contributing to two different voices (see the notes that are circled with a thin line); likewise for player 6 (circled with a bold line). Player 4 in this example contributes to all three voices at different times (indicated in the figure with rectangles). The individual musical "voices" emerge from the composite of the whole ensemble, not from any single individual's efforts. Thus, even when performing distinctly Western music, diatonic *angklung* ensembles give primacy to Sundanese musical characteristics—mutual cooperation, acting in harmony, and recognition of individual contributions to the whole—and hearken back to cooperative *angklung* ensembles of the past, in which melodies emerged from the careful interlocking of several simple ostinatos.

As Daeng and his disciples proliferated *angklung* groups throughout the region, a firm *pakem* (set of conventions) arose governing repertory and stage decorum. Participants in *angklung* performances, mostly young people of middle school and

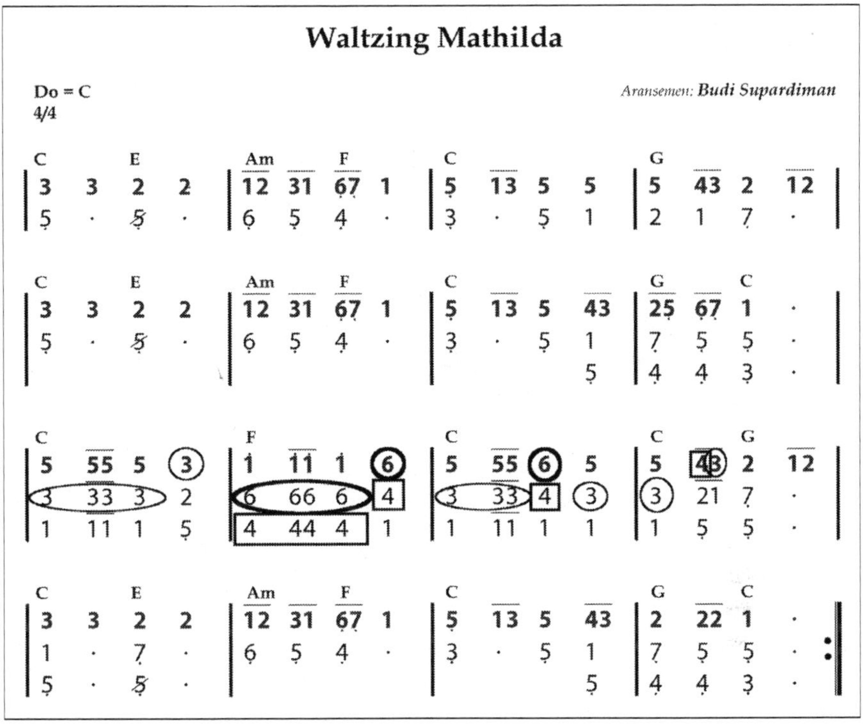

Figure 1.3 *Angklung* arrangement of "Waltzing Mathilda" demonstrating how a single *angklung* player contributes to multiple voices.

high school ages, typically wore simple school uniforms. Each student was responsible for playing a single *angklung.* According to Handiman Diratmasasmita, an *angklung* maker who performed with Daeng's *angklung* ensemble in the early 1960s, the repertory included mostly well-known patriotic Indonesian songs (*lagu wajib*), such as "Satu Nusa, Satu Bangsa" (Liberty Manik), "Meninjau Alam," and Ismail Marzuki's "Hallo Bandung," arranged for four parts by Daeng (pers. comm., May 7, 2013). For foreign visitors, the Indonesian repertory was supplemented by *lagu-lagu monumental*—light classical pieces or excerpts, Broadway tunes, and pop standards that were well known to global audiences. The first of these was Johann Strauss's "An der schönen blauen Donau" ("Blue Danube Waltz," Op. 314; Sumarsono and Pirous 2007, 136)—an arrangement that remains part of the *angklung* ensemble's standard repertory into the present. The musicians were expected to memorize their parts for performances.

As *angklung* performances became a fixture of diplomatic events in the 1950s and 1960s, Daeng developed a way for foreign audiences to participate. After the children's group finished their performance, he handed out *angklung,* one for each audience member, marked with pitch numbers. Then he explained (using the English skills he had developed during an extended trip to Australia in 1955) how to play them. Finally, he unfurled a poster of notation, which the foreign guests could follow with ease (ibid., 155–156). Soekarno no doubt hoped that communal *angklung* playing would embody cooperation among the assembled diplomats, just as it had for Sundanese farmers for centuries. It is impossible to determine whether this "*angklung* diplomacy" had any immediate effects, but it certainly provided a pleasurable and memorable experience for the assembled foreigners, and helped to increase international awareness of the instrument and its cooperative nature.

At some point, Daeng or one of his disciples learned Kodaly hand signals and adapted them for use in these audience participation demonstrations. They changed a couple of the hand positions, however, to eliminate gestures that were considered impolite in Sundanese society (E. Budi, Rochim, et al. 2013), and included a quick lesson in the hand signals as part of the demonstration.

Several of Daeng's students found their own ways to promote the study and performance of *angklung*. In 1967, Udjo Ngalagena (a student of Daeng's and a longtime *angklung* enthusiast) opened a workshop in Padasuka (on the eastern edge of Bandung), with the goal of introducing local children to *angklung*. Before long, the workshop developed a show, aimed at tourists, that featured the children performing a variety of music and dance numbers, encompassing both Sundanese and diatonic tonal systems. Over the decades, the institution has proved very successful. Currently called Saung Angklung Udjo (*saung* refers to a rustic shed for storing crops), its daily shows, presented in a covered amphitheater, draw impressive crowds of mostly European visitors, who also shop for bamboo souvenirs in a large gift shop. The show features Sundanese gamelan and dance, a short excerpt of *wayang golek* (doll puppet theater), and a variety of bamboo musical ensembles, including *angklung*. The shows always culminate with an audience participation section. Saung Angklung Udjo has become one of the Bandung area's major tourist draws and was even featured on CBS Television's *The Amazing Race* when the show visited Bandung for their 2013 season. The producers selected Saung Angklung Udjo, along with ram fights and the bird market, as iconic local attractions, for season 23, episode 9, "Part Like the Red Sea" (airdate November 24, 2013; see http://www.cbs.com/shows/amazing_race/episodes/212650).

In 1972, students at the Institut Teknologi Bandung (ITB; Bandung Institute of Technology), one of Indonesia's best technical schools, established Keluarga Paduan Angklung (KPA). They continue to promote *angklung* performance through performances and competitions into the present. Another of Daeng's students, Obby Wiramihardja, established Masyarakat Musik Angklung (MMA; Angklung Music Society) in 2002, which is billed as a continuation of Daeng's Badan Koordinasi Musik Angklung (BKMA; Body for the Coordination of Angklung Music). Later in the first decade of the 2000s, ITB alumnus Budi Supardiman established the Angklung Web Institute (AWI; *awi* is the Sundanese word for "bamboo") to provide resources for *angklung* study and performance in Bandung and via the internet. Daeng's student Handiman continues to fabricate *angklung* at his workshop on Jl. Surapati in Bandung.

Beyond the *Pakem*

One of Bandung's signature moments in the early history of the Indonesian state was the city's hosting the Asian-African Conference in 1955, at which representatives of twenty-nine newly independent Asian and African nations met to discuss their roles in a rapidly decolonizing world. Everything about the event pointed toward Indonesia's emergence as an independent, modern nation with an important role to play in the nascent nonaligned movement. The site of the conference was the former meeting hall of the Dutch colonial Sociëteit Concordia, a center for Dutch culture in the colonial period. This spectacular Art Deco masterpiece, built in 1926, was rechristened as Gedung Merdeka (Independence Building) after its 1955 renovation. Commandeering and renaming such a monument to the grandeur of centuries of Dutch colonial presence made the site an especially appropriate one for the Asian-African Conference. Among other activities, the delegates were treated to *angklung* performances at President Soekarno's request. Daeng himself was regrettably studying abroad in Australia and unavailable for the event, but his disciples made a favorable and lasting impression on the foreign diplomats.

To commemorate the twenty-fifth anniversary of the conference, Daeng and his disciples engineered a truly *massal angklung* event in 1980 involving a projected one thousand *angklung* players. The enthusiastic *angklung* club at ITB, founded a few years before, provided a solid base of performers for the event. To train a thousand players, a number of local schools initiated, resurrected, or amplified their *angklung* ensembles, including Sekolah Menengah Atas Negeri 3 (SMAN3, the state-sponsored middle school 3), which in subsequent years became known for the enthusiasm and quality of its *angklung* playing. Some educational materials, including Winisasmita and Budiaman's *Angklung: Petunjuk Praktis* (*Angklung*: Practice Hints; 1978), were prepared and published to aid in the effort. The sheer size of the undertaking created a sense of excitement among the population, and record-breaking mass *angklung* performances have been a popular undertaking ever since. Recent events include one in Washington, DC, in 2011 with 5,180 participants (http://www.indonesia.travel/en/news/detail/437/indonesia-breaks-guinness-world-records-largest

-angklung-ensemble-in-washington-dc), and another in Beijing in 2013 with 5,393 participants (https://www.youtube.com/watch?v=c8YmjIgx_os). *Guinness Book of World Records* judges verified the number of participants for both of these events. More recently, for the sixtieth anniversary of the Asian-African Conference, 20,000 *angklung* players gathered in Bandung (http://www.thejakartapost.com/news/2015/04/23/bandung-breaks-angklung-world-record.html; https://www.youtube.com/watch?v=s86b8JPi2HI). A perennial repertory choice for these massive events is "We Are the World" (composed by Michael Jackson and Lionel Richie).

The archetypal *angklung* performance practice sets out a principle of one player, one *angklung*. At some point, however, individual players began to be responsible for shaking two, three, even four instruments. Although most photographic evidence from the 1950s suggests that one-player-one-*angklung* was the norm for stage ensembles in the early decades of independence, photographs in the 1978 *Angklung: Petunjuk Praktis*, as well as specific guidelines on pages 55–58 for how to efficiently assign multiple *angklung* to players, suggest that two or three *angklung* per person was part of the *pakem* for advanced groups by the late 1970s.

The ITB and SMAN3 clubs continued to pursue *angklung* performance even after the *massal* performance was over. As the years wore on, SMAN3 alumni returned to their alma mater to impart the skills they had developed, resulting in an increasingly high level of musicianship as alumni passed along their experience, tricks, and expertise. The ITB club sponsored a biannual competition for local groups, providing an incentive for pushing beyond the *pakem*, which had solidified to include a few time-worn pieces, such as the "Blue Danube Waltz," "Besame Mucho," and various Indonesian patriotic songs, the notation for which was copied and recopied by each generation (Danoesoebroto 2007, 258–260). ITB and SMAN3 presented daring arrangements of contemporary global pop hits, such as "New York, New York" (as made popular by Frank Sinatra).

The oral tradition holds that more conservative *angklung* enthusiasts, including Udjo Ngalagena, did not approve of expanding the repertory beyond the *pakem* established by Daeng. Others justified the expansion of the repertory by pointing out that Daeng himself experimented with a variety of repertories for the ensemble and was interested in expanding its instrumentation (Danoesoebroto 2007; Yayan Udjo, pers. comm., May 13, 2013). One of Udjo's sons, Daeng Udjo, eventually became a proponent of creating new arrangements for *angklung*, eventually winning his more conservative father to the cause (Rita Milyartini, pers. comm., April 19, 2013). Currently, just about anything goes, and creative arrangements of classical, traditional, and popular songs are regarded as integral components of the *angklung* repertory.

These new arrangements take full advantage of the extended and fully chromatic range of Daeng's largest *angklung* sets, as well as the extended pitch vocabulary afforded by assigning as many as four rattles to each player. Ensemble directors use distribution guidelines for assigning *angklung* to individual players to avoid *bentrok* ("clashes")—an awkward situation where a single player is required to play two *angklung* at the same time, or two different *angklung* in rapid succession. Daeng's student Hidayat Winitasasmita developed guidelines for distribution that provides for two players of each of the main twenty-eight *angklung* (f#3–a#5), plus one player for each of the bass *angklung* (g2–f3). Each player controls *angklung* from several different octaves, but which are not likely to be combined harmonically at any time or need to be played in sequence. For example, player 1 controls the g2, f#3, and f4, which are not likely to be played simultaneously in any key and are also not likely to be played sequentially in any key, either. If, in rehearsal, a *bentrok* arises, despite these guidelines, then one of the two players leaves the conflicting note out, or else the *angklung* distribution is adjusted slightly.

Some recorded renditions of "New York, New York," easily available via YouTube, provide an idea of how arrangers and performers negotiated complex pop/jazz harmonies and dramatic key changes without *bentrok*.[1] The goal is to have each player appear relaxed and not overtaxed.

Sundanese Values in *Angklung* Music

When I first encountered diatonic *angklung* music as an outsider in the 1980s, its gentle, inoffensive timbre and tremolo-filled arrangements epitomized for me the sort of cultural "grey out" decried by Alan Lomax, which, he predicted, would "fill our human skies with smog of the phony and cut the families of men off from a vision of their own cultural constellations" (1972).

For its Indonesian proponents, however, diatonic *angklung* provides a uniquely Javanese antidote to the dangers of cultural grey out. The *angklung* repertory consists entirely of "covers"—adaptations of songs from other repertories, including light classical, easy listening, and Indonesian patriotic songs; there is virtually no call and no market for original compositions. *Angklung* expert Budi Supardiman told me that most audiences, whether Indonesian or foreign, become interested only if they hear tunes they recognize (pers. comm., July 24, 2013).

The practice of covering songs in American popular music has a checkered history; since the mid-nineteenth century, beginning with minstrelsy, white performers have appropriated African American music and made it more palatable—and more profitable—by "covering" the markers and associations of blackness that white audiences might find repugnant through rearrangement (Johnson 1996, 231). More recently, the practice of covering has been analyzed as a fundamental element of the aesthetics of rock, through which performers establish and extend their authority (Solis 2010). It is precisely the *angklung* ensemble's capacity to "cover" Western songs—draping them with an unmistakably local musical timbre and, in doing so, appropriating the song's cultural capital—that give *angklung* music its power and enabled its enduring popularity. An *angklung* performance asserts Sundanese ownership of imported music and projects a thoroughly modern Sundanese identity to its audiences, whether they are local, Indonesian, or international.

When asked to defend the playing of diatonic Western music on *angklung* during an oral examination I observed, a university degree candidate replied that *angklung* music provides Sundanese musicians the opportunity to play abroad and to share Sundanese culture with the rest of the world. Her examiner challenged her: Why should we share Sundanese culture on the West's terms? Why can't we present Sundanese music as it actually is? The student countered that people everywhere are drawn to something that is familiar; once their attention was captured, the unfamiliar timbre of the *angklung* provided an opening for cultural interchange.

Not only does the sound of the *angklung* continue to evoke the landscape of West Java for listeners, the mechanics of the ensemble further long-standing Sundanese values of cooperation and modesty. The careful distribution of *angklung* among all members of the ensemble ensure that everybody has a role to play, but that nobody stands out. The careful avoidance of *bentrok*—"clashes"—that might disrupt the ensemble both sonically and visually—suggests that these expressions of *gotong royong* (the spirit of cooperation that is one of Indonesia's most treasured values) remain at the center of diatonic *angklung* performance practice.

Although *angklung*'s association with traditional Sundanese values and the spirit of cooperation is still in evidence in such performances, it is no longer the literal embodiment of cooperation that expresses a Sundanese identity. Rather, it is the *sounds* of the *angklung* that have come to index both cooperative behaviors and their underlying social values. This abstraction opens a space for versions of *angklung* that provide a single performer the capability to perform complex music alone, in displays of virtuosity rather than of mutual collaboration, yet still conjure images of Sundanese tradition. Various kinds of *angklung* chimes provide a single performer the capability to perform complex music alone, in a display of virtuosity rather than of mutual collaboration. Yayan Udjo (another one of Udjo Ngalagena's sons) showed me three prototypes of various "keyboard" *angklung* he developed. The first model mounts a collection of *angklung* that cover several chromatic octaves in a rack that allows the performer to grasp and shake each rattle. The *angklung* are mounted upside down, with their bases just above waist height, so the player can perform standing up. A second model provides a sort of keyboard; each key connects to a mechanism that briefly shakes the appropriate *angklung*; Yayan noted that this version did not capture well the *angklung*'s characteristic tremolo. In 2013, his latest keyboard innovation simulated tremolo by activating the *angklung* with rods mounted with rubber bands; by pushing down on the "key," the *angklung* shakes by itself (pers. comm., March 13, 2013).

His original inspiration for building these instruments was to provide a way for ladies' groups to perform *angklung* without looking undignified on stage. The *angklung* chimes allow the ladies to perform without obscuring their matching formal outfits. Beyond the ladies' groups, however, Yayan hopes to meet the needs of individuals who want to have fun by themselves, to have the freedom to play whatever they want without relying on others, to provide an opportunity to learn about how music works in the privacy of their own homes. He dreams of a day when every household will have a keyboard *angklung* instrument, instead of a piano, for musical self-expression (pers. comm., March 13, 2016).

Yayan's experiments are not the first. Dinda Satya Upaja Budi (2013) reports that others created keyboard *angklung* chimes as early as the 1980s. Sumarsono and Pirous mention that a Dutch musician, Mr. Diks, created a keyboard *angklung* called the *diksophone* in the 1970s (2007, xxxi).

A similar *angklung* chime is the output device for an innovation that strays even further from the spirit of *gotong royong*—*angklung robot*. One such automated *angklung* is the research project led by Eko Mursito Budi, a professor of mechanical engineering at Institut Teknologi Bandung (ITB, the Bandung Institute of Technology), Indonesia's preeminent technical university (see E. Budi, Rochim, et al. 2013; E. Budi, Suhada, et al. 2013). The mechanics of tremolo (which are surprisingly subtle and difficult to accomplish without human control) is a popular research problem for mechanical engineers throughout the world. Budi has experimented with three different actuating mechanisms: a solenoid, a rotating motor that reverses over and over, and a railroad-type cam action. The last one seems to work the best; the solenoid is too rough, the rotating wheel takes too much energy. He has developed not only a tremolo-producing robotic *angklung* but also a software interface, called *klungdroid*, to easily input and play back arrangements to his robotic device. Robotic *angklung* have been installed in a variety of locations, including the West Java provincial governor's office in the famous Gedung Sate, and various hotel lobbies, to produce the sounds of West Java at the touch of a button (see fig. 1.4).

To understand how this twenty-first-century innovation—devoid of imme-

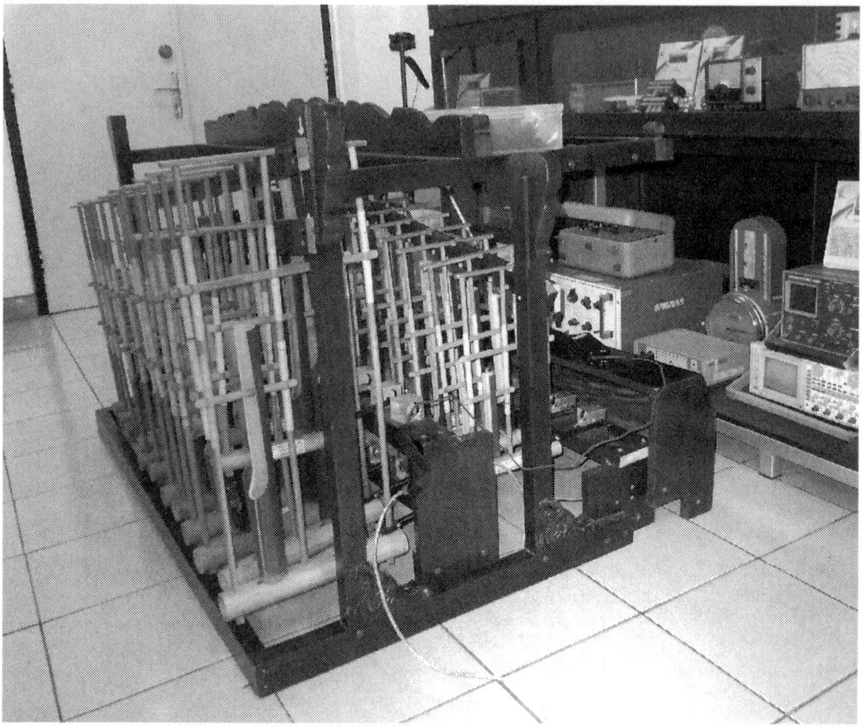

Figure 1.4 *Angklung Robot* (in Eko Mursito Budi's laboratory at ITB). Photo: Henry Spiller.

diate human action—might still recall traditional Sundanese values, I return to the concept of "covering." Twentieth-century *angklung* ensembles covered international songs with unmistakably Sundanese timbres and cooperative musical processes to assert local authority over modernity. They also laid a foundation for twenty-first-century disembodied *angklung* sounds to assert local control, authority, and ownership of technological innovations such as robotics and sampling, even when physically decoupled from any literal mimesis of Sundanese values. Although *angklung robot* strays from the basic value of *gotong royong*, it nevertheless reinforces the voice of bamboo as a sonic evocation of the relationship of Sundanese people to the landscape of West Java, and to the egalitarian, cooperative social structures that sustain them. Throughout the *angklung*'s wide-ranging travels—from the rice fields to the cities, from beggars to international "*angklung* diplomacy," and from West Java to Malaysia, Australia, Europe, and the United States—the use of bamboo contributes to the ongoing creation and maintenance of a uniquely Sundanese cultural identity, especially in a modern world.

Note

1. For example: an instrumental version from Temen AWI Angklung Orchestra (https://www.youtube.com/watch?v=H5fW1jEcpEw); the ITB group with a chorus (https://www.youtube.com/watch?v=hM4phPVbwCk); Angklung Hamburg (https://www.youtube.com/watch?v=rydGw0lr1O4). The video component of a version performed by a robot *angklung* features a note-by-note view of *angklung* notation (https://www.youtube.com/watch?v=jTyh7FIspF4).

References

Aprianti, Yenti. 2007. "Bambu: Dari Kelahiran Hingga Kematian Urang Sunda." *Kompas*, July 28.

Atmadibrata, E., N. H. K. Danumiharja, and Y. Sunarya. 2006. *Khazanah seni pertunjukan Jawa Barat.* Bandung: Dinas Kebudayaan dan Pariwisata Jawa Barat.

Baier, Randall. 1985. "The Angklung Ensemble of West Java: Continuity of an Agricultural Tradition." *Balungan* 2, no. 1–2: 8–16.

Benite, Zvi Ben-Dor. 2011. "Modernity: The Sphinx and the Historian." *American Historical Review* 116, no. 3: 638–652.

Bolman, B. C. 2006. "Wet Rice Cultivation in Indonesia: A Comparative Research on Differences in Modernization Trends." Master's thesis, Wageningen University.

Budi, Dinda Satya Upaja. 2013. "Perkembangan (Instrumen) Angklung." Paper delivered at Seminar Alat Musik Nusantara (Seminar on Musical Instruments of the Indonesian Archipelago), Museum Negara Sri Baduga, Bandung, Indonesia, June 19.

Budi, Eko Mursito, Ari Angga Rochim, Hermawan K. Dipojono, Andrianto Handojo, and Joko Sarwono. 2013. "Musical Gesture Recognition for Interactive Angklung Robot." Third International Conference on Instrumentation Control and Automation (ICA), Bali Indonesia, August 28–30. http://ieeexplore.ieee.org/stamp/stamp.jsp?tp=&arnumber=6734062.

Budi, Eko Mursito, Asep Suhada, Hermawan K. Dipojono, Andrianto Handojo, and Joko Sarwono. 2013. "Improved MIDI Message for Robotic Angklung Choir." Second International Conference on Informatics Engineering & Information Science. Kuala Lumpur: The Society of Digital Information and Wireless Communications.

Caturwati, Endang. 2013. "Angklung and Local Wisdom Values." Unpublished manuscript.

Danoesoebroto, Sudjoko. 2007. "Memperkaya Angklung Daeng." In *Membela Kehormatan Angklung: Sebuah biografi dan bunga rampai Daeng Soetigna*, edited by Tatang Sumarsono and Erna Garnasih Pirous, pp. 256–262. Bandung: Yayasan Serambi Pirous.

Ekadjati, Edi S. 1995. *Kebudayaan Sunda (Suatu Pendekatan Sejarah).* Jakarta: Pustaka Jaya.

Haas, H. W. M. de. 1964. "Oud bamboe schud-instrument maakt furore in Indonesië." *De Tijd-Maasbode*, December 14, p. 5.

Hermawan, Deni, Abun Somawijaya, Dinda Satya Upaja Budi, Ucu Mulya Santosa, and Iyon Supiono. 2012. "Angklung Sunda Sebagai Wahana Industri Kreatif Dan Pembentukan Karakter Bangsa" (Sundanese Angklung as a Vehicle for Creative Industries and the Formation of a National Character). Unpublished manuscript.

Johnson, Maria V. 1996. "'You Just Can't Keep a Good Woman Down': Alice Walker Sings the Blues," *African American Review* 30, no. 2: 221–236.

Keen, Palmer. 2015. "Ritual Rattles; Cipta Gelar's Angklung Dogdog Lojor." *Aural Archipelago* (blog), http://www.auralarchipelago.com/auralarchipelago/2015/8/6/mytx5inrp0w9ahx67rsgigv79p4kup. Accessed August 6, 2015.

Lomax, Alan. 1972. "An Appeal for Cultural Equity," *World of Music* 14: 3–4, 9.

Lubis, Nina H. 1998. *Kehidupan kaum ménak Priangan 1800–1942*. Bandung: Pusat Informasi Kebudayaan Sunda.

Masunah, Juju, Rita Milyartini, Oya Yukarya, Uus Karwati, and Deni Hermawan. 2003. *Angklung di Jawa Barat: Sebuah Perbandingan* (Angklung in West Java: A Comparison). Jakarta: Pusat Penelitian dan Pengembangan Pendidikan Seni Tradisional.

Solis, Gabriel. 2010. "I Did It My Way: Rock and the Logic of Covers," *Music and Society* 33, no. 3: 297–318.

Sumardjo, Jakob. 2005. "Mitos Nyi Pohaci." *Pikiran Rakyat*, January 29.

Sumarsono, Tatang, and Erna Garnasih Pirous, eds. 2007. *Membela Kehormatan Angklung: Sebuah biografi dan bunga rampai Daeng Soetigna* (Defending Angklung's Honor: A Biography and Anthology of Daeng Soetigna). Bandung: Yayasan Serambi Pirous.

Tryana, Tino. 2011. "Pertunjukan Angklung Buncis Dalam Acara Seren Taun di Kecamatan Cigugur Kabupaten Kuningan." Universitas Pendidikan Indonesia (UPI) thesis.

UNESCO Convention for the Safeguarding of the Intangible Cultural Heritage. 2010. "Nomination File No. 00393 for Inscription on the Representative List of the Intangible Cultural Heritage in 2010: Angklung Indonesia."

Wessing, Robert. 1977. "The Position of the Baduj in the Larger West Javanese Society." *Man* (new series) 12, no. 2: 293–303.

Wilken, G. A. 1912. "Het Animisme bij de volken van den Indischen archipel." In *De Verspreide geschriften van Prof. Dr. G. A. Wilken*, ed. F. D. E. v. Ossenbruggen. Semarang: G. C. T. van Dorp.

Winitasasmita, Mohd. Hidaya, and Drs. Budiaman. 1978. *Angklung: Petunjuk Praktis* (*Angklung*: Practice Hints). Jakarta: PN Balai Pustaka.

Wiramihardja, Obby A. R. 2007. "Sejarah Angklung" (Angklung History). Masyarakat Musik Angklung. https://angklungmusicsociety.wordpress.com/sejarah-angklung.

———. 2011. *Panduan Bermain Angklung* (A Guide for Playing Angklung). Jakarta: Masyarakat Musik Angklung.

Wolf, Eric R. [1982] 2010. *Europe and the People without History*. Berkeley: University of California Press.

Yampolsky, Philip Bradford. 2013. "Music and Media in the Dutch East Indies: Gramophone Records and Radio in the Late Colonial Era, 1903–1942." PhD diss., University of Washington.

Zainal, Mohd Ridzuwary Mohd, Salina Abdul Samad, Aini Hussain, and Che Husna Azhari. 2009. "Pitch and Timbre Determination of the Angklung." *American Journal of Applied Sciences* 6, no. 1: 24–29.

Zanten, Wim van. 1995. "Aspects of Baduy Music in Its Sociocultural Context, with Special Reference to Singing and Angklung." *Bijdragen tot de taal-, land- en volkenkunde* 151, no. 4: 516–543.

CHAPTER 2

Soundtracks for the Masses

TRANSMEDIATING INDIA IN *DANGDUT* FILMS OF INDONESIA

Andrew N. Weintraub

Blending Malay, Indian, Middle Eastern, and American musical elements, Indonesian *dangdut* swells with the sounds of distant times, places, and people. Like their musical ancestors in the traveling *bangsawan* and *komedi stambul* theater troupes, and the various Malay bands (*orkes Melayu*) that settled in the urban supercultures of the colonial Netherlands Indies, *dangdut* musicians of the 1970s mixed and remixed the songs, vocal styles, instruments, and performance practices that surrounded them.[1] As a form of entertainment, communication, and sociality, *dangdut* enabled people to speak a common musical language. Structuring that feeling of movement and sound, *dangdut*'s persistent drumbeat, pulsating bass lines, sinewy melodies, and cyclic harmonic forms coalesced in *dangdut*'s signature dance—*goyang pinggul*—"swinging one's hips [from side to side]." In the late twentieth century, in step with a top-down political formation that attempted to shape those diverse people, languages, and cultures into a centralized polity, and a commercial media industry that spread the music from westernmost Sabang to easternmost Merauke, *dangdut* became part of Indonesia's national culture.

However, the construction of national music in Indonesia is often essentialized for the strategic purpose of setting it apart from former colonizers and contemporary nation-states (for political and economic stakes, including intellectual property ownership and rights). From an Indonesian perspective, the notion of cultural hybridity is not necessarily celebrated in ideologies of the nation, for better or worse. Therefore, I was not completely surprised when an Indonesian journalist asked me: "If *dangdut* is 'Indonesian music,' how do you—a professor—account for the fact that so many *dangdut* song melodies are copied (*jiplak*) from Indian film songs? How can *dangdut* be considered 'our' music?"[2] I answered that the sound of *dangdut* (and its predecessor *orkes Melayu*) was, indeed, deeply influenced by Bollywood film songs.[3] Since the 1950s, due to the popularity of Bollywood films in Indonesia, it was common for Indonesian composers to take a melody from a Bollywood film and create new lyrics in Indonesian.[4] But the journalist's question presented only two alternatives: *dangdut* was either Indonesian or not (that is, Indian or Indonesian). The article was published with the following headline: "Prof. Andrew Weintraub: Dangdut Is Indonesia's Original Music!"[5] Several other newspaper articles aimed to show that *dangdut* was essentially Indonesian—and not Indian or other.[6]

There are several problems here. First, as *dangdut* singer and composer A. Rafiq told me, originality is a tricky business. Referring to other kinds of performing arts symbolically coded as national, he asked: "What is Indonesia's original art form? *Wayang* [puppet theater] is from India! *Kroncong* [string band music] is Portuguese!" (A. Rafiq, pers. comm., July 18, 2005). Second, the meaning of a song is not located in its sound alone; rather, the "meaning of texts or objects is enacted through practices of reception" (Appadurai, quoted in Ginsburg, Abu-Lughod, and Larkin 2002, 6). Third, the published quote attributed to me that *dangdut was* Indonesian made it sound as if the production of *dangdut* could be understood fully and singularly within the boundaries of the nation-state: "Dangdut is originally Indonesian, because it has Indonesian characteristics that are not found in Melayu or Indian music, namely themes of songs that are specific to the lives of Indonesians."

Press conferences are not about subtlety, and neither are news headlines. The appropriation of Indian songs by Indonesian composers grew into the wildly popular genre *dangdut*, a music that is rooted in Indonesian (national) places and spaces. *Dangdut* was created by, about, and for Indonesians; in this sense, it was "Indonesian music." As I have previously described in some musicological detail, Indian songs were decontextualized as a medium for recontextualizing Indonesian ideas, values, and meanings (Weintraub 2010, 57–75). However, this was not something new, as Indian-derived sonic elements, images, and body movements, as well as stories and characters, had been part of Indonesian performing arts for centuries. Further, the process of blending sonic elements across fuzzy national borders is embedded in the evolving meanings of "Melayu," a term used to signify such concepts as region, culture, and ethnic identity in the modern nation-states of Brunei, Indonesia, Malaysia, the Philippines, Singapore, Thailand, and East Timor.

In this chapter, I examine the sounds, images, and narratives of "*dangdut* films" (*film dangdut*) as an important yet underacknowledged context for framing meanings about social class, gender, and Islamic modernity in Indonesia in the 1970s and 1980s.[7] *Dangdut* films "ruled" Indonesia's cinemarket between 1977 and 1981 (Frederick 1982, 123). The music and films of India, specifically Bollywood films, loom large in the genre of *dangdut* films: Indian film music shaped the development of a new musical genre called *dangdut*, which then gave rise to a new genre of Indonesian film. Films were constructed around individual songs, and the songs were central to the narrative meanings of the films. In *dangdut* films, Indonesians used the storytelling devices in Indian films to tell their own stories to masses of ordinary Indonesians (*rakyat*) who could relate to them as their own. I will explore the sound and meaning of "India" for Indonesian musicians and consumers as "a place of transit, not of residence" (Clifford 1992, 96). How did these displaced images and sounds from across the Indian Ocean help to imagine a sense of place for Indonesians? What was formed in this crucible between India and Indonesia? How did the assemblage of "*dangdut* and Indian film" articulate meanings specific to the lives of Indonesians?[8]

Anthropologists of media have noted that theories of cultural imperialism, globalization, or "flow" do not capture the complexities and disjunctures of transnational mass media traffic. "Transnational media . . . do not float over regions of the world and land like alien spaceships in 'a culture'" (Mankekar and Schein 2012, 6). Transnationalism, like globalization, is not something that happens *to* a culture. Rather, Purnima Mankekar proposes a "transnational analytics" (Grewal et al. 1999) to analyze media "in terms of their bumpy and uneven trajectory as emerging from, converging with, and even bypassing multiple sites across the world" (Mankekar 2008, 147). *Dangdut* did not come from an Indian taproot and then spread to Indonesia. Rather, the social construction and meaning of *dangdut* took place in contact zones between India and Indonesia, and in the movement across different spatial and temporal registers (sometimes bumpy and sometimes smooth). Further, India—as discourse and practice—did not go away after *dangdut* formed; its presence is strongly felt in the production of media and the listening and viewing practices of contemporary Indonesia.

In his writings, as well as in graduate seminars at the University of Hawai'i, Ricardo D. Trimillos stressed that music often comes bundled with other communicative aesthetic media. Meaning emerges out of those bundled multimedia texts in the context of reception. As such, the study of music cannot be separated from, for example, the study of dance, theater, and/or film. This is especially salient in narrative forms, where different media are used to tell a story. I will use the term "transmedia" to elaborate on the nature and meaning of this communicative practice in several ways. First, songs from Indian films were transmediated into Indonesian *dangdut* songs, and then those songs were transmediated into a new genre of *dangdut* films. Second, "transmediation" refers to a mode of storytelling in which different kinds of media work together to tell a story. Similar to the conventions of Bollywood film (Thomas 1985), music and dance are integral to the cinematic, narrative, and visual contexts of *dangdut* films. Third, "transmedia" refers to a kind of marketing that relies on synergy between media products. For example, a film and its soundtrack are independent products, but they are codependent upon each other.

India and Indonesia

Deeply rooted traveling cultures between India and Indonesia can be traced to maritime trade routes that transported people, language, religion, and drama across the Indian Ocean some two millennia ago. The close relationship between India and Indonesia can be encapsulated in the following points:

1. Indonesia as a crossroads of "traveling cultures" between India and China.
2. The notion that Indonesians (especially on Java and Bali) see themselves as related to ancestors whose religion was a mix of Hindu and Buddhist practices. The living traditions of Hindu-Buddhist-inspired art forms include *wayang* (puppet theater), dance, and related arts.
3. The inclusion of many Sanskrit words into Indonesian (Bahasa Indonesia).
4. The discourse and history of Islam coming from Gujerati traders from India via Samudra (Aceh), although this is highly contested territory (Ricklefs 1993, 12).[9]
5. A history of traveling *bangsawan* and *komedi stambul* theatrical troupes in Southeast Asia, which incorporated stories from India, as well as music, dance, and martial arts (Tan 1993; Cohen 2006).
6. The prominent roles taken by Sukarno and Nehru in the Asian-African Conference of 1955 that solidified bonds between Indonesia and India as nonaligned nations.
7. The popularity of the Ramayana and Mahabharata television series in 1991/1992 and the film *Kuch Kuch Hota Hai*, which achieved box office success in Indonesia in 2001.
8. The shared idea of a "parallel modernity" in which Indonesians look to Indian films to learn how to negotiate between tradition and modernity. Brian Larkin's work on Indian film reception in Nigeria is applicable here: "the choice of wearing Indian or Western-style clothes, the use of English by arrogant upper-class characters or by imperious bureaucrats, even the endemic corruption of the postcolonial state, are all familiar situations with which Hausa [or Indonesian] viewers can engage" (Larkin 1997, 413).
9. Identification by Indonesian film viewers with Indian actors, stories, and scenes because they are culturally familiar.

Indian Film in Indonesia

Drawing from Brian Larkin's observation [in Africa] that African media is not made up solely of the media African people produce, but the media they consume. Similarly, Indian films must be considered part of the Indonesian cinematic and musical world (Larkin 2008, 196). However, the most prominent scholars of Indonesian cinema have paid little attention to their presence or influence (Heider 1991; Said 1991; Sen 1994; Heeren 2012). The following section provides some background on the history of Indian films in Indonesia.

In 1932, the film *Noorjehan* (1931, dir. Ezra Mir) was advertised as the first sound film from India to be shown in Indonesia ("Advertisement Nur Jehan" 1932).[10] In the 1950s, after Independence, Indian films dominated the Indonesian film market (Said 1991, 102). Biran (2008, ix) notes that "[s]ince 1952 the marketing of our films were being pushed aside by the production of neighboring countries. Then [it was] subdued completely by the marketing of Indian films." Producer Djamaludin Malik and director Usmar Ismail, the two founding fathers of Indonesian film in post-Independence Indonesia, both supported and rejected Indian film production and consumption at different times. For example, Malik, the head of the Persari Studio, hired the writer and director B. K. Raj to make the film *Janjiku* (My Promise, 1956), which was essentially a remake of a popular Indian movie (Said 1991, 42).[11] Malik is famously quoted as saying, "If the public wants Indian, we'll give them Indian until they're sick and tired of it" (quoted in Said 1991, 42).[12] Director Usmar Ismail, who formed his own company, Perfini, directed the film *Korban Fitnah* (1961) using the Indian-sounding pseudonym P. L. Kapoor, which is also the surname of the film family/dynasty in India of the 1950s. However, both producers supported quotas in 1956 to restrict the number of Indian film imports, and then a full closure of all studios in 1957 to protest their market dominance (Sen 1994, 31).

Cultural critic and poet Goenawan Mohamad draws on Bollywood film to emphasize the assimilation of Hindi language with family life in Indonesia and beyond (1984, 15). Films became so deeply embedded in Indonesian culture that: "Certain Bombay stars were considered hot in our homes: the beautiful Shakila, the handsome mustachioed Mahipal, and Raj Kapoor, who pedicab drivers and school kids used to call 'Rai Kapur.' Hindi language even entered the vocabulary of our local cafes: *nehi* became 'no,' and *sukriya* became 'thank you'" (ibid., 15). Mohamad links the film *Awaara* (1951) and its famous song "Awaara Hoon" to the genre of *dangdut*: "At RRI Jakarta [the national radio station in Jakarta], Abdul Harris sang in his baritone voice a song for which no one knew the origins, 'Awarahum' [*sic*]. That song would be popular thirty years later as 'Larilah Hai Kudaku' (Run, my horse). A type of new music that would be called 'dangdut' was born in the Republic of Indonesia" (ibid., 15).

Fans attended the same film over and over so that they could memorize the songs; they were not just spectators, but "addicts" (*pencandu*) of Indian film ("Film India Pernah Merebut" 1974). Musicians borrowed Bollywood film song melodies in the 1950s in the "proto-*dangdut*" genre of orkes Melayu (Malay orchestra).[13] An early recorded example of this process is the song "Termenung" (Daydreaming, ca. 1960), which is based on "Chhup Gayaa Koii Re Duur Se Pukaar Ke" sung by Lata Mangeshkar (1957).[14] The song was made popular by Ellya Khadam, who modeled her vocal style, stage movements, and costumes after Indian singers and film actors. Orkes Melayu grew into *dangdut*, even though the naming of the genre as *dangdut* did not occur until the early 1970s.

Certain theaters were known to show Indian films. For example, at the eight-hundred-seat Rivoli Theatre in central Jakarta, which began showing Indian films in 1952, spectators were arriving in "droves" in the early 1970s ("Penggemar Film India" 1971). In 1976, Jakartans referred to the Rivoli, National, and Apollo movie theaters as "Indian Halls" ("Film India di Indonesia" 1976). Artists, intellectuals, and critics maintained that the popularity of Bollywood was drawing spectators away from Indonesian films, thus harming the national film industry. Filmgoers were more familiar with Indian film stars compared to Indonesian ones ("Giprodfin Mau Disuap" 1974). Therefore, the Department of Information again placed import quotas on Indian films in 1974 ("Quota Import Film India Diturunkan" 1974). Even the art films or "festival films" of the 1970s were adopting elements from Indian film. In 1976, all of the ten finalists for FFI '76 (Festival Film Indonesia) in Bandung had a vocalist and long song sequences, inciting critic Eddy D. Iskandar to ask, "are Indonesian films modeled on Indian films?" (Iskandar 1976).

What accounts for Indonesians' appreciation of Indian films? They were presented in a different language, whose characters belonged to a different religion, culture, and sociopolitical context. One possible answer is that film, especially musicals, transcended language: the musical format enabled people to enjoy the films without understanding the language (Manuel 1993, 42).[15] But this does not explain what it was about the films that was so attractive to them. In fact, Bollywood films reportedly contained everything that viewers wanted: "Indian film . . . has every element that people of all stripes wish for in a film: fighting, humor, crying, a husband caught red-handed, and then released by the police; a shooting, car-chase, singing (when people are happy and when they are sad), romance, you name it. . . . All types of scenes are represented. The only thing missing is porn" (Mazwien 1977).[16]

Perhaps the stars of *dangdut* films can shed some light on this topic. As a child growing up in the 1950s, Rhoma Irama (b. 1947) listened to Bollywood songs broadcast on the radio across the Indian Ocean from Radio Ceylon. By the time he began watching Indian films as a teenager in Indonesia, he was already familiar with the music. Rhoma Irama reflects on the films of his childhood:

> I liked Indian films better than Western films. They touched me more deeply. The acting was outstanding. We could relate to the stories because they mirrored our own cultural values: politeness, loyalty, and relationships, for example, between a husband and wife, or children and their parents. A mother was treated with great respect. They didn't kiss in the movies. They expressed love. In those films, love is something so great and beautiful. It is praised from every angle and to the highest degree. Love is a gift expressed in profound ways. I've never seen a Western film about love that touched me so deeply. (pers. comm., August 6, 2016)

Dangdut star A. Rafiq (1949–2013) came from a musical theater family. His uncle led the *sandiwara* (theater) troupe Palestina in Semarang, where A. Rafiq grew up wanting to be a film star. In Semarang, he met visiting artists from "Tangkiwood," a name given to the area of Tangki in West Jakarta during the 1950s due to its large concentration of film actors. A. Rafiq drew liberally from Indian film to develop his music and his stage performance. His big hit "Pandangan Pertama" (1978) was based on "Pyar Ka Saaz Bhi Hai" from the film *Asli Naqli* (1962). In performance, A. Rafiq took his dance moves and stage demeanor from Indian film, among other things (namely Chinese martial arts and Elvis Presley). He transmediated film and music in live musical performances: "My stage show was filmic. I talked like I was in a film. It was like people were watching a film on stage" (A. Rafiq, pers. comm., July 18, 2005).

Elvy Sukaesih (b. 1951) wanted to be a film actor, not a singer (pers. comm., July 20, 2005). Like her predecessor Ellya Khadam, Elvy Sukaesih modeled her vocal style, dance, facial movements, stage movements, and costumes after Indian singers and film actors. She learned songs and musical ornaments (*cengkok*) from listening to Indian film recordings. Elvy's winks, hips, and shoulder movements were as much a part of this construction as the songs that she adopted from Indian film songs.[17] In performance, she not only "transvocalized" Indian songs, but also "transmediated" the Indian body in dance sequences (see below).

The popularity of Indian films in the 1970s, as well as the popularity of Indonesian songs derived from Indian film songs, led to the development of *dangdut* films, discussed in the following section.

Dangdut Films

The scant number of articles specifically about *dangdut* films have not been produced by film scholars, largely because film scholarship in Indonesia has ignored cult films, B-movies, and exploitation films (Imanjaya 2014, i). The most advanced study of *dangdut* films is historian William Frederick's seminal article about *dangdut* superstar Rhoma Irama and some of his early films (pre-1982).[18] In another fine article, Bettina David addresses the popularity of the 1990s blockbuster *Kuch Kuch Hota Hai*, drawing on the metaphor of "intimate neighbors" to describe the close and overlapping relationship between Bollywood film, its music, and *dangdut* in mainstream media discourse (2008).[19]

The genre of *dangdut* film capitalized on the popularity of *dangdut. Dangdut* films are musical films starring *dangdut* singers as actors, in which their songs are played back and lip-synced by the actors.[20] The first *dangdut* film was *Oma Irama Penasaran* (1976), whose title combined musician Oma Irama's name with the hit song "Penasaran" (1974).[21] *Dangdut* films were popular in the late 1970s and 1980s, although one can find examples in the 1990s to the present (see table 2.1).

Table 2.1 shows a list of *dangdut* films categorized by main actor/*dangdut* singer. *Dangdut* films often featured live performances of the artists playing music on stage. Films became central to the popularity of the artist and the meaning of the music. *Dangdut* films gave singers a way to dramatize a character in ways that musical recordings did not. Rhoma Irama stated that "all this time my fans can only hear my voice. With film, they can see and hear who I am" ("Benarkah" 1981, 45). In his films, he typically portrayed himself, using his own name. A. Rafiq and Elvy Sukaesih did the same. The dominant actor in the genre is Rhoma Irama, who starred in twenty-eight films between 1976 and 2014.

Dangdut films were patterned after Indian film genre conventions. Indonesian producers, directors, writers, and artists borrowed the style of storytelling in Indian film to tell stories that would appeal to Indonesian audiences. Audiences were familiar with the look and feel of Indian films, and recognized them in *dangdut* films. They are musicals, with 5–6 songs (and often several dance scenes). The implausible sequence of events, heightened emotions, defined positions of right and wrong, and emphasis on action (martial arts, violent encounters) place them squarely within the melodramatic idiom. Film advertisements mirrored those of Indian films (fig. 2.1 and fig. 2.2).

Their narrative form is similar to popular Hindi films, "characterized by the sharp delineation of good and evil, the use of coincidence, an excess of emotion, and the privileging of moral conflicts over psychological ones" (Ganti 2004, 137). Similar to a *masala* ("spice") film, a *dangdut* film "mixes the genres

Table 2.1 Leading Actors and *Dangdut* Films, 1976–2014

Rhoma Irama	*Elvy Sukaesih*	*Latief M.*	*A. Rafiq*	*Camelia Malik*	*Mansyur S.*
Gitar Tua Oma Irama (1977)	Assoy (1977)	Hujan Duit (1977)	Pandangan Pertama (1978)	Colak-colek (1979)	Khana (1980)
Darah Muda (1977)	Penasaran (1977)	Warung Pojok (1977)	Milikku (1979)	Jangan Coba Raba-Raba (1980)	
Rhoma Irama Berkelana I (1978)	Cubit-Cubitan (1979)		Karena Dia (1979)		
Rhoma Irama Berkelana II (1978)	Mana Tahan (1979)		Dari Mata Turun ke Hati (1979)		
Begadang (1978)	Kerinduan (1979)		Cantik (1980)		
Raja Dangdut (1978)	Gaya Merayu (1980)				
Cinta Segitiga (1979)	Irama Cinta (1980)				
Camelia (1979)	Senggol-Senggolan (1980)				
Perjuangan dan Doa (1980)	Mandi Madu (1986)				
Melodi Cinta Rhoma Irama (1980)					
Badai di Awal Bahagia (1981)					
Sebuah Pengorbanan (1982)					
Terjebak Dalam Dosa (1983)					
Satria Bergitar (1984)					
Cinta Kembar (1984)					
Pengabdian (1984)					
Kemilau Cinta di Langit Jingga (1985)					
Menggapai Matahari (1986)					
Menggapai Matahari II (1986)					
Nada-Nada Rindu (1987)					
Bunga Desa (1988)					
Jaka Swara (1990)					
Nada dan Dakwah (1991)					
Tabir Biru (1993)					
Dawai 2 Asmara (2010)					
Sajadah Ka'bah (2011)					
Sajadah Ka'bah 2 (2014)					

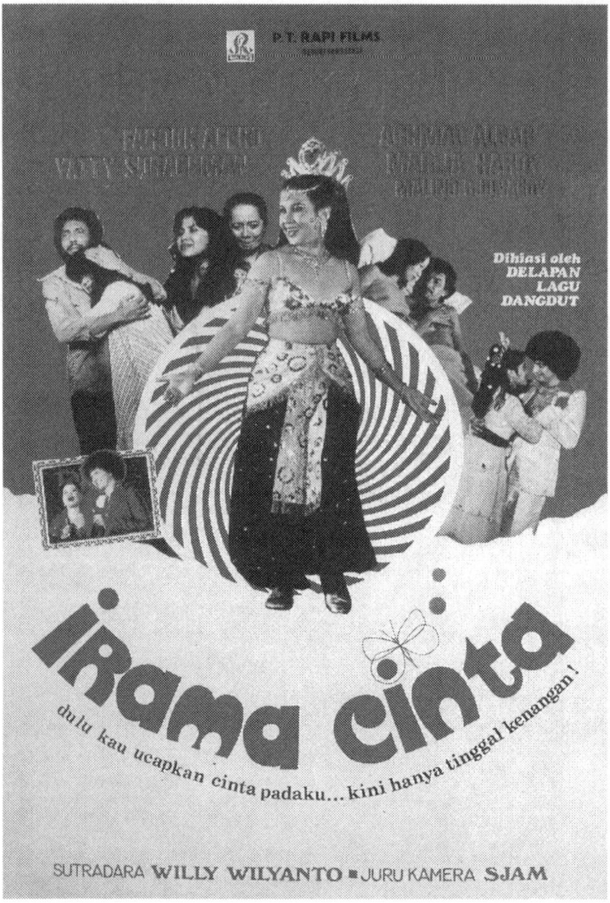

Figure 2.1 Film poster for *Irama Cinta* (1980).

of romance, melodrama, action, musical and comedy within the same film" (Larkin 1997, 411) in order to appeal to intergenerational audiences. Indonesian audiences appreciated these predictable storytelling techniques.

The films of A. Rafiq, like *dangdut* music, were thought to be copied from Indian films (Mousli SL 1980b, 36). It was not uncommon for a distributor to hire a director to adapt a novel, or to hire a popular novelist to write a script. However, most of the films were not technically "remakes" of Indian films, but they were constructed by piecing together story elements around songs that were already familiar to audiences (a kind of "bricolage" approach). The stock characters of Indian films made them easy to follow as moral guides. The formulaic nature of films, criticized by scholars, enabled these films to be appreciated by viewers as a genre, although the meanings generated by film were not monolithic.[22]

The films were made to be consistent with the desires and aspirations of ordinary people (*rakyat*), the majority market of filmgoers (those classified as "the middle class and below"). Rhoma Irama uses the popular term *singkong bukan keju* ("cassava not cheese") to differentiate the *dangdut* film audience according to social class: "We are aware of the socioeconomic gap among audiences. We are aware that the market or orientation is the middle class and below. That means that when we make a film we have to make cassava and not cheese. We are not making films for film festivals, we are not making films to win prizes. It is because of that social gap that we have intentionally simplified the dialogue" ("Lebih Jauh" 1988).

People would come to watch the films, to hear the music, and to be entertained. This is not to say that *dangdut* films were all the same, or that people viewed them using the same aesthetic or evaluative criteria. For example, some fans went simply to watch their idols sing new songs (this was before the era of video clips), while others came for the stories. *Dangdut* singers had their own fans, who would flock to the films of their idols (and not necessarily to others' films).

Dangdut films were widely disseminated in movie theaters as well as in makeshift outdoor screenings in villages, where the films were projected onto screens or sheets (*layar tancap*), and second-run movie theaters (*misbar*). *Dangdut* films were considered B-movies (low budget), which is (perhaps) why they have been largely ignored by serious film scholars (Imanjaya 2014). They could also be considered "cult" films, characterized by dedicated fans, repeated viewings, and fans who memorized the dialogues (Imanjaya, pers. comm., June 7, 2016).

Films were often named after the title of a new song. Like Indian films, *dangdut* films helped to promote an artist's songs on film soundtrack albums (known as STF, or "soundtrack film"). The soundtracks were released on cassette before the film. If the soundtrack was successful, people would go to see the film. Audiences attending the films were able to sing along with the songs during the screening because they had heard them before. Transmedia marketing created synergy among commercial products: the soundtrack attracted people to watch the film, and the film advertised the soundtrack. Rhoma Irama's songs were banned from national media TVRI and RRI from 1977 to 1988 (Weintraub 2010), and so he used film as a medium (along with live concerts and recordings) to promote his new songs. He stated that "my films exist solely as a way to get closer to my fans" (Des 1977, 42). The genre of film musicals offered him a novel way to distribute his music.

The similarity of *dangdut* films to Bollywood films is apparent in the song sequences. As in Bollywood, film and music co-structure the narrative in *dangdut* films. As producer Budhi Sutrisno told me, "songs are a part of the dialogue of a film" (pers. comm., August 6, 2016). Songs are essential because they provide a space to do things that cannot be done in the narrative.

The songs were often composed beforehand and inserted into a story (*tempelan*), but they could also be composed especially for the film.[23] When composed before the film, they played an important role in generating the plot structure. Songs did not simply enhance the narrative or the emotion depicted in the film; they were generative.[24]

If music and film are intermedial, how do they intertwine to produce narratives and meanings? In the following sections, I present the music and narrative of three films, *Raja Dangdut* (1978), *Pandangan Pertama* (1978), and *Irama Cinta* (1980), to reveal the similarities with Bollywood film and to demonstrate the ways in which *dangdut* films tell Indonesian stories about class, gender, and religion. I will provide a brief summary of the film and then analyze selected songs and their relation to the narrative. Audio and video of the films and songs discussed in this chapter are available on YouTube. Readers are encouraged to refer to the recordings while contemplating the points addressed in the text. How do the song sequences function in various ways to construct or enhance the narrative? What kind of Indonesian stories do they tell?

Raja Dangdut (The King of Dangdut, 1978)

As the title suggests, *Raja Dangdut* (The King of Dangdut, 1978) depicts Rhoma Irama as a leading figure (a "king") of *dangdut* music. The film shows him composing songs, performing with his band Soneta in front of screaming fans à la Beatlemania, and enjoying his wealth and celebrity status. As the author of the script, this "auteur" film reflects Rhoma's personal creative vision to communicate messages about Islam (*dakwah*) in a modern way. For example, he dresses in Arab clothing and communicates messages in Islamic-themed songs (*lagu dakwah*) in a style that blends psychedelic rock and *dangdut*. He viewed film as a commercial medium for articulating Islamic messages (*dakwah*): "*Dakwah* is at the heart of all my films. But the films must be packaged with human interest —love, action, humor, song—so that people will accept the message. The goal is *dakwah*, but people won't respond unless it is packaged with human interest" (pers. comm., August 6, 2016).

Ida, a devoted fan of *dangdut*, has been writing letters to Rhoma, but they never reach him. Ida is beautiful, simple, honest, devoutly religious, and comes from humble beginnings. Her mother, a widow, sells vegetable salad from a small food stand in Kampung Melayu (Melayu Village), an underclass urban *kampung* (neighborhood) located on the eastern margins of Jakarta.[25] After finally reading one of Ida's letters, Rhoma is struck by her beauty and innocence and they fall in love.

Mira completes the love triangle, a common trope in *dangdut* films (and Bollywood). Rhoma's mother has chosen a relative, Mira, to be Rhoma's wife in order

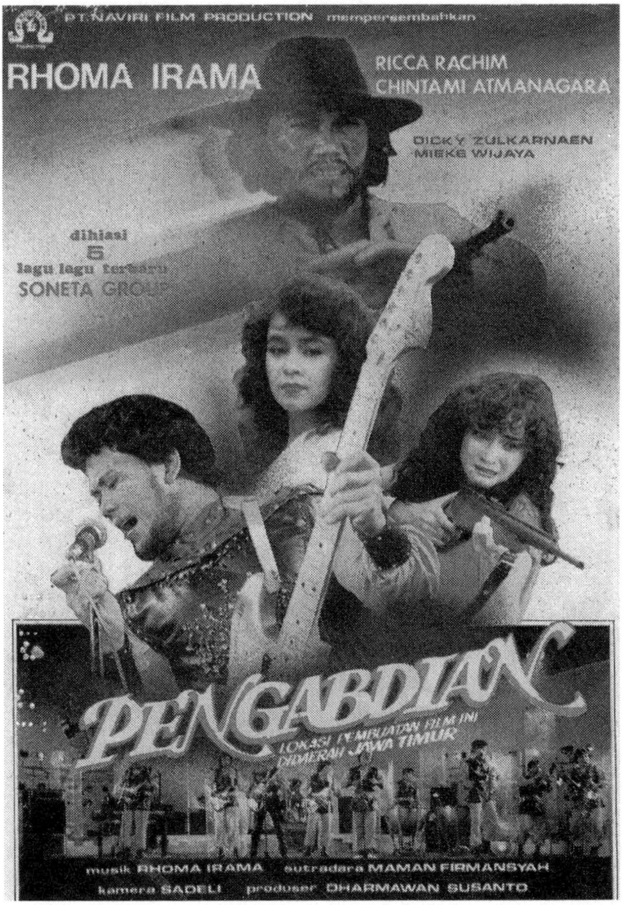

Figure 2.2 Film poster for *Pengabdian* (1984).

to guarantee that the wealth will stay in their aristocratic family. Mira is depicted as a manipulative, spoiled city girl whose social standing is higher than Ida's. Mira signifies "modern"; she wears low-cut shirts, drinks alcohol, and loves going to discos. Although Rhoma demonstrates his obedience to elders, he goes against the family by telling his mother that he wants to marry Ida rather than Mira.

Rhoma's mother and Mira decide to consult a *dukun*, a ritual healer/shaman associated with traditional pre-Islamic Javanese beliefs. The *dukun* concocts a special tea that is supposed to make Rhoma forget about Ida. However, Mira accidentally drinks it and tragedy ensues. After an argument with Rhoma, Mira leaves the house on her motorcycle and is struck by a car, coincidentally, in front of the school where Ida teaches religious classes. Ida helps Mira get to the hospital, but it is too late. On her deathbed, Mira finally gives permission for the marriage of Rhoma and Ida.

The film plays with the tension between Indonesian (Javanese) tradition and Western modernity in order to ultimately present Rhoma Irama's counter-narrative of Islamic modernity as a "third space" (Bhabha 2004, 55). Islamic modernity is portrayed in several ways. Despite his celebrity status, Rhoma remains religious, patient, and respectful to elders. He is shown doing his daily prayers and uses Arabic phrases like "Alhamdulillah" ("Praise be to God") and "Assalamuwalaikum" ("Peace be upon you"). He criticizes Mira for wearing clothes that reveal her *aurat* (parts of the body that must be covered, according to certain schools of Islamic thought). In one scene, he fights off Mira's sexual advances and lectures her (and the audience) that sex before marriage is forbidden by Islam. When Mira insults Islam, he slaps her violently to the ground. In Rhoma Irama's representation of Islamic modernity, resisting temptation even justifies violence against women.

Two song sequences enable the message of Islamic modernity to emerge, somewhat apart from the plot. After rejecting Mira's sexual advances, Rhoma visits Ida to reiterate his commitment and to tell her that he must leave the next day to perform some concerts in Kalimantan. Cut to a cave where Rhoma and his band Soneta, dressed in white robes, are performing the song "La Ilaha Illallah" (There is no God but Allah), which seems to bear little relation to the story. This is an early example of *lagu dakwah*, songs that present an Islamic message. Before the song begins, Rhoma pronounces the lines from the last verse of the *surah* (chapter) *Al-Ikhlas* in the Qur'an.[26] The sung lyrics elaborate the pronouncement that Allah is unique and incomparable. The song demonstrates Rhoma's resolve to one God, and the video portrays him as a religious leader. During the performance of the song, the film intersperses shots of Rhoma the musician and Rhoma leading a group of believers through the desert. They pass by a man worshipping human-looking statues (gods) and the camera cuts from Rhoma the musician to the rumbling of an earthquake, causing destruction to the statues.

The film builds on the picturization of "La Ilaha Illallah" by showing the fallacy of honoring religious deities other than Allah. The next scene shows Mira and Rhoma's mother plotting to consult the *dukun*. The comedic scene that follows depicts the *dukun* expressing himself in the Jakarta style of the Indonesian language. A reversal takes place: despite their desire to be modern, Mira and Rhoma's mother are the ones shown to be backward.

In the following scene, Mira visits Ida and warns her to stay away from Rhoma. The song "Malapetaka" (Catastrophe) sets the stage for the impending conflict. Every disaster is caused by the behavior of human beings, who bring the wrath of God. Everything happens for a reason, and human beings can learn from these catastrophes. The film builds on "La Ilaha Illallah" and "Malapetaka" by showing the calamity that will befall those honoring deities other than Allah.

The ambiguous boundaries between tradition and modernity allow the counternarrative of Islamic modernity to emerge. For example, it is Mira, the modern girl, who suggests that they consult a *dukun*. Rhoma accuses his mother of being traditional ("feudal") when she insists that he marry Mira in order to strengthen their aristocratic family lineage. He tells her that the colonial era is dead and there is no place for such a feudalistic attitude. Rather, he stands up for the *rakyat* (the people) who represent the future of the country. On one hand, his transgressive attitude threatens the established social order, but on the other hand, his actions support the greater good.

Restricted by tradition (family and social class standing), the coupling of Rhoma and Ida seems implausible. The tension between tradition and modernity generates the theme of "forbidden love," in which the obstacles facing the lovers are cultural (parents, family, and tradition) and economic (rich vs. poor). The film is driven by their desire, and against all odds, the lovers succeed. Islamic modernity reconciles Islamic faith with modern Western values of romantic love and modern lifestyles. Islam unites them, as it is God's will that determines the future.

The story places viewers in familiar situations relating to individual desire and collectivity (mainly family). Characters from the *kampung* serve as a point of identification for spectators who identify with underclass living conditions and poverty. Spectators also identify with the star, who is not one of them, but is on their side. For example, Rhoma is perceived as someone who speaks up to power, whether it be parents or greedy businessmen. Audiences identify with Rhoma's struggles, which are marked as authentic because they come from his real life experience. He gains the sympathy of the filmgoing masses, who identify with Rhoma's struggles as their own.

Pandangan Pertama (At First Sight, 1978)

In *Pandangan Pertama*, A. Rafiq plays Rafiq, a goat herder in the mountains of West Java who is content to pass the days tending his animals and singing and playing his flute. His songs and flute playing attract the attention of Santi, a successful female singer from Jakarta who is on holiday nearby. One cannot miss the allusion to Krishna, the Hindu deity who attracted female maidens with the divine sound of his flute. Rafiq and Santi meet and fall in love. Santi invites Rafiq to come to the city to be with her. He is hesitant but eventually agrees. His younger sister Ratih cannot stand the thought of losing him, and threatens to kill herself, but they make a promise to stay together as a family (and she eventually meets her husband, Arifin, in the city as well).

Santi urges her manager, the villain Prana, to give Rafiq a chance to sing at a performance in Jakarta. Prana is in love with Santi, and so he agrees, but he devises all sorts of ways to eliminate Rafiq (that ultimately fail). For example, Prana sets up Rafiq to fail in his first performance onstage (but he succeeds). Prana's henchmen chase Rafiq's car off the road and he ends up in the hospital (but he survives). They kill Santi's father, and Rafiq is suspected and chased away (but he is proven innocent and the killers are caught). In a last-ditch effort to get rid of Rafiq, Prana attacks him backstage, but Prana is killed by an electrical fire in the rafters while trying to escape.

The hero Rafiq is young, charming, handsome, affable, virtuous, and artistic. He begins the film as an awkward country bumpkin and eventually learns to thrive in the big city. However, the film is not about his character development.[27] Even though his outer life has changed, his inner values have not: he remains virtuous and innocent throughout the film. Rafiq's move from the countryside to the city represents a process of ruralization (Krause 2013), in which the social values of rural and urban places are recombined in creative ways. Rafiq brings the rural values of honesty and virtue to the city. The foil for Rafiq is the villain Prana, who is vicious, violent, rude, and lascivious. By winning Santi, Rafiq conquers the evil Prana, who stands for the corrupt values of the city. But this is not strictly a teleology of rural to urban. Rather, it is the combination of Rafiq conquering the city and also adapting to its modernity that complicates this move. The message here is that the rural and the urban are one national space with a shared set of goals. These places can be united into one national space, just as the two lovers can be united across class difference.

The main action is Rafiq's move from his laid-back bucolic existence in the countryside to the city, where all sorts of complications ensue in a very short time. The countryside is beautiful and pure and simple. It is associated with the past, the place that Rafiq leaves behind. On the other hand, the city is full of possibilities and stands for the future: in the city, Santi and Rafiq can be together. She tells him that she has money, a car, and a house where he can live, and his sister Ratih can find a husband there. But the city is full of problems. People lie and cheat and kill to get what they want. These spaces come together in the village, the site of romantic love and sexuality. Santi is urbane, sophisticated, and cosmopolitan, whereas Rafiq is simple, naïve, and unrefined. The hero and heroine could not be more different, but that helps the plot advance. The romance hinges on the main characters coming from, and then overcoming, different class positions.

Music, through the *suling* (bamboo flute), creates the bond between the countryside and the city. When Rafiq plays the *suling* in his village as he is daydreaming or taking a break from his work, its *pelog*-style melodies are plaintive and highly ornamented.[28] The style of playing is reminiscent of Sudanese *kacapi suling* (zither flute ensemble). He brings the *suling* to the city as a reminder of home. However, when he plays the *suling* in the city, its diatonic tones and timbre resemble the side-blown flute used in *dangdut* (also called *suling* or *seruling*). Therefore, the sound of the *suling* indexes the two different spaces and also serves as a way to bring them together.

Songs mark Rafiq's transformation from country bumpkin to successful entertainer. Prana deviously arranges for Rafiq to sing at a show before his stage act is ready. In his first performance onstage, he simply stands and sings the song "Pandangan Pertama." The camera is positioned at chest level the entire time, interspersed with shots of the audience reacting negatively. It seems as if Prana's plan has succeeded. The audience members become restless and start booing him and shouting for him to get off the stage. But Santi enters and hands him his flute, and when he plays it onstage, he feels confident. After playing the intro to "Pandangan Pertama" on the flute, he and Santi sing it as a duet and dance together. Rafiq begins moving his body vigorously. As if acting in an Indian film, he shimmies across the stage, spins, shakes his hips and shoulders, and strikes the A. Rafiq pose: legs apart, eyes and mouth open, shoulders back, chest out, arms bent, and hands at chest level pointing forward. In this rendition of the song, the camera captures his whole body, including his bell-bottom pants that would become known to spectators as "A. Rafiq pants." The crowd goes wild.

The next scenes illustrate his rise to fame and Prana's demise. The "Pandangan Pertama" melody plays intermittently throughout the film in different tempos and arrangements.[29] In the last song sequence, Rafiq has conquered the city. He strikes an Elvis-like figure in his white jumpsuit with wide collar and tight pants. Adoring female fans in the audience plant kisses on his face during the performance.

Irama Cinta (The Rhythm of Love, 1980)

In *Irama Cinta* (The Rhythm of Love), Elvy Sukaesih portrays two roles: the obedient wife and the "Queen of *Dangdut*" (Ratu Dangdut). Onstage, her life is complete. She has a successful career as an entertainer, a devoted singing partner, and lots of fans. But offstage she is unhappy. Her unemployed husband, Farouq, spends his time drinking, gambling, and having affairs with other women. He beats her regularly, but she never protests. He eventually loses everything she has earned, including their house and family heirlooms. Farouq causes her to enter a mental hospital, while he is forced to live on the side of the road before he decides to ask forgiveness. Elvy accepts his apology.

In the narrative sections, Elvy plays a long-suffering, obedient wife who will do anything for her husband. She never expresses dissent or contests his decisions. The song sequences are quite different. In these "dream sequences" (Gopalan 2002), Elvy is in love with her singing partner, played by rock musician Achmad Albar. As they drive through the mountains from one gig to the next, they fantasize about their lives together. In the song sequences that follow, they sing about their growing love as the scene shifts from a beach to a mansion, a public park, and a romantic dinner date. Following the conventions of Indian film (Skillman 1988, 153), they change costumes frequently within each song sequence. In their hearts they will always be together, even if not in reality.

In a particularly striking scene, the space of music and dance are noteworthy. This scene contrasts with what happens in the rest of the movie. If the previous scenes represent the lack of possibilities and censure, this one represents hope and freedom of expression. After Farouk beats Elvy for money, she imagines herself as an Indian dancer at court, and she is finally able to express her feelings. As Farouk whips her in front of a king and his consort, she sings the Indian-inspired song "Pecut" (Whip). In contrast to the real-life scenes where she tends to avert her gaze, she now looks directly at Farouk (with disgust). Pointing at him (an indication of anger and assertiveness), she warns him not to torture her ever again. In the song, she is finally able to use words that express her emotions: *siksa* (torture), *sakit* (pain), and *derita* (suffering). Viewers finally get a sense of her desire, expressed as something that she "does not *want*" (*tak mau*). She can no longer carry the burden of the law (marriage) and asks to be released, just as the whip releases its power on her body.

Elvy announces that she has buried her feelings (in her body) for too long. Therefore, in this scene, Elvy's dance movements are the most sexualized among all the scenes in the movie (including the scenes where she is performing onstage as the *dangdut* queen). On one hand, her dancing body can be viewed as an offering (to the king) from Farouk who wields the whip that controls Elvy's movements. But on the other hand, Elvy's body is expressing an inner self that has been dormant for so long. This is demonstrated in the instrumental interlude, where she moves her body across a greater range of space than any previous scene. Facing the king, she sits on her knees and then extends her body backward as she shakes her shoulders. Her head extends back as her hair falls to the ground, and her expression turns from one of pain to great intoxication and release. A shot of the king shows him gazing at her with lust, as she is finally able to embody and express her feelings.

As people moved across the Indian Ocean, the South China Sea, and the Pacific Ocean and through the archipelago of some seventeen thousand islands, they mixed and remixed what was around them. In contemporary Indonesia, Bollywood film and Indonesian popular music have been deeply intertwined since the 1950s, when Indonesian composers began using Bollywood film songs as the basis for constructing their own songs, combining Indian melodies and Indonesian lyrics in novel ways. Rather than standing in the way, the transnationalization of Bollywood film as a cultural technology provided a way to tell Indonesian stories through *dangdut* films.

Although rarely discussed by film scholars, *dangdut* films are important for the history of film, if only because they were preferred by the majority of filmgoers during the late 1970s and early 1980s. Despite raising the ire of critics, *dangdut* films should be praised for "realizing the dreams of the film industry to place Indonesian-made films in a dominant position nationally... [and] for never losing money" (Yoyo 1980). *Dangdut* films made in the 1970s are still occasionally shown on television, and fans post YouTube videos lip-syncing the dialogues to Rhoma Irama films.[30] The songs are still played in concerts and on recordings by the original artists (notably Rhoma Irama), but also as covers by other bands.[31]

The influence of Indian entertainment did not go away; it is thriving in television serials (*sinetron*) that transmediate Indian shows into Indonesian settings. The main family of television producers, led by Raam Punjabi, is of Indian descent, leading some clever individuals to create a pun on the name of television channel TPI (Televisi Pendidikan Indonesia, which means "Indonesian Educational Television") to Terminal Pilem India (which means "Indian Film Terminal"). Therefore, it is necessary to understand India and Indonesia as part of one fluid space, rather than two separate places, and as part of an evolving historical relationship.[32]

Indonesian scholars and critics of the 1970s tended to dismiss commercial or "lowbrow" films, as opposed to films coded as serious art or contemplation and directed by auteurs.[33] Indonesian journalists criticized Indian films because the actors would break into song whether the mood of the character was sad (*sedih*) or happy (*gembira*): *"sedih menyanyi, gembira apalagi"* ("Perfilman di India" 1972). Scholars and critics dismissed *dangdut* films for being predictable, and for not challenging audiences to think beyond a "good versus evil" mentality. In the 1977 Indonesian Film Festival "the jury criticized and condemned most Indonesian popular films that had sexual and sadistic scenes" (ibid., x). They were produced by "dream merchants" and did not reflect the realities of Indonesian life (Said 1991, 3). Critics denounced their commercial and formulaic qualities of melodrama, which they called *cengeng*—overwrought, emotionally excessive, stimulating bodily pleasure (through shifting emotions like chills down one's spine or crying), and hence not intellectual (although one could argue that the split between mind and body was a false one). One article referred to *dangdut* films as an epidemic (*wabah*) that would hurt the worldwide perception of Indonesian national film (Iskandar 1980, 7).

According to critic Salim Said, the national character (literally, *wajah Indo-*

nesia, or "Indonesian face/countenance") was missing from most Indonesian films of the late 1970s (1991). These films were based on foreign models, therefore "the Indonesian face" was missing (the "real" face). Film scripts were authored by producers and either copied or assembled from foreign movies. He noted that films by contemporary Indonesian producers (a) were solely for entertainment; (b) failed to portray the realities of Indonesian life; (c) were formulaic; (d) emphasized "sex, wealth, violence, exaggerated sadness"; and (e) did not represent Indonesian dreams. Said did not discuss *dangdut* films per se, which is odd, given that *dangdut* films were so popular. Interestingly, Said focused on Hollywood as the medium (genre) that replaced the "Indonesian face" with a foreign face, but he did not mention the "Indian" face of Bollywood. Perhaps this was because the relationship between Indian and Indonesian films is a vexed topic, one that is considered a "love-hate relationship" or an "open secret" (Ekky Imanjaya, pers. comm., June 7, 2016). Director Ami Priyono put the matter more bluntly: "What's the fuss? As far as finding identity, Indonesian national film has an Indian character. To make films that are truly Indonesian [*berwajah betul-betul Indonesia*] is difficult...because, for a long time, so many outside influences have been incorporated into our national culture" (quoted in Yoyo 1980).

I have argued that, on one hand, *dangdut* films represented a version of the "Indonesian face," albeit not the face recognized or desired by Said and his fellow critics. But it was a face that appealed to a wide spectrum of Indonesians across class, racial, and gender divides.[34] *Dangdut* films as a category of films were not considered overly sexual, violent, or sadistic (although these kinds of scenes were used at times for particular effects). Further, they depicted both wealth and poverty on screen and they portrayed social inequalities. On the other hand, one can understand Said's position that films did not show the complexity of Indonesian life. The three films discussed in this chapter mounted a critique of wealth accumulation through the portrayal of villains as Westernized secular elites, "feudal" parents, cosmopolitan children, and conniving businessmen. Values associated with this cast of characters include greed, violence, and casual attitudes about sex, whereas the values associated with heroes and heroines in *dangdut* films include family ties, sacrifice, and love. In these films, a strictly dualistic portrayal of good and evil does not capture the complexity of Indonesian everyday life, nor does it allow individual characters to develop because they are too busy realizing their essential(ized) moral positions.

Under these conditions, *dangdut* films became soundtracks for the masses: not only background music, but active agents in guiding what it meant to be Indonesian. Despite being denigrated by scholars and film critics, *dangdut* films were some of the most commercially successful and widely known films of their era. It is time to take a look at these films, and to understand them on their own terms. I argue that Indian film and music did not somehow get in the way of Indonesians telling their own stories. On the contrary, film was the site where people could register their ideas, aspirations, and anxieties about the future. It was precisely under the conditions of transnationalism and transmediation that these meanings "took place" in the space between India and Indonesia.

Notes

I am grateful to Shalini Ayyagari, Ekky Imanjaya, and Intan Paramaditha for comments on earlier drafts of this chapter.

1. *Bangsawan* and *komedi stambul* troupes played a hybrid repertoire of Malay, Chinese, Indian, Middle Eastern, and European music (Tan 1993, 73; Cohen 2006). Malay bands (*orkes*) include *orkes Melayu*, *orkes gambus*, and *orkes harmonium* (Weintraub 2010). Historian Anthony Reid defines the "urban superculture" in nineteenth-century cities of the Netherlands Indies as a "Malay-speaking urban population of mixed origins" (2001, 305).

2. Three other terms that characterize this phenomenon are *plagiat* (plagiarized), *meniru* (imitated), and *sadur* (adapted).

3. Although Indian film is made up of many popular cinemas, the vast majority of Indian films that were shown in Indonesia in the 1950s were Hindi-language films made in Bombay (Mumbai). Therefore, I will refer to them as Bollywood.

4. In a similar case from Nigeria, Hausa musicians take Indian film tunes and change the words to sing songs that praise the prophet Mohammed (Larkin 2002).

5. https://indonesiaproud.wordpress.com/2012/05/06/prof-andrew-weintraub-dangdut-musik-asli-indonesia/ (May 6, 2012).

6. http://www.antarajatim.com/lihat/berita/86820/dangdut-bukan-musik-melayu-atau-india (May 1, 2012). See also: http://archive.kaskus.co.id/thread/14221023/0/dangdut-bukan-dari-india (May 1, 2012).

7. For my discussion, I will use the term "*dangdut* film," a translation of the term "*film dangdut*" mentioned in several articles by journalist "Mousli/Mousley SL" in 1980 (1980a; 1980b; 1980c; 1980d).

8. For more about the transnationalization of Indian films, see Kaur and Sinha (2005); Iordanova et al. (2006); Gopal and Moorti (2008); and Roy and Huat (2012).

9. It is popularly believed that Islam was brought to the island of Java by the *wali sanga*, the nine saints who used music and theater to propagate Islam (Dijk 1998).

10. Indonesia's first sound film, *Terang Boelan* (1937), featured *kroncong* (string band music).

11. According to Said, it was not successful (1991, 102), a point echoed by Heide (2002, 134). However, according to the website Film Indonesia, it was "an Indonesian box-office hit": http://catalogue.filmindonesia.or.id/movie/title/lf-d009-56-130689_djandjiku.

12. The original citation is Usmar Ismail (1954, 30).

13. The song "Kudaku Lari" ("My horse runs"), alluded to in the quote above, was actually heard in two films: *Kumala Dewa Dewi* (1952) and *Perkasa Alam* (1954). The story of singer A. Harris (b. 1927), who starred in *Perkasa Alam*, illustrates the crossover between

film and music. Harris, who served as an assistant camera operator for the Japanese during the war, joined a theatrical *sandiwara* troupe, and, after serving in the army during the revolution, he belonged to the *orkes Melayu* group Sinar Medan from 1951 to 1953. He worked in Singapore with the Shaw Brothers, who had been making films for the Indonesian and Malaya market since the late 1930s (Cheah 2001, 196). A. Harris would go on to direct Rhoma Irama's first *dangdut* film, *Oma Irama Penasaran* (1976).

14. "Termenung" is a song on the album *Kafilah* (Irama LPI 17537) accompanied by Orkes Kelana Ria. "Chhup Gayaa Koii Re Duur Se Pukaar Ke" was composed by Hemant Kumar for the film *Champakali* (dir. Nandlal Jaswantlal, 1957).

15. One reviewer went so far to say that "because Indian films are so easy to 'digest,' spectators do not even need to use their brains to get the meaning and enjoy the film" ("Film India di Indonesia" 1976).

16. The question of what constitutes "porn" on screen was a subject of debate; other reviewers noted that Indian films appealed to Indonesian audiences precisely because they had sex scenes (Halimi 1973).

17. A good example is the film "Intan Berduri" (at 1:17:15). http://www.nonton.com/play/classic/indonesia/comedy-drama/intan-berduri/11842.

18. In an article about Islamic cinema in Indonesia, Imanda (2012) devotes one paragraph to Rhoma Irama.

19. Other neighboring film industries, notably Hong Kong, have had an important impact on Indonesian film, but are not discussed in this chapter.

20. These were not the only Indonesian films that featured *dangdut* music. Ellya Khadam, who bridged the genres of *orkes Melayu* and *dangdut*, lip-synced songs in many films of the 1960s and 1970s. Comedy films starring the wildly popular Benyamin Sueb and the trio Warkop DKI also featured *dangdut* songs and *dangdut* singers; for example, the first Warkop DKI film *Mana Tahan* starred singer Elvy Sukaesih (1979). But these films were not *dangdut* films. Others featured *pop Indonesia*, Western-inspired pop music.

21. Oma Irama later changed his name to Rhoma Irama; R. H. stands for "Raden Haji"; *raden* is an aristocratic title and *haji* refers to a male who has made the pilgrimage to Mecca.

22. For example, see director Wim Umboh's comment about producers assembling Indonesian film scripts from bits and pieces of imported films (Said 1991, 4).

23. Other films feature *dangdut* singers as characters, but these are not "*dangdut* films" (e.g., *Matahari-matahari*; *Ateng minta kawin*; *Detektif Dangdut*).

24. Kalinak (1992, 20–31).

25. Kampung Melayu was formerly a Dutch settlement of ethnic Malay inhabitants. As a form of Melayu music, *dangdut* is popular there.

26. At the time of the song's release, traditionalist Muslim leaders protested against the *surah* being inserted into a song. However, Rhoma replied that it is clearly spoken and not sung. Further, the text was not accompanied by instrumental music. Religious leaders accused him of commercializing Islam; in addition, they protested against his wearing Arab clothing onstage, including the long shirt (*gamis*) and turban (*serban*). For the film *Perjuangan dan Doa* (Struggle and Prayer, 1980), he had to get permission from the Indonesian Council of Ulamas (Majelis Ulama Indonesia, MUI) (see Frederick 1982). These criticisms only ignited his popularity.

27. *Dangdut* films, like most Indian films, emphasize "moral ordering" over narrative resolution (Thomas 1985).

28. Sundanese *pelog* refers to a tuning system with large and small intervals that can be approximated in a Western diatonic tuning using the pitches <g, f#, d, c, a>.

29. As one comment on YouTube points out, "'Pandangan pertama' memang sulit dilupakan" ("'Pandangan Pertama' is indeed difficult to forget"). https://www.youtube.com/watch?v=GaDPrEUZZvQ (accessed September 17, 2016).

30. For example, a dialogue from the film *Gitar Tua* (1977) by YouTube sensation Yoga SP was viewed over 1.2 million times during a three-year span, 2013–2016 (https://www.youtube.com/watch?v=ew_SdDtJzAY), accessed July 16, 2016.

31. For example, "Pandangan Pertama" was covered by the wildly successful rock group Slank for the film *Get Married* (dir. Hanung Bramantyo, 2007).

32. A funny but accurate essay describes six ways that Indonesian television dramas (*sinetron*) are similar to Indian film: (1) the main characters get into an accident and fall in love at first sight; (2) after a car or motorcycle accident, the main character appears with a bloody wound on the forehead; (3) the police arrive after the fight is already over; (4) there are many close-up shots, often alternating between characters in a scene; (5) a character stands up and silently reflects while looking off into the distance; and (6) characters appear at home in full makeup (Tetalogi 2015).

33. This situation is changing, as described by Imanjaya (2014, ii).

34. I am referring to the symbolic mixture of Malay, Indian, Arab, and European musical elements in an industry primarily controlled by Chinese producers. Further, as stated by former Jakarta governor Basuki Tjahaja Purnama (aka Ahok), the films of Rhoma Irama were very popular and influential among the Chinese community where he grew up (Siswanto and Ummi Hadyah Saleh 2016).

References

"Advertisement Nur Jehan." 1932. *Doenia Film and Sport* 4: 11–16.

"Benarkah Film *Dang-Dut* Rontok?" 1981. *Selekta* no. 1053 (November 23, 1981): 45.

Bhabha, Homi. 2004. *The Location of Culture*. Abingdon, Oxfordshire, UK: Routledge Press.

Biran, Misbach Yusa. 2008. . . . *Oh, Film!* Jakarta: Kepustakaan Populer Gramedia.

Cheah, Philip. 2001. "Film in Singapore From 1972: The Reconstruction of a Film Industry." In *Film in South East Asia: Views from the Region*. Hanoi: SEAPAVAA.

Clifford, James. 1992. "Traveling Cultures." In *Cultural Studies*, ed. Lawrence Grossberg, Cary Nelson, and Paula Treichler, pp. 96–116. New York: Routledge.

Cohen, Matthew. 2006. *The Komedie Stamboel: Popular Theater in Colonial Indonesia, 1891–1903*. Athens: Ohio University Press.

David, Bettina. 2008. "Intimate Neighbors." In *Global Bollywood: Travels of Hindi Song and Dance*, ed. Gopal, Sangita and Sujata Moorti, pp. 179–199. Minneapolis: University of Minnesota Press.

Des. 1977. "Wawancara Mini dengan Oma 'Superstar' Irama." *Aktuil*, March 7: 42.

Dijk, Kees van. 1998. "Dakwah and Indigenous Culture; The Dissemination of Islam." *Bijdragen tot de Taal-, Land- en Volkenkunde* 154, no. 2: 218–235.

"Film India di Indonesia: Mulai Turun Pasarannya?" 1976. *Sinar Harapan*, March 27. [Collection of Sinematek Indonesia, *KU-1976*.]

"Film India Pernah Merebut Hati Publik Indonesia." 1974. *Kompas*, May 21. [Collection of Sinematek Indonesia, *KU-1974*.]

Frederick, William. 1982. "Rhoma Irama and the Dangdut Style: Aspects of Contemporary Indonesian Popular Culture." *Indonesia* 34: 103–130.
Ganti, Tejaswini. 2004. *Bollywood: A Guidebook to Popular Hindi Cinema*. New York: Routledge.
Ginsburg, Faye, Lila Abu-Lughod, and Brian Larkin, eds. 2002. *Media Worlds: Anthropology on New Terrain*. Berkeley: University of California Press.
"Giprodfin Mau Disuap." 1974. *Merdeka*, January 27. [Collection of Sinematek Indonesia, *KU-1974*.]
Gopal, Sangita, and Sujata Moorti, eds. 2008. *Global Bollywood: Travels of Hindi Song and Dance*. Minneapolis: University of Minnesota Press.
Gopalan, Lalitha. 2002. *Cinema of Interruptions: Action Genres in Contemporary Indian Cinema*. London: British Film Institute.
Inderpal Grewal, Akhil Gupta, and Aihwa Ong. 1999. "Asian Transnationalities: Media, Markets, and Migration." *Positions: East Asia Cultures Critique* 7, no. 3: 653–655.
Halimi, Iim. 1973. "Perkembangan Baru Dalam Film2 India." *Yudha Sport and Film*, May 5. [Collection of Sinematek Indonesia, *KU-1973*.]
Heeren, Katinka van. 2012. *Contemporary Indonesian Film: Spirits of Reform and Ghosts from the Past*. Leiden: KITLV Press.
Heide, William van der. 2002. *Malaysian Cinema, Asian Film: Border Crossings and National Cultures*. Amsterdam: Amsterdam University Press.
Heider, Karl. 1991. *National Culture on Screen*. Honolulu: University of Hawai'i Press.
Imanda, Tito. 2012. "Independent versus Mainstream Islamic Cinema in Indonesia: Religion Using the Market or Vice Versa?" In *Southeast Asian Independent Cinema: Essays, Documents, Interviews*, ed. Tilman Baumgartel. Hong Kong: Hong Kong University Press.
Imanjaya, Ekky. 2014. "An Introduction: The Significance of Indonesian Cult, Exploitation, and B Movies." *Plaridel* 11, no. 2: i–xi.
Iordanova, Dina, et al. 2006. Special Issue: Indian Cinema Abroad: Historiography of Transnational Cinematic Exchanges. *South Asian Popular Culture* 4, no. 2.
Iskandar, Eddy D. 1976. "Filem Indonesia Sekarang Corak Filem India?" *Berita Buana*, April 14. [Collection of Sinematek Indonesia, *KU-1976*.]
———. 1980. "Film *Dang-dut* Merosot?" *Vista* 507 (May): 6–7.
Ismail, Usmar. 1954. "Sari Soal dalam Film-film Indonesia." *Star News* 3, no. 5 (September 25): 30.
Kaur, Raminder, and Ajay J. Sinha. 2005. *Bollyworld: Popular Indian Cinema through a Transnational Lens*. New Delhi: Sage Publications.
Krause, Monika. 2013. "The Ruralization of the World." *Public Culture* 25, no. 2: 233–248.
Larkin, Brian. 1997. "Indian Films and Nigerian Lovers: Media and the Creation of Parallel Modernities." *Africa* 67, no. 3: 406–440.
———. 2002. "Bandiri Music, Globalization and Urban Experience in Nigeria (La musique bandiri, globalisation et expérience urbaine au Nigeria)." *Cahiers d'Études Africaines* 42, no. 168: 739–762.
———. 2008. *Signal and Noise: Media, Infrastructure, and Urban Culture in Nigeria*. Durham, NC: Duke University Press.

"Lebih Jauh dengan Rhoma Irama." 1988. *Kompas*, May 29.

Mankekar, Purnima. 2008. "Media and Mobility in a Transnational World." In *The Media and Social Theory*, ed. David Hesmondhalgh and Jason Toynbee. London: Routledge.

Mankekar, Purnima, and Louisa Schein. 2012. "Mediations and Transmediations" (esp. "Rethinking Asia," pp. 13–16). In *Media, Erotics, and Transnational Asia*, ed. Purnima Mankekar and Louisa Schein, pp. 1–32. Durham, NC: Duke University Press.

Manuel, Peter. 1993. *Cassette Culture*. Chicago: University of Chicago Press.

Mazwien. 1977. "Kenapa Film India Menarik?" *Berita Buana*, July 21.

Mohamad, Goenawan. 1984. "Catatan Pinggir: Goyang." *Tempo*, June 30, p. 15.

Mousli SL. 1980a. "Sutradara Yopie and Danu Umbara Tentang Filem Dangdut." *Aktuil* 12, no. 13 (April 21): 58–59.

———. 1980b. "Achmad Rafiq." *Aktuil* 12, no. 14 (May 5): 36–37.

———. 1980c. "Mengapa Drama Dangdut Sukses?" *Aktuil* 12, no. 20 (July 28): 36.

———. 1980d. "Minat Menonton Filem Dangdut Merosot." *Aktuil* 13, no. 2 (November 24).

"Penggemar Film India Berdujun-dujun ke Riyoli Theatre." 1971. *Dunia Film*, March 2. [Collection of Sinematek Indonesia, *KU-1971*.]

"Perfilman di India: Maju Dengan Bantuan Besar Dari Pemerintah" 1972. *Harian Kami*, December 2. [Collection of Sinematek Indonesia, *KU-1972*.]

"Quota Import Film India Diturunkan." 1974. *Minggu Merdeka*, March 3. [Collection of Sinematek Indonesia, *KU-1974*.]

Reid, Anthony. 2001. "Understanding Melayu (Malay) as a Source of Diverse Modern Identities." *Journal of Southeast Asian Studies* 32, no. 3: 295–313.

Ricklefs, M. C. 1993. *A History of Modern Indonesia since c. 1300*. 2nd ed. Stanford, CA: Stanford University Press.

Roy, Anjali Gera, and Chua Beng Huat, eds. 2012. *Travels of Bollywood Cinema: From Bombay to LA*. New Delhi: Oxford University Press.

Said, Salim. 1991. *Shadows on the Silver Screen: A Social History of Indonesian Film*. Jakarta: Lontar Foundation.

Sen, Krishna. 1994. *Indonesian Cinema: Framing the New Order*. London: Zed Books.

Siswanto and Ummi Hadyah Saleh. 2016. "Hidup Ahok Ternyata Pernah Dipengaruhi Film Rhoma Irama." (March 30). http://www.suara.com/news/2016/03/30/195102/hidup-ahok-ternyata-pernah-dipengaruhi-film-rhoma-irama. Accessed September 27, 2016.

Skillman, Teri. 1986. "The Bombay Hindi Film Song Genre: A Historical Survey." *Yearbook for Traditional Music* 18: 133–144.

Tan, Sooi Beng. 1993. *Bangsawan: A Social and Stylistic History of Popular Malay Opera*. Singapore: Oxford University Press.

Tetalogi. 2015. "Film India vs. Sinetron Indonesia, Keduanya Ternyata Mirip!" (August 31). http://www.boombastis.com/india-vs-indonesia/37736. Accessed September 27, 2016.

Thomas, Rosie. 1985. "Indian Cinema: Pleasures and Popularity." *Screen* 26, no. 3–4: 116–131.

Weintraub, Andrew N. 2010. *Dangdut Stories*. New York: Oxford University Press.

Yoyo. 1980. "Sulit Mencari Film Nasional yang Betul Berwajah Indonesia." *Suara Karya Minggu*, March 23.

Films and Songs Discussed in This Chapter

Burnama, Jodi (director). *Pandangan Pertama* (PT Panorama Film [Merry Gultom], 1978), 35 mm film, YouTube video, posted by "VidkaChannel-1 By Abdu," December 10, 2015. https://www.youtube.com/watch?v=WrRjHwj3cnw

Firmansjah, Maman (director). *Raja Dangdut* (PT Cipta Permai Indah Film, 1978), 35 mm film, YouTube video, posted by "MrHarvan89," August 13, 2011. https://www.youtube.com/watch?v=oqZvJu_X3IY

Irama, Rhoma (composer and singer). "La Ilaha Illalah," YouTube video, posted by "Mahapatih Rifa'i Irama," January 28, 2011. https://www.youtube.com/watch?v=uPl1j14BEiw

Rafiq, A. (singer). "Pandangan Pertama," YouTube video, posted by "njendra 01," June 27, 2015. https://www.youtube.com/watch?v=BIsSL37RRCI

Sukaesih, Elvy (singer). "Pecut," YouTube video, posted by "anjar setiawan," March 24, 2016. https://www.youtube.com/watch?v=9ODN3dgdeV8

Wilianto, Willy (director). *Irama Cinta* (PT Rapi Film [Sabirin Kasdani], 1980), 35 mm film, YouTube video, posted by "Indonesian Music Lover," May 19, 2015. https://www.youtube.com/watch?v=7XAJY2q5ktg

CHAPTER 3

Localizing Global Sound Worlds in Bali and Lombok

David Harnish

BALI and Lombok, neighbor islands east of Java, have been subject to globalizing sound worlds for centuries if not millennia. Successive cultural periods in Java contributed arts and sound elements to both islands, which also encountered Chinese, Arab, Malay, and European (especially Dutch) musical and cultural ideas. Bali, moved into the global economy by the Dutch by the 1930s, has interacted with circulating musics particularly over the last hundred years; the island's status as exotic paradise has attracted foreign capital, artists, and recently the formation of a California-style "yoga culture" with spas, New Age–ish music, and vegan and raw foods diets. Traveling melodic and rhythm concepts inspired many Balinese gamelan composers and musicians to innovate their musics (often for fierce gamelan competitions), though the resulting sound has generally remained "Balinese" with the borrowed ideas submerged in gamelan textures (see Harnish 2000, 2005; Bakan 1999; Tenzer 2000). I identified a change in this process of adapting external or global elements from this inspiration-level influence, where the resulting sound is still "Balinese," to more unadulterated globalization and imitative adoption in the early twenty-first century, symbolized by the ubiquity at that time of undifferentiated Teletubbies dolls and merchandising (Harnish 2005, 119). Balinese economic, cultural and musical expressions became cross-fertilized by transnational trends, and are more compartmentalized and globally oriented than at any time in the island's history.

Lombok's history and external stimuli have been distinct from Bali's, even though Javanese influences were once equally pronounced and the island was colonized by Balinese forces for nearly two hundred years (until 1894). Unlike in Bali—and without arts academies and with a much smaller tourist industry—influences from the Western world have been muted and generally unwelcomed. One primary distinction has been in the realm of religion: Islam on

Lombok (practiced by 95 percent of the populace) and Hinduism on Bali (practiced by just over 80 percent). Many more Arab and Malay ideas are in circulation in Lombok, which formerly had a pattern of adaptation similar to Bali for artistic and religious practices. Over time, a purist position has been promulgated by Muslim leaders, reducing or eliminating the syncretism associated with traditional practices and discouraging the emulation of non-Islamic trends; while traveling sounds from Western countries are discouraged, those from the greater Malay world and particularly from Arab countries are eagerly accepted. Monies from outside Lombok, including from Saudi Arabia, have poured in for the ever-increasing mosques and Islamic schools (*madrasah* and *pesantren*). Along with swelling urbanization, this reformist agenda has terminated many earlier music forms and caused substantial changes in others.

This chapter provides an overview of these phenomena, explores selected forms (jazz and indie musics in Bali, and *gambus* lute and *zikrzamman* Sufi-style music/dance in Lombok), and compares how external/global musical sounds have been adapted, acculturated, or used by agents on these islands in distinct ways. While media—mainstream commercial media, zines, internet (common in Indonesia for twenty years)—have been the main vehicles of traveling musical sounds, local agents have either imitated, adapted, or innovated those musics to fit their localities and sensibilities.

Musics Traveling to Indonesia

In the prehistoric and early historic periods, sounds and musics came to Southeast Asia with cultural exchange and trade missions from India, China, the Arab world, and neighboring areas. Many ideas were absorbed, including language and terminology used for gamelan elements; philosophizing; arts ideation and forms; writing systems; religions and religious ideologies; iconography and graphic design; political systems of courts, priests, temples and armies; currency (e.g., *kepeng* or Chinese coins); and narrative forms (epics such as Ramayana and Mahabharata, and Chinese stories such as Ken Arok). Missionaries and leaders—including at least several of the legendary Muslim Wali Sanga (credited with spreading Islam), who were foreign born—brought sound worlds and ideas to the islands. The Dutch colonialists—as well as the British (briefly) and the Portuguese[1]—brought and implanted Western musics, arts, and political ideas. Indonesia also became home to diasporic groups such as Chinese and Yeminis, who brought their cultures, musics, and sensibilities with them.

Into the twentieth century, the Dutch controlled the media and "Western" sounds such as hymnody, military music, and then jazz became prominent in parts of the country; meanwhile, musical sounds continued coming into the coastal areas, primarily from India and the Arab world. While Javanese and then Balinese intellectuals launched journals (monitored by the colonialists), the Dutch initiated radio and external companies began taking music recordings primarily for local sale (see Murphy 2013). Japanese forces expunged the Dutch in 1942, introducing new military musics (which did not take hold locally), and these forces withdrew at the end of World War II.

As in other countries, the rapid development of Indonesian mass media accelerated the process of constructing the nation-state (see Appadurai 1995), and radio became a force for unity and nationalism in the 1950s as journals, magazines, and newspapers became tools for the country (Harnish 2013, 107). Government arts academies opened gradually throughout Indonesia—first in Java and then elsewhere, including Bali, though never in Lombok—to centralize and modernize music and the arts. Films, imported from India and elsewhere, were disseminated to cities for middle- and upper-class citizens, and then a nascent Indonesian film industry arose. Western popular music was largely banned, particularly in the latter years (early 1960s) of Indonesia's first president, Sukarno.[2] But, a number of artists nevertheless managed to form underground scenes around U.S. and British rock bands and musics.

The second president, Suharto, opened up the country to foreign capital before the end of the 1960s and released this prohibition.[3] This new era of media coincided with the rapid development of an audiocassette industry, with studios forming to record and market recordings and inexpensive playback technology (i.e., cassette players) suddenly available. In addition to encouraging greater Indonesian musical activity and business, this fostered the arrival of a much larger number of external musics, albeit overwhelmingly pirated. Cheaply made foreign films, including B-films from the United States, could be played in urban cinemas. These developments barely reached Bali—apart from the recording industry, which was quick to market local gamelan recordings—but would not get into Lombok for another decade.

In the 1970s, television viewing became common in Bali (initially acquired by hamlets for group watching; television arrived later in Lombok), used again at first as a tool for nation building and modernizing. Traveling sound worlds from a variety of media sources were coming into Bali; musicians, sometimes for academic study or teaching gamelan and sometimes with gamelan troupes, were also going out into the world (the United States, Australia, Europe, and then Japan) and returning with new ideas for music. Later in that decade emerged a radical style at the arts academy, a result of embodying sounds (and direct studying) outside of Bali, labeled *musik kontemporer* (contemporary music),[4] which discarded most "traditional" Balinese elements, was personal (rather than community, i.e., gamelan) expression, often embodied themes (religious or political), and can be considered avant-garde (see Harnish 2000; Mc-

Graw 2013). This is likely the first music style to represent the Teletubbies analogy above, where traveling sounds no longer "sound" traditional or as if they have belonged in Bali.

The internet became available in Bali by or just before the late 1990s as *warnet* (internet cafés) emerged to serve locals and tourists; these cafés were ubiquitous by 2000. In 2001, the Indonesian government recognized the need to overcome "the digital divide" and prioritized communication technologies, and Indonesian youth were quick to master those technologies, which have largely served cell phones rather than computers since few in Indonesia can afford a computer, and initiate web-based social networking. Around 2003, I realized that Balinese youth had joined virtual communities of fans devoted to particular styles—for example, grunge—or to particular bands, such as Rage Against the Machine or Green Day, and that many knew much more than I did about those styles and bands. Young people in Bali and Lombok were sharing musics by then, and a whole world of music was at their fingertips. And, these people inspired me as I wrote the Teletubbies article.

Traveling Musics into Bali

Jazz was the first global popular style disseminated throughout Indonesia (see Harnish and Wallach 2013; McGraw 2012). Filipino musicians often staffed jazz bands, along with Chinese Indonesians and a smattering of "ethnic" Indonesians. A number of musicians, all of them in urban areas, made careers as jazz musicians. World War II shattered these careers, which sometimes took up again in the 1950s. Bubi Chen (1938–2012) took Indonesian jazz into the 1960s and beyond. Jazz was always considered a "sophisticated" and somewhat respected type of popular music preferred by cultural and economic elite (see Wallach 2008b: 30), though the style did not become popular in Balinese urban centers until much later. Until the 1970s–1980s, jazz was usually considered authentic only if performed in the global and original styles, rather than localized. Fusion or hybrid musics based on jazz or rock seem to have initiated in the 1970s. Guruh Sukarnoputra, who spent years in Bali and was the son of the first Indonesian president Sukarno, pioneered combining Balinese music elements (metallophones mostly) in a rock music context (see Sutton 2010, 188–189). Krakatau was the first Indonesian jazz band to hybridize their music by combining West Javanese/Sundanese gamelan instruments and tonality with synthesizer, fretless bass, and trap drum set (see Harnish and Wallach 2013).

Though there were efforts to fuse Western instruments and elements with Balinese instruments in the Pop Bali style and in experimental music, the first major artist to hybridize jazz and gamelan was "shredding" guitarist I Wayan

Balawan (b. 1973), who has combined a rock lineup (guitar, bass, drums) with select gamelan instruments (metallophone, bamboo xylophone, drums, gong-chime) and also adds metal and other styles into his music (see Harnish 2013). Balawan played gamelan *gong kebyar* in his home village of Batuan as a youth; he was fascinated with speed, volume, and power in the music. This fascination took him to the guitar after hearing friends' audiocassettes of rock music at age eight and led him to speed metal in the 1980s, then to jazz (after hearing the furious jazz fusion guitarist John McLaughlin) in around 1992. Thus, speed, volume, and power linked these diverse music experiences together. Though Balawan is of common caste, his family was wealthy and he had the opportunity to study at the Australian Institute of Jazz in Sydney while he continued meshing these styles together. His music and the scene it organizes in Bali are cosmopolitan in the sense that they acknowledge pluralism, are simultaneously local and translocal (Turino 2000, 7), engender cross-cultural understandings, and "modernize tradition" for his fans (Harnish 2013, 3). He has used his agency—the capacity to act independently, make free choices (see Barker 2005) and to understand conditions and chart a forward pathway—to localize the global and globalize the local. His fan base is broad, though those attending his concerts tend to be middle-class, tech-savvy, and internationally oriented Balinese; he also has fans abroad (primarily Europe and Australia) and expatriates within Bali. As in all styles of popular music, social networking is widespread and essential; Balawan has been posting and communicating with his fans since the early 2000s on his cell phone. While Balawan's story is unique—and made possible by financial and social capital—he has inspired other artists, who have either remained more true to style (e.g., jazz, rock, or metal) or similarly experimented with hybridity.

Another type of hybrid music appeared in Bali in the mid- to late 1990s: Bali spa music. This music is meant to accompany massage or meditation and is soft in dynamic level, thin in texture, and euphoric without tension or dissonance. This entire movement—spas, yoga, and public meditation—was developed by expatriates from California, who set up establishments at first around the Ubud area to serve tourists who seek spiritual retreat or relaxation. A few local musicians (e.g., Joseph Vijay and Kadek Narantha), often working with the Maharani label, combined nature sounds, light gamelan metallophones, flute, occasional piano or sitar, and/or tabla into a New Age–ish mixture, presumably built on 1980s American New Age music, meant to induce a meditative state. Sometimes West Javanese gamelan *degung* (small bronze gamelan) or *kecapi suling* (flute with zithers) music is included in Bali spa, played and meant to signify a spiritual Bali. Local music stores even developed an extensive section of hundreds of recordings dedicated to Bali spa, demonstrating that the music had a clientele outside of the spa. Bali spa, to my knowledge, has never been performed live for an audience, but some events—such as the annual Bali Spirit Festival—host some artists whose works have a New Age feel and nurture spiritual experience or meditation in a translocal fashion. What I find fascinating about this movement is that Bali has been transformed into a spa, yoga, and spiritual retreat for Westerners and East Asians, as identified by this iconic music style. And none of these represent Bali before the 1980s.

Reggae, punk, rock, and metal have been in Bali since the 1980s–1990s; these styles, the largest respective scenes in Southeast Asia, have been attractive to young men and (to a lesser extent) women due to their subcultural "formal stability" and conservation as a "living tradition" (Wallach 2008a: 99).[5] Youth had access to globally circulating musics through radio, tourists, occasional concerts, and the active trading (and pirating) of audiocassettes with friends. Social networking has been crucial to maintain and expand these scenes regionally, nationally, and internationally. During the early years of these styles, bands emulated the original artists (e.g., Bob Marley, Green Day, Metallica). The emphasis on covering music closely, including singing in English, seems to have compelled scholar Emma Baulch to suggest in her groundbreaking work (2007) that the artists of these styles "gesture elsewhere" in their respective music scenes and that emulating those musics was important to create the proper scene. Rebekah Moore, who wrote the landmark work on the indie music scene (2015), argues that these musics are (and have been) firmly implanted in Bali and, in fact, are Balinese and intertwined with lived experiences and Balinese identities.[6] Cover tunes are still usually sung in English, but original songs can be in Balinese or Indonesian language. Musicians and bands created their own music industries via recordings largely in their own studios (major labels have had little interest in Balinese metal, punk, or indie bands, except for the punk band Superman is Dead) and shared freely among themselves and with fans. Occasionally bands, such as Eternal Madness, add Balinese elements (interlocking parts, pentatonicism) to ground the music in their locality, but only few bands make an effort to "sound" local. Some (particularly indie) bands, such as Navicula (as explicated by Moore 2015), have a social or environmental agenda, and their songs undermine the individualism of commercial musics and are meant to encourage social change and environmental activism.

The music scenes above involve deep hanging out (*nongkrong*; lit., to squat) that emerges directly from local and village notions of socializing (Wallach 2008b: 20) and the "mutual tuning in" (awareness of a vivid present together) (Moore 2015, 257) found also in the Balinese *desa/kala/patra* (place, time, circumstance) contextualization of social and religious experience. Similar to their countries of origin, the globally circulating styles of punk, indie, and metal are dominated by men. *Nongkrong*, however, is also a largely male domain of socializing and is often the practice that first leads boys to form an interest in music (ibid., 177); as in many cultures, women face social restrictions that prevent more active involvement. This *nongkrong* cultural pattern of socializing, found in music studios and in scenes and backstage, informs nearly all music-related activities (Wallach 2008b, 167) and is a primary activity for scene building in metal, punk, rock, and indie (Moore 2015, 182). Thus, while these globally circulating styles foster cross-cultural or transcultural understandings, they have simultaneously embodied traditional forms of socializing and made waves by instigating change and newly meaningful, local lifeways.

Traveling Sound Worlds to Lombok

As I outlined above, Lombok was "behind" Bali when it came to technologies, communications, institutions, tourism, infrastructure, and overall aid or attention from the national government. Many people I have known, particularly in the 1980s, have felt that Jakarta (the location of the federal government) neglected them and believed Lombok to be a backwater island either not worthy for or unable to handle investment. The burgeoning tourism in 1980s Bali, however, signaled that tourists could potentially pour over into Lombok, and major corporations and the government quickly took steps for the construction of hotels, restaurants, and other infrastructure to further develop the industry. Thirty years later, many of the tourist projects on Lombok intended for Westerners—largely unfulfilled—now serve Arabs and Malaysians, and the Westerners have been moved offshore to the smaller Gili islands, where they can wear skimpy clothes and party without offending Islamic sensibilities—and where whatever impacts of the music they play can be restricted to those islands.

Muslim evangelists came to Lombok, then partially Hindu and Buddhist, from Java in the sixteenth century, and later introduced and used Javanese Sufic performing arts with Islamic content, such as the shadow play *wayang kulit*,[7] as a means of converting local populations (see Harnish 2011); the resulting style, *wayang* Sasak, falls into the category of *musik tradisional* (traditional music). Later that century, more orthodox groups came not only from Java but also from Sulawesi and Sumbawa, perhaps introducing non-Javanese, Islamic forms in Arabic language, such as *burdah* (hymn singing in Arabic by a group of men, often hajjis, accompanying themselves with *rebana* frame drums), *hadrah* ("presence," poetic remembrance of devotional songs and praises in Arabic by a brotherhood), and *zikrzamman* (men, usually in a brotherhood, chanting a cappella in Arabic and performing synchronized movements); these three fall into the local and regional category of *seni music Islam* (Islamic musical arts).

Sasak kingdoms in Central and East Lombok converted fairly rapidly, which in turn benefited their relationships with Bugis, Arab, and other Muslim traders who controlled much of the seagoing market. Balinese inhabitants were moving into West Lombok and by the seventeenth century controlled that area of the island. In the eighteenth century, Balinese forces defeated the Sasak kingdoms to unify the island under royal Balinese rule. The Balinese brought bronze gamelans with them to Lombok. Gamelans were present in Lombok, but few of them included bronze metallophones and multiple gongs. Over time, Balinese influence, which sometimes involved Balinese and Sasak musicians playing together, inspired Sasak musicians to form bronze Sasak gamelans, particularly in West Lombok, where the majority of Balinese communities were located. One ensemble, in fact, became known as *gamelan gong* Sasak, a gamelan gong-type ensemble (found all over Bali) played by Sasak musicians using a combination of Sasak and Balinese terminology for the music and the instruments. Lombok, then, was a receiver of sounds traveling from Java, Bali, other Indonesian islands, and the greater Malay and Arab worlds.

In the late nineteenth century emerged *kemidi rudat*, a musical/theatrical genre found in various forms throughout Indonesia performed in the Malay language (see Cohen 2006).[8] Based on "1,001 Nights" (or "1,001 Arabian Nights"), the Sasak *kemidi rudat* includes songs, dances, humor and drama in which the young noble hero "travels with his warriors, fights non-Islamic rulers or demons, woos a princess, and demonstrates his good character" (Harnish 2011, 92). Clown characters extemporize the plot, narrative, and action in Sasak language. This hybrid style, combining elements of the Javanese form, the Turkish form, the Malay or Acehnese form (*rudat*, the folk dance; also found in West Javanese *pesantren* schools), and Sasak elements joined *wayang* Sasak as a *musik tradisional* form—with Islamic content but not *seni musik* Islam.

Though there were some music developments (mostly local and without traveling sounds), the peoples of Lombok were deeply impoverished under Dutch colonization (1894–1942), which was actually made worse under the Japanese since the Japanese armies needed ever-increasing resources. Independence just before 1950 brought a new infusion of Javanese influence—in terms of politics and governance (and a Javanese governor), civil law, arts policies, education, and so forth. It also brought new Balinese influence because Lombok and Bali were grouped into the same province until 1958, when Lombok joined Sumbawa (a neighbor island to the east) to form the Nusa Tenggara Barat province. Islam and *seni musik* Islam continued to grow in importance as the "traditionalists," called Wetu Telu (Three Stages, nominal Muslims), gradually declined in numbers.

The Sasak, overall, were once more tolerant and Sufi in orientation (one important sect was Naqsybandiyah), and practiced a syncretic faith combining *adat* (local customary laws), belief in Allah as God and Muhammad as His

Prophet, and, above all, ancestor worship (see Harnish 1988). Throughout the twentieth century, the practice of Islam (guided by teachers/leaders called *Tuan Guru*) became increasingly conservative and reformist, orientations aided by such organizations as the local Nahdlatul Watan (NW) and the national Muhammadiyah. Religious practice, once pluralistic (particularly in West and North Lombok, the main areas of Wetu Telu), hardened during Dutch colonization, the early independence period, and the supposed communist coup in Java (1965), which led to extreme and often vigilante violence throughout the country. At that time, Wetu Telu were immediately threatened and began following *Tuan Guru* for their own protection. It is a mistake, however, to assert that Islam—as a religious force—simply terminated musics, because the religion also inspired a number of forms from the seventeenth to nineteenth centuries (most of the *musik tradisional* forms)—largely shaped by traveling musics from Java and the greater Malay world—that either proselytized for Islam or presented Islamic content (see Harnish 2011).

One day in Lombok in 2012, I had a chance to meet a group of musicians through a friend who were hanging out at a food stall, one of their spaces on the outskirts of the regional capital of Mataram for meeting, socializing, performing, and celebrating their marginality. They identified themselves and their music—primarily singer/songwriter style and acoustic guitar-based—as "indie." These were mostly sidelined middle-class male youth, who marked themselves with tattoos, wore very long hair, and did not embrace the notions of society and religion promoted by their parents and mosque communities. In our conversations, it was clear that these musicians' path toward creating a scene with other young people was full of socioreligious obstacles. This small community of mostly middle-class males sheltered in a coffee stall next to the Arts Section of the provincial government Education and Tourism Ministry (where they feel protected) is far outside the norms of Sasak society. Music with Western elements, apart from the generic pop style, and particularly styles like indie, punk, and metal—with their positions of resistance and alternative dress and behavior—is shunned. These musicians have been unable to follow the success of indie bands in Bali; they haven't developed anything like their own mini industry with studios, recordings, clubs, social networking, or fan base. Further, I have never seen nor heard of metal or punk bands in Lombok. Public norms of decorum may be one explanation for this absence, but the religiosity and drive for orthodox behavior likely accounts for restrictions on these kinds of expressions.[9]

Interestingly, the most successful puppeteer of the provincial shadow-puppet play *wayang* Sasak over the past forty years, Lalu Nasib (also spelled Nasip), spearheaded experiments combining Western instruments (guitar, bass, trap drums) with Sasak instruments in 1980s–1990s audio clips and music videos.[10]

Around the same time, a Sasak version of Javanese/Indonesian *dangdut* (see Weintraub 2010) arose featuring religious or romantic songs generally sung in the Sasak language. Sasak musicians and music producers reportedly studied Javanese *dangdut* audiocassette recordings, mixed local ideas and the Sasak language, and marketed the music in local food stalls. From the 1990s onward, this style further divided into "religious" and "romantic" songs and also appeared for sale in more upscale shopping centers; the latter style, now sometimes labeled *lagu* Sasak (Sasak songs) or Sasak *alternatif*, added synthesizers, often removed all other instruments (i.e., completely digital with samples of some Sasak instruments), and in up-tempo settings used skank offbeat patterns familiar to ska. The lyrics are overwhelmingly in the Sasak language, as the music is not exported to other Indonesian islands. Music videos of this two-part style generally show chaste young men and women in traditional dress singing longingly to each other.[11] To my knowledge, few live gigs of this style occur—*lagu* Sasak does not depend upon a gig market—though the more religious songs (sometimes the *dangdut*-inspired style known as *qasidah* Sasak), sung occasionally in Arabic (or featuring certain phrases in Arabic), are often performed around religious holidays.

A combination of traditions—some local, others Balinese or Javanese—led to the music/dance form called *aleh-aleh*, including elements from the Sasak folk style *kecimol* (which no longer exists), Balinese *joged nakal* ("naughty" *joged* [not the classic social form], featuring a woman dancing in a sexually provocative way with partners in turn) and Javanese *dangdut* (often featuring women dancing erotically to hybrid music [from Hindi films, Malay coastal bands, and rock; see Weintraub 2010]). The *aleh-aleh* dance features young, presumably single women who sing and select male partners for improvised dancing. The movements can become erotic, depending on the partner, with seduction and thrusting and touching pelvises or doggy-style/twerking motions. The music seems to be a hybrid of the former *kecimol* and *dangdut*, and the dance is a hybrid between *joged nakal* and *dangdut*. *Aleh-aleh*, which emerged about twenty years ago, is a folk style that often is engaged for weddings and celebrations. Not surprisingly, it is not favored by reformist Muslims, who, for the most part (and for reasons beyond the scope of this chapter) blame Balinese for its existence in Lombok.

The "Arab"—generally considered sacred and assumed to be related to the Prophet (local Arabs are often called *sayyid*, indicating descent from the Prophet)—has been highly valued in Lombok for a hundred years and is an icon of sacred power and moral action and ideation. This aura has given the *musik seni Islam* forms (and just about every context of Arabic) a special power and place in society; the sounds of these imported styles signify the "Arab" generally, represent a religious purity relating to the Arab world (primarily

Mecca and Medina) and legitimize Islamic practice. All of these forms originate outside of Lombok—not necessarily Yemen or other Arab country; some believe the origins might be India—and were introduced during Islamization, presumably in an earlier century (likely the nineteenth century, though some Sasak teachers insist on locating origins in the sixteenth century). One very recent form, perhaps around the onset of this century, semi-qualifying for the *seni musik* Islam category is *nasyid*, an imported Malaysian form (originally Arab) usually featuring a group of young men (boy band–ish) looking neat and pious singing songs in a combination of Arabic and Sasak (rarely Indonesian), while accompanying themselves on *daf* or *rebana/terbang* tambourines.

Zikrzamman (remembrance of the time), a men's a cappella style, is perhaps the best-known Sufi-related form of *seni musik* Islam in Lombok. Developed both within brotherhoods at mosques and at some *pesantren*, it is a variant to the *dhikr* (remembrance, repetition) performance styles found elsewhere in Indonesia and throughout much of the Islamic world. A ritual and not a "performance," *zikrzamman* is usually performed in mosques on Thursday nights, on Islamic holidays (Maulud, Idul Fitri, surrounding the hajj), and occasionally during the day for less religious occasions. The texts come from the unique *Barzanji*, a series of stories about Muhammad and his sayings, that some say was first compiled in Banten, West Java (Harnish 2011, 93–94). The music within some brotherhoods consists of nine distinct sections that modulate to different scales as in Arabic *maqamat* traditions. Men sit in two lines and sing (often responsorially) through nine long song segments with associated choreography that can often lead to trancelike states.

The *musik tradisional* forms, including here *wayang* Sasak and *kemidi rudat*, have been discredited and neglected by political leaders in Lombok. The current, though outgoing, governor, Tuan Guru Bajang, rather infamously denies opportunities for "traditional" Sasak music and dance to be performed. He prefers only *seni musik* Islam forms, Arabic poetry, and Quranic recitation. Interestingly—and I think due to the repetitive, trancelike movement and Sufi connections (discredited in today's more reformist Lombok)—*zikrzamman* is only rarely practiced today in mosques and has been abandoned by many *Tuan Guru*. Thus, the music/dance forms that were introduced to proselytize for Islam, e.g., *wayang* Sasak, and at least one of the *seni musik* Islam forms, *zikrzamman* (and *hadrah* and *burdah* both also have Sufi roots), are either discouraged or delegitimized.

The *gambus*, a lute that traveled to Indonesia from Yemen, is in general a marker of Arab ethnicity and of the Islamic social imagination (Capwell 2011, 198) throughout Indonesia. While played in ensemble or solo for Arab Indonesian wedding celebrations or to accompany the Malay-style *zapin* dance, where its function is primarily secular, it is imbued with Islamic spirituality (see Berg

2011). In much of Indonesia, including Lombok, its sound is an index of Islam and thus positive moral values. The original instrument in pre-reformist Lombok was called *penting*, and it was performed solo by rural musicians or in Sasak folk ensembles such as *cilokaq*; as Lombok turned more strongly toward Islam, the instrument's shape transformed into the Arab model, *penting* was dropped, and the instrument assumed enhanced Islamic associations. It is believed locally that the *gambus* proper was brought to Lombok not by Arabs but by Bugis traders and musicians from South Sulawesi.

Over the years, I occasionally saw *gambus* musicians, often in *cilokaq* or the now-obsolete *kecimol* folk ensembles that accompany songs in Sasak language[12] rather than in Arabic; the solo style, on the other hand, usually features Arabic (keeping with the Bugis and Yemini roots), rather than Sasak. Then one day in 2012, I visited a unique *gambus* player in Beruak, East Lombok, who is dedicated to maintaining the older tradition in Lombok. Despite the Islamic associations of the instrument and music, this musician, Amaq Sadar, who has been a *cilokaq* musician, performs solo, improvised Sasak folk music, maintaining a pre-reformist style of music that is nearly obsolete, on an instrument associated with Bugis and Arabs given to him by the Sultan of Yogyakarta after a competition in Java. His songs are about rural wisdom, offering guidance for children and youth, and some are love songs. Amaq Sadar doesn't know Arabic, has little interest in learning, and states that Sasak was the older language of religious instruction and is still fitting for *gambus*. His is a unique talent to improvise meaningful songs either humorous or wise. He is undeterred by the traveling Arabic language and religious songs that are so ubiquitous and associated with his instrument.

The following day in Central Lombok, I attended a *zikr* ceremony commemorating a one-hundred-day-old death and an anniversary of a mosque, where the discourse vacillated from Arabic to Sasak to Indonesian, though the ritual language was strictly Arabic. This *zikr* was unrelated to *zikrzamman* (though both terms refer to "remembering") and did not include group singing or movement, and this undifferentiated ritual, performed all over the Islamic world, is now substituting for the localized and inner-directed *zikrzamman*, representing something like a Teletubbies analogy of translocal practice replacing local processes of adaptation.

Bali and Lombok (historically and up until today) encountered different traveling musics and reacted differently to those musics, and local agents took different actions. Bali embraced select traveling musics from the West, from India, and from Java, though not from the Islamic world. Lombok embraced traveling musics from the Arab and Malay worlds, though not those originating in Europe or in the United States circulating globally.

Since it is located directly next to Java (as close as 2.4 kilometers), Bali received more Javanese (and Indic) influences, musics, and peoples through Java's Hindu-Buddhist years (until the fifteenth and sixteenth centuries).[13] These developments led to the formations of new gamelans, other performing arts, court ideologies, new ideas about caste, and so forth. Due to a variety of circumstances, Bali became somewhat isolated over the next few centuries from both the Javanese Islamic courts and the incursions of Dutch imperialism. Then, rather suddenly in the early twentieth century, soon after the Dutch crushed the last Balinese resistance (1908), the Western world discovered Bali and thrust upon it notions of exotic paradise. The twenty-first-century yoga and spa trend demonstrates that romantic essentializing is ongoing.

The early twentieth-century external focus on Bali ushered in one hundred years of first colonialism (until the mid-1940s) and then neocolonialism (post 1950), extensive tourism, romance, fantasizing, interaction, appropriation, collaboration, and change. The pattern for acculturating or assimilating the vast traveling musics coming to the island was a unique process of localization: of taking foreign sounds, incorporating them into gamelan elements, and essentially Balinizing them so that the original traveling sounds could no longer be heard. Over the last fifty years, globally circulating musics entered Bali en masse—first via pirated audiocassettes and underground scenes and then via the internet and social networking—capturing local imaginations in fresh ways, leading to hybrid formations (e.g., Balawan's music), and emulations of rock, metal, and punk, and then to localization of these forms and their subcultural positions of marginality and resistance. During the early part of the twenty-first century, translocal styles became more undifferentiated and less Balinized and new, more globally oriented Balinese took them as their own. During these same fifty years, Balinese musicians studied abroad and acquired new ideas to bring back to Bali, leading to the creation of the *musik kontemporer* avant-garde style, and collaborations with foreign artists inspired other new music and dance forms (see Harnish 2005).

Though the island nearly abuts Bali (about thirty-five kilometers away), Lombok's history and the processes for addressing traveling musics are entirely different. Lombok never was identified as a tropical paradise by Westerners, and tourism was muted and thus never had a large influx of Western influences; it has been a backwater area when compared to Bali and never received the attention and resources of the national government; and, importantly, Sasak society has not been accommodating to outsiders and practiced a religion (Islam), controlled by local religious leaders (*Tuan Guru*), that largely insulated Lombok from traveling sounds and ideas from outside the Malay/Islamic world. Javanese influence is apparent: rulers were often lesser siblings from families in Java, court systems were modeled on Javanese ideas, and Javanese-style Islam with Sufic roots was the first practiced. Javanese and then Balinese influences led to the developments of some gamelans, arts terminologies, and language (the "high" Sasak language); Bali remained as a cultural example of what Sasak leaders do *not* want Lombok to become (see Harnish 2011).

Traveling musics did enter Lombok, however, and local musicians did adapt ideas for their own use. Musics from the Arab world (perhaps via India or other Indonesian islands in some cases) initiated forms such as *zikrzamman*, musics from the greater Malay world created *kemidi rudat* (originating in Turkey) and others such as *nasyid*, and more popular forms came from Java (e.g., *dangdut*), which led to *dangdut* Sasak and influenced some of the developments of *lagu* Sasak and the social dance form *aleh-aleh*. Amaq Sadar enacted something that I had not seen before: he took a Bugis/Arab instrument (*gambus*) and used it not to further Islam in an Islamizing society, but to maintain an earlier folk tradition, rejecting the traveling sound world of the *gambus*. Meanwhile, though the desire and the marginality are there, the indie music scene is struggling to survive, and such styles as metal and punk are virtually nonexistent. The door to traveling musics is not closed in Lombok, though it is not as wide open as in Bali and it seems to be ajar solely toward the Arab and Malay worlds. Further, though it is a generalization, its people do not seem to be as passionate about musics in the world as contributing to their own identities. Music does not thrive quite like it does in Bali.

The developments on both islands are related to the cultural sensibilities of their peoples and the agencies of their leaders and musicians—and, of course, to those particular traveling musics that have come to their respective shores. Due to differing histories, the structures of their societies, the religious orientations of their peoples, and the strategies for managing new sounds (and the sources of those sounds), some traveling musics are ultimately adapted, others are emulated and often localized in a search for scenes, and still others are rejected. In both cases, these strategies for dealing with the greater world reflect their pasts and presents, characters, and identities of these respective peoples in Indonesia within the archipelago in island Southeast Asia.

Notes

1. Portuguese influence led directly to the formation of the early popular music *kroncong* (also the name of a small chordophone similar to 'ukulele) in coastal Indonesia. This style never became very popular in Bali or Lombok.

2. There seems to have always been a concern that Western popular musics and ideas (and lifestyles) would have too large an influence on Indonesian youth. Sukarno was also trying to balance leftist and rightist forces and tended to veer left.

3. This action did not at all undo radio censorship, which remained firmly in place to

monitor political, religious, and erotic expressions until Suharto's fall at the end of the 1990s.

4. The Javanese counterpart is *komposisi baru* (new compositions). Javanese and Balinese new music composers have sometimes collaborated or competed at events in Java.

5. Though Wallach was describing punk, the same ideas apply well to the other styles, particularly metal.

6. Moore's argument aligns with my contention that the Teletubbies in the early twenty-first century were indicative of unadulterated globalization—finding a cultural foothold on Bali disconnected with previous adaptation patterns or the "Balinizing" of external influences.

7. The stories consisted of the *Serat Menak,* a cycle of tales featuring Amir Hamza, the uncle of Prophet Muhammad.

8. This Sasak form developed out of *Komedie Stamboel* (*Stambul*, that is Turkish/Istanbul, commercial entertainment), with perhaps some elements of *rudat*, a dance widespread in the archipelago sometimes including Southeast Asian martial arts (*pencak silat*) movements.

9. I have heard of Sasak rock and reggae bands on Lombok's Gili islands (largely visited by partying tourists) but doubt that these bands could play in Lombok proper.

10. One of Nasib's musicians told me that the Western elements were meant to "spice up" (modernize) Sasak music. Nasib, who has an entrepreneurial spirit, may have had profit motive in mind as well.

11. See, for example, https://www.youtube.com/watch?v=r_ntJfw99yg.

12. Amaq Sadar and his host for our visit, Syaeffudin, informed me that *cilokaq* is taught in two schools of East Lombok, which demonstrates a commitment by some to maintain rural Sasak folk traditions.

13. There was a migration of Hindu Javanese, most of them privileged elite, during the late years of the Majapahit empire (collapsed around 1500) and the ensuing years.

References

Appadurai, Arjun. 1995. "The Production of Locality." In *Counterworks: Managing the Diversity of Knowledge*, ed. R. Fardon, 204–255. London: Routledge.

Bakan, Michael B. 1999. *Music of Death and New Creation: Experiences in the World of Balinese Gamelan Beleganjur.* Chicago: University of Chicago Press.

Barker, Chris. 2005. *Culture Studies: Theory and Practice.* London: Sage.

Baulch, Emma. 2007. *Making Scenes: Reggae, Punk, and Death Metal in 1990s Bali.* Durham, NC: Duke University Press.

Berg, Birgit. 2011. "'Authentic' Islamic Sound? Orkes Gambus Music, the Arab Idiom, and Sonic Symbols in Indonesian Islamic Musical Arts." In *Divine Inspirations: Music and Islam in Indonesia*, ed. D. Harnish and A. Rasmussen, 207–240. New York: Oxford University Press.

Capwell, Charles. 2011. "From 'Dust' to Platinum: Global Currents through the Malay World of Musical Islam." In *Divine Inspirations: Music and Islam in Indonesia*, ed. D. Harnish and A. Rasmussen, 197–206. New York: Oxford University Press.

Cohen, Matthew. 2006. *The Komedie Stamboel: Popular Theater in Colonial Indonesia 1891–1903.* Athens, OH: Ohio University Press.

Harnish, David. 1988. "Religion and Music: Syncretism, Orthodox Islam, and Musical Change in Lombok." *Selected Reports in Ethnomusicology* 7: 123–139.

———. 2000. "The World of Music Composition in Bali." *Journal of Musicological Research* 20: 1–40.

———. 2005. "Teletubbies in Paradise: Tourism, Indonesianization, and Modernization in Balinese Music." *Yearbook for Traditional Music* 37: 103–123.

———. 2011. "Tensions between Adat (Custom) and Agama (Religion) in the Music of Lombok." In *Divine Inspirations: Music and Islam in Indonesia*, ed. D. Harnish and A. Rasmussen, 80–108. New York: Oxford University Press.

———. 2013. "The Hybrid Music and Cosmopolitan Scene of Balinese Guitarist I Wayan Balawan." *Ethnomusicology Forum* 22, no. 2: 188–209.

Harnish, David, and Jeremy Wallach. 2013. "'Dance to Your Roots': Genre Fusions in the Music of Indonesia's Krakatau." *Asian Music* 44, no. 2: 115–134.

McGraw, Andrew. 2012. "The Ambivalent Freedoms of Indonesian Jazz." *Jazz Perspectives* 6, no. 3: 273–310.

———. 2013. *Radical Traditions: Reimaging Culture in Balinese Contemporary Music.* New York: Oxford University Press.

Moore, Rebekah. 2015. "Indie Music in Post-Bomb Bali: Participant Practices, Scene Subjectivities." PhD dissertation, Indiana University.

Murphy, David. 2013. *Longing for the Past: The 78 RPM Era in Southeast Asia.* Memphis, TN: Dust to Digital.

Sutton, R. Anderson. 2010. "Gamelan Encounters with Hybridism." *Journal of Popular Music Studies* 22, no. 2: 180.

Tenzer, Michael. 2000. *Gamelan Gong Kebyar: The Art of Twentieth-Century Balinese Music.* Chicago: University of Chicago Press.

Turino, Thomas. 2000. *Nationalists, Cosmopolitanisms, and Popular Music in Zimbabwe.* Chicago: University of Chicago Press.

Wallach, Jeremy. 2008a. "Living the Punk Lifestyle in Jakarta." *Ethnomusicology* 52, no. 1: 98–116.

———. 2008b. *Modern Noise, Fluid Genres: Popular Music in Indonesia, 1997–2001.* Madison: University of Wisconsin Press.

Weintraub, Andrew N. 2010. *Dangdut Stories: A Social and Musical History of Indonesia's Most Popular Music.* New York: Oxford University Press.

CHAPTER 4

"Molihua"

CULTURE AND MEANING OF CHINA'S MOST WELL-TRAVELED FOLKSONG

Frederick Lau

THE American saxophonist Kenny G is no stranger to contemporary Chinese audiences.[1] A generation of Chinese has grown up listening to his music on the internet, in live concerts, and through various legal and sometimes illegal channels since the 1990s. Of his voluminous musical output, his 1989 instrumental hit "Going Home" is perhaps the most well-known piece in present-day China. This song is often blasted through speakers in public places such as shopping malls, schools, train stations, gyms, and marketplaces at the end of each day to signal the closing of the venue or ending of an event, or simply telling people it is time to leave. This phenomenon of inscribing new meaning to existing music prompted *New York Times* writer Dan Levin to write an article with the whimsical title "China Says Goodbye in the Key of G: Kenny G" (Levin 2014).

What is fascinating about this phenomenon is not so much that the Chinese fall in love with American tunes, as evidenced in the lingering popularity of John Denver's "Take Me Home, Country Roads"[2] and Céline Dion's "My Heart Will Go On."[3] Rather, it is the propensity of traveling music to acquire new, shared meanings about what these songs stand for in the Chinese soundscape that merits our attention. How does a simple tune become so familiar and acquire such powerful meanings when it is adopted by a new culture? What are the conditions that necessitate the process of inscription, and why? Clearly, the Chinese audience heard "Going Home" very differently than the American audience did. Prompted by the title, the Chinese interpreted "Going Home" as "it is time to go home from work." Consequently, instead of focusing on Kenny G's musicality, command of the saxophone, and signature timbre, listeners hear a contextualized signal to disperse. In this sense, Kenny G's sonic utterances were resignified through the filters of Chinese ears and social milieu and the cultural ethos of the new millennium. Understanding the Chinese meanings of

"Going Home" cannot be separated from the sentiments and desires of 1990s China at a time when the country was eager to embrace Western culture and values to fill the void after decades of isolation from the rest of the world due to the Cultural Revolution (Rofel 2007). Exploring how music travels and is adopted by another culture requires comprehending the cultural logic and tension of time, place, history, and politics, and music as a means for drawing people into a network of cultural circulation, imagination, and desire.

This article tracks the journey of a Han Chinese folksong through different times and spaces. Widely known as "Jasmine, "Jasmine Flower," or simply "Molihua," this folksong is perhaps one of China's most well known and frequently traveled folksongs inside and outside China to date. Its popularity is seen in its frequent appearance in traditional Chinese and international music concert circuits, concerts by pop bands and solo singers, scholarly debates, new choral arrangements, and state-sponsored events as an emblem of national pride. Like Kenny G's "Going Home" in China, "Molihua" has come to mean different things as it moves across different cultural and temporal and domains. The parallels between their journeys are striking. But it also highlights the peculiar multidirectional impact of globalization that involves movements of cultural commodity from the center to the margin and vice versa as in the case of Kenny G in China and "Molihua" in the West.

The version of "Molihua" that most people know today is one of many versions of the song with the same title. The folksong was first documented in staff notation in the late eighteenth century by John Barrow (1764–1848), an assistant to the British diplomat George Macartney (1737–1806). Barrow recorded this piece and presented it and his personal impression about Chinese music in his book *Travels in China* (Barrow [1804] 2010). The piece began to circulate in Europe, and in 1924 Giacomo Puccini (1858–1924) incorporated it in his opera *Turandot*. Consequently, this version of the tune made a grand entrance onto the world stage and gained widespread international popularity. Since then, "Molihua" has emerged not only as the best-known Chinese folksong abroad; its global fame has also prompted Chinese musicians, composers, and cultural workers to view it as a significant national musical and cultural icon in China. The tune's multiple existence and image is subject to what I call the politics of desire and imagination. It is a process that engages the production of new subjectivity, construction of ethnicity, articulation of difference, and the formation of nationhood. Music is one of several important cultural sites in which desire and imagination are crystalized in practice. In this chapter, I explore these processes and conditions that enabled a little-known Chinese folksong to travel so widely and assume such an influential status. Why and how did the circulation of the tune, in turn, impact the culture that produced it?

The national and international notoriety of "Molihua" demonstrates a cultural phenomenon in existence long before Appadurai's concept of cultural flow was in vogue and cultural hybridity was celebrated as the coming of age of cosmopolitanism and a trademark of the millennium lifestyle (Appadurai 1996; Turino 2000). Musical exchange between China and the outside world can be dated to as early as the Tang dynasty (618–907) with the arrival of Nestorian Christian hymns (Tao 1994, 2). The adoption of early Christian culture and music signified the greatness of the Tang empire through accepting outsiders rather than the Tang succumbing to the pressure of outsiders. With the increasing number of missionaries coming to China, more and more European music was brought in not only for religious purposes but also for the expansion and building of European empires. Based on this historical foundation, the gravitation toward "Molihua" by insiders and outsiders calls attention to what Radano and Olaniyan succinctly describe as the audibility of music as components in a process of modernization: "Critical musical practices (and, indeed, the very activity of critical listening to radical art) are never simply and merely oppositional. What Richard Middleton names 'the voice of the people' was and is 'constitutive of modernity itself (modernity as it actually developed), its role not only reactive but also productive…'" (Radano and Olaniyan 2016, 9). It is by focusing on how and why sound is produced and heard that one can pinpoint the conditions and social dynamics that enable the formation of auditory culture.

Following their theoretical insights, I focus on four stops along the journey of "Molihua" to examine how this folksong has been reconstituted, utilized, resignified, and capitalized on in various contexts. I want to highlight the waves that underpinned the piece's consumption and production in order to reveal the complexity between cultural contexts and types of knowledge, agency, and power that shaped the meaning of each of its manifestations. In the following, I first describe the origin and brief history of the folksong "Molihua" before moving on to describe the circumstance behind the ascendance of "Molihua" onto the global stage. In the last part of the essay, I outline the elevation of "Molihua" as an emblem of national pride back home and its frequent appearance and veneration on the national stage, which is no doubt inspired by its international fame and recognition. Then, I delve into the interest that Chinese musicians and scholars have shown in this tune and explore possible reasons for the intensity of their interest. I suggest that the fascinating journey of "Molihua" as a traveling music tacitly enshrines and affirms it as one of the greatest pieces of Chinese music. By analyzing its changing image and reception, I argue that a shifting meaning of "Molihua" is predicated on what it represents against cultural expectations, history, desire, imagination, and the ever-changing economic and political relationship of China to the rest of the world.

In the Beginning: "Molihua" and Regional Identity

"Molihua" originated as a folksong from East Central China in Jiangsu and Zhejiang Province, around the city of Shanghai, Suzhou, and Hangzhou. In popular perception, this regional folksong (*difang minge*) has become a significant and powerful icon of regional *jiangnan* (south of the Yangtze River) identity. It is not surprising that many Chinese can hum a few measures of this song or at least have heard the name, which is the same as one of the popular green teas in southern China. Similar to the history of many Chinese regional folksongs, the exact origin of "Molihua" is unknown. However, based on textual evidence, some scholars speculate that it first appeared during the Qing dynasty (1644–1911).

Also known as *Xianhuadiao* (Fresh Flower Melody), "Molihua" belongs to the Han Chinese folksong tune type called *xiaoqu* or *xiaodiao* (small song or short melody): usually multistanza in form and with uniform phrase structures and equal numbers of words. Based on their study of the lyrics and content, some scholars surmise that this type of song has an even longer history that precedes the Qing dynasty (Zhongguo Yinyue Chubanshe Bianjibu 1985, 272). As a folksong found across the country, "Xianhuadiao" or "Molihua" exists in many regional variations, each bearing certain music characteristics resemblance to the core *xiaodiao* musical and structural features but with influences based on regional flavors at the local musical level (ibid.).

According to Jiang Mingdun, a scholar of Chinese folksong, the basic structure of "Molihua" is made up of a simple four-line stanza, based on the traditional Chinese musical structural ideal of *qi-cheng-zhuan-he*, roughly translated as (1) *qi-* introduction, (2) *cheng-* continuation, (3) *zhuan-* transition, and (4) *he-* synthesis. According to ethnomusicologist Alan Thrasher, this principle is the guiding principle employed in traditional literature and poetry (Thrasher 2008, 123). But he also warned that this pattern is mostly an ideal, and it is often unclear how it is employed in actual practice. This basic formal structure of "Molihua" is contested by its variations in other regions and this structural ideal cannot always convincingly explain many versions of the song.

In northern China, this tune is sometimes called "Lameihua" (Waxed Plum Blossom) or "Yumeihua" (Jade Plum Blossom). The melody of the southern variant is generally conjunct and stepwise, conforming to the overall stereotypical lyrical quality of music from southern China. The melodic contour of the northern variations, on the other hand, is disjunct and contains big leaps. Jiang claims that because the northern songs are used to accompany dancing, the northern melody is generally more rhythmic than the southern version (Jiang 1982, 237). It is also sometimes absorbed into regional song and dance form such as *yangge* (field songs) or Southwest *huadangdiao* (lantern songs) and as instrumental pieces in narrative genres (ibid.).

Besides melodic differences, the southern and northern variations of this song also differ in terms of the lyrics and content. The northern versions tell a longer story and its content varied from place to place. Some stories were taken from literary classics such as *Xixiangji* (Romance of the Western Chamber)[4] or the *Shuihuzhuang* (Water Margin),[5] one of the four great Chinese novels from the sixteenth century. For example, the version of "Molihua" in the Changli area of Hebei Province differs from its southern counterpart by containing more melodic embellishments that accommodate longer phrases and extra words and passages. Since it is a genre in the northern part of the country, it adopts a musical style in line with the typical northeastern music style, which is livelier and rhythmic and contains disjunct melodies. Some versions contain more padding notes to accommodate more words and melismatic passages in order to enhance dramatic effect. Despite their origin and structural similarity, different versions of "Molihua" have been used as icons of regional identity and style.

In the past, both northern and southern versions of "Molihua" have served as icons of regional identity and style, but the ten-line stanza format found in the south has been incorporated as a national icon because of its association with the Han majority. In the discourse of Chinese ethnicities, the Han consider themselves as the dominant group above other minority groups, and Han culture is often portrayed as a uniform entity and superior. This monolithic narrative not only buttresses the Han-centric ethos of the empire; it also reinforces the predominance of Han music over the music of other groups. "Molihua" has been skillfully inserted into the Han narrative as a symbolic strategy to reaffirm the superiority of the Han majority over the ethnic minority, who were traditionally known in China as "barbarians." Versions of this song have been included in textbooks, popular songbooks, scholarly publications, and popular entertainment. The cultural regime of knowledge that codifies "Molihua" is too obvious to ignore.

Within China, "Molihua" represents regional identity and has become the source of many new musical creations. In a European context, the song's image and flavor was drastically transformed.

European Exotic Gaze on "Molihua"

Before the nineteenth century, European knowledge about Chinese music was rather scanty. Fragmented accounts of Chinese music were mostly documented by missionaries, diplomatic convoys, explorers, scholars, and travelers whose views were inevitably framed by European musical ideals, aesthetics, and cultural stereotypes of the time (Tao 1994). Starting with the Jesuit priest Matteo Ricci (1552–1610) during the beginning of the seventeenth century, missionaries and priests often reported on Chinese music after their visits to China and especially about their interaction with the Chinese imperial court. One of the earlier tunes that Europeans encountered was a folksong titled "Chinese Air" contained in French philosopher Jean-Jacques Rousseau's *Complete Dictionary of Music* (1768). This so-called folksong was collected in China by the French Jesuit missionary Joseph-Marie Amiot (1718–1793) and also subsequently published in a book by another Jesuit priest, Jean-Baptiste du Halde (1674–1743), who compiled an encyclopedia of the history, culture, and society of the country. The irony is that du Halde never set foot in China, yet few questioned the tune's authenticity, accuracy, and reliability.

Among the European accounts of Chinese music, the most reliable ones were recorded by Jesuit priests Matteo Ricci and Jean-Joseph-Marie Amiot, who spent a considerable amount of time in China. Ricci was often credited as the first Jesuit priest to introduce Western music to China by offering Western instruments to Qing emperor Kangxi (1654–1722) and subsequently bringing Chinese music to Europe. Despite his evangelical mission, Ricci opened the first door in educating Europeans about Chinese culture, music, and science. The other significant contribution was made by Amiot, who was sent as a missionary to China in 1750. While in China, he was able to live at the Qing court and was believed to have been close to Emperor Qianlong (1711–1799). Among Amiot's writings, his *Mémoires concernant l'histoire, les sciences et les arts des Chinois* (1776–1791) (Memoirs Concerning the History, Sciences, and Arts of the Chinese) is perhaps one of the most influential sources on Chinese music of the time.

The focus of these early reports was unique and largely on theoretical matters, temperaments, acoustics, and issues related to music as science rather than on presenting the actual music or musical practices. This partial view of music prompted Meredith Schweig to remark, "In the European imagination, 'Chinese music' became a unified concept that belied the many regional, historical, and functional differences among the various musical traditions practiced in China" (Schweig 2013). Consequently, the idea that there is only one type of Chinese music was perpetuated in Europe. This essentializing view gave a false impression of Chinese music as monolithic and bounded, something easily grasped and readily quantified (ibid.). This view has become a false premise for all music from China, including the tune "Molihua."

The story of "Molihua" in Europe provides another aspect of how this song is being viewed and understood. In 1792, the British empire appointed diplomat George Macartney (1737–1806) to lead the first convoy to China in order to promote trade with the Chinese Qing government. Macartney led the first convoy to Beijing in 1792 with a large British delegation on board a sixty-four-gun man-of-war, the HMS *Lion*. Although the embassy was ultimately not successful in achieving its primary aim to open trade with China, numerous unexpected benefits were attained, including firsthand assessment of the strength of the Chinese empire and its people and culture, and an in-person meeting between Macartney with the Qianlong emperor. This encounter paved the way for the British Empire to consolidate its power in setting up treaty ports in places such as Shanghai, Canton, Amoy, Ningbo, and Hong Kong during the nineteenth century.

After making a journey to Beijing, Macartney embarked on a journey traveling from the capital to the southern seaport of Canton (Guangdong Province) in order to survey the potential for setting up trading opportunities. He was accompanied by his assistant John Barrow (1764–1848), who was a comptroller of the convoy attached to the first British embassy to China from 1792–1794. After the completion of the trip, Barrow returned to London and in 1804 published his famous *Travels in China*, in which he recorded his impressions along the way. In this fascinating travelogue, he provided vivid descriptions of all aspects of life, culture, and ritual in China. In addition to describing what he saw, Barrow also provided commentary. His remarks toward ethnic others are informative and revealing of the Eurocentric biases of the time.

Barrow's view on Chinese music was not flattering. He went to great lengths to describe the different instruments, from percussion to string instruments, and point out the differences between the sounds produced in Chinese and European music. Without referring to specific pieces of music, he states that "the merit of a performance should seem to consist in the intenseness of the noise brought out of the different instruments" (Barrow [1804] 2010, 314). He continues to say, "Their (Chinese) instruments, it is true, are sufficiently varied, both as to shape and materials, but I know of none that is even tolerable to a European ear" (ibid., 315). In chapter 20 of his book, he further denigrates Chinese music by describing it as unscientific and a commodity: "It [music] does not seem to be cultivated as a science: it is neither learned as an elegant accomplishment, nor practiced as an amusement of genteel life, except by those females who are educated for sale, or by such as hire themselves out for the entertainment of those who may be inclined to purchase their favours" (ibid., 313).

Barrow further bemoans the lack of emotion in performance in a reference to "Molihua": "I never heard but one single Chinese who could be said to sing with feeling or plaintiveness. Accompanied with a kind of guitar, he sung the following air in praise of the flower *Moo-lee*, which it seems, is one of the most popular songs in the whole country. The simple melody was taken down by Mr. Hittner, and I understand has been published in London, with head and tail-pieces, accompaniments, and all the refined arts of European music; so that it

316 TRAVELS IN CHINA.

China. I have therefore given it in its unadorned ſtate, as ſung and played by the Chineſe, together with the words of the firſt ſtanza, and their literal tranſlation.

MOO-LEE-WHA.

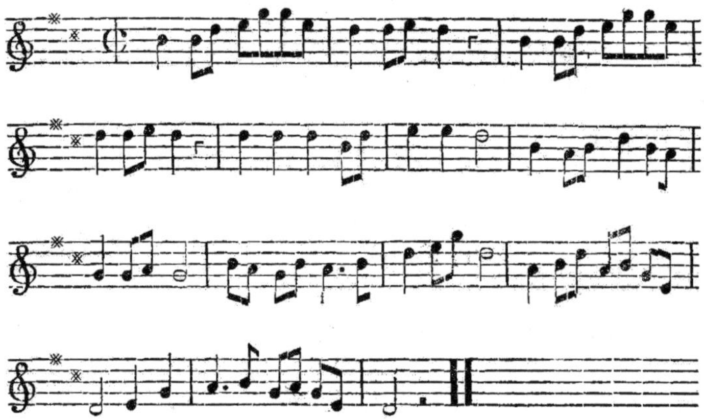

MOO-LEE-WHA.

I.

[1]Hau [2]ye-[3]to [4]ſien [5]wha,
[6]Yeu [7]tchau [8]yeu [9]jie [10]lo [11]tſai [12]go [13]kia
[14]Go [15]pun [16]tai, [17]poo [18]tchoo [19]mun
[20]Twee [21]tcho [22]ſien [23]wha [24]ul [25]lo.

II.

(a)

Figure 4.1 (a, b) Music of "Molihua" from Barrow ([1804] 2010).

II.

[1]Hau [2]ye [3]to [4]Moo-[5]lee [6]wha
[7]Man [8]yuen [9]wha [10]kai [11]ſoy [12]poo [13]quee [14]ta
[15]Go [16]pun [17]tai [18]tſai [19]ye [20]ta
[21]Tai [22]you [23]kung [24]kan [25]wha [26]jin [27]ma.

Literal Tranſlation.

I.

How [1]delightful [2]this [3]branch of [4]freſh [5]flowers
[6]One [7]morning [8]one [9]day it was [10]dropped [11]in [12]my [13]houſe
[14]I the [15]owner will [16]wear it [17]not [18]out of [19]doors
[20]But I [21]will hold the [22]freſh [23]flower [24]and be [25]happy.

II.

How [1]delightful [2]this [3]branch of the *[4]Moo-[5]lee* [6]flower
In the [7]full [8]plot of [9]flowers [10]blowing [11]freely [12]none [13]excels [14]it
[15]I the [16]owner will [17]wear [19]this [18]gathered [20]branch
[21]Wear it [22]yet [23]fear, the [25]flower [24]ſeen, [25]men will [27]envy.

I have thought it not amiſs to ſubjoin a few other airs of the popular kind, which were written by the ſame gentleman at Canton, who made the drawings of their muſical inſtruments.

I

(b)

ceases to be a specimen of the plain melody of China. I have therefore given it in its unadorned state, as sung and played by the Chinese, together with the words of the first stanza, and their literal translation" (ibid., 316). Ironically, Barrow's less than complimentary remarks didn't damage the reputation of "Molihua." In 1884, this tune began to appear in a Japanese music anthology called *The Music Notation of Ocean and Mountain* as the Japanese elite considered Chinese music and especially music of the Ming and Qing dynasties (*Minxingaku*) as a product of high cultural value. Many Japanese were learning the Chinese instrument *genkkin* (*yueqin*, a round-bodied plucked lute from China) to indicate their taste and class. The popularity of "Molihua" not only grew overseas, it also caught the attention of the imperial Qing court. In 1896 the song was used as a temporary national anthem by the Qing Chinese officials in Europe almost a quarter century before Puccini incorporated it in his opera *Turandot*.

"Molihua" and the Emergence of "Great Nation"

Beginning in the latter part of the twentieth century, the image and function of "Molihua" changed drastically. In contemporary China, this regional folksong has ascended to a status that no one could have ever anticipated. The once humble folksong, viewed as a marker of regional identity in traditional China and an object of exotic gaze in the eyes of eighteenth-century Europeans, has been transformed into an iconic symbol of the Chinese nation in contemporary China. Obviously this is a big leap for "Molihua," and it didn't happen in a vacuum (Melvin 2016).

The reputation of "Molihua" as a song known in Europe, used by the famous opera composer Puccini in his world-renowned opera and recorded in many overseas publications, inadvertently raised the song's value. Soon after Puccini's opera *Turandot*, the composers Herbert Stothart and Edward Ward used "Molihua" in the Hollywood movie *The Good Earth* (1937), based on American novelist Pearl Buck's *The Good Earth*, which won a Pulitzer Prize in 1932. In the film, the tune "Molihua" seemed to conjure up the majestic notion of family and the ethics of hard work and honesty, quintessential virtues of Confucianism.

In the new millennium, "Molihua" has become a popular tune that many musicians and composers like to incorporate into their work. One only needs to search the internet for the title "Molihua" to know that there are many hits with this name. In 2006, the song was elevated even higher and secured a place as intangible cultural heritage on a UNESCO list of recommended songs together with a few traditional pieces of the *guqin*, an instrument of the literati (Ying 2008). The fate of "Molihua" seemed to shift into high gear toward the end of the twentieth century, when composer Tan Dun was commissioned before 1997 to write a symphony to commemorate Hong Kong's rejoining China as a special administrative region. In his 1997 "Heaven, Sky, Man" symphony, he chose "Molihua" in addition to using local Hong Kong musical material, bronze bell, and other Chinese musical elements as the basis of his composition. Although the collage nature of this piece was obvious to many Chinese listeners, the meaning and symbolism of the adopted music material was controversial. Critics felt that the dominance of the People's Republic of China government over the former colony was symbolically inscribed through "Molihua" playing above and on top of the other musical material (Yu 2004).

International exposure for "Molihua" doesn't stop here. At the closing ceremony of the 2004 Summer Olympics in Athens, when Beijing was introduced as the host of the 2008 Olympic Games, the Chinese team launched into an elaborate and spectacular performance using "Molihua" as the centerpiece together with other Chinese dances and traditional musics (Price and Dayan 2008, 202). At the 2008 Beijing Olympic Games, Tan Dun again was chosen among many nominations to compose music for the ceremonies. He and another composer, Wang Hesheng, again adapted "Molihua" as the basis of the piece. In this piece, the tune was played on ancient bronze bells and jade chimes in order to imitate the instruments used in ancient court ritual orchestra. According to Tan, who remarked at a press conference to announce his chosen piece, "'Molihua' is such an iconic piece it is almost a cultural symbol of China, so everybody thought it was a great choice" (Cui 2008). He went on to say that "From Puccini to the Beijing Olympics, this melody is a gift from the Chinese people to the world's athletes." Tan, whose opera *Tea: A Mirror of Soul* (2002) made its Chinese debut in Beijing in 2008, said he was looking forward to his music being a key for the world to understand Chinese philosophy. A four-part composition, co-written by Tan and Wang Hesheng, a composer with the army orchestra, would be played before, during, and after each of the 302 medal ceremonies. The main melody, which Tan described as "glorious, heartwarming and full of respect," was recorded using the digital recording of a 2,450-year-old bell set excavated from a site in Hubei. The organizer of the head of the Beijing Organizing Committee for the Olympic Games' culture and ceremonies department Zhao Dongming even stated that "Molihua" was selected as the music for the medal ceremonies from more than four thousand pieces submitted over the previous four years by amateur and professional composers from around the world, saying: "This piece of music reminds you of the gold medals for the Beijing Olympics, which are made of gold and jade" (Cui 2008). The same piece of music was reorchestrated as a piano showpiece performed by the internationally famous Chinese pianist Lang Lang (b. 1982) at another high-profile international event the 2010 Shanghai Expo opening ceremony.

With all the international attention given to "Molihua," famous Chinese soprano Song Zuying (b. 1966), who is well known for singing in the traditional Chinese style, decided to use the name "Molihua" as the theme of her 2006 solo Kennedy Center concert in Washington, DC. She called her concert "What a Beautiful Jasmine" (*Haoyiduo meilide Molihua*), which is the first line of the song. Her promotional video proudly announced: "She came from the East and she came from China. She has a sweet voice to sing praises to the glory of the great nation. She has a great smile for people who are moved by today's China. Let's come together to share this glorious moment." Here the singer, her glorious voice, her country, and what she represented were all conflated in the notion of the jasmine flower via "Molihua."

While the meaning of "Molihua" was becoming more nationalistic, a small episode about this tune adds another dimension to the story about "Molihua." The 2010 Tunisian Revolution was called the Jasmine Revolution by the media. During the uprising, President Zine El Abidine Ben Ali was forced out by popular protests. Inspired by the events in Tunisia, in 2011 the pro-democracy protestors in China dubbed their protest as the Jasmine Revolution. Although the protest was quickly squelched, the term "Jasmine Revolution" was immediately banned from the Chinese internet. A quick search on the internet in Chinese for "Hu Jintao sings 'Mo Li Hua'" turns up video posted long before the Tunisian unrest, showing the Chinese president (from 2003 to 2013) singing along with a group of African performers, then telling them how important the song is where he comes from (Scocca 2011). However, a video featuring the Vienna Boys Choir singing "Molihua" was banned in China, although it is still in circulation outside China. It was thought that the government at that time did not want the association of "Jasmine" with revolution to be advertised as an example to inspire any social unrest in China.

Validation by outsiders not only expanded the reputation of "Molihua" but also symbolically transformed it from being a regional folksong to national music that everyone should know, admire, and treasure. This form of resignification and meaning inscription is precisely what Lisa Rofel argues is at the core of China's contingent, piece-by-piece reconfiguration of its relationship to a postsocialist world (Rofel 2007). The desire of creating and constructing of new subjectivity is part of the process of negotiating what it means to be modern and cosmopolitan in the new millennium.

"Molihua": Topic of Intense Research and Scholarly Debate

The recent hype about "Molihua" doesn't stop with composers and performers. It has also ignited the interest of scholars and students of Chinese music inside China, as evidenced by the recent publication of articles, MA theses, and PhD dissertations focusing on this tune. Many of these scholarly works examine the melody, lyrics, structural semantics, and melodic content in order to ascertain the authentic origins of this tune.

In these works, scholars have gathered a treasure trove of information about the tune. Unbeknownst to John Barrow, we now know that the earliest "Molihua" lyrics appeared during the Ming dynasty Wanli period (1563–1620). Despite this written documentation, "Molihua" remained mostly as a regional folksong. Interestingly, scholars who have studied the lyrics tend to view it as a piece of folk literature and focus entirely on the poetry and its structure. They rarely mention the melody, let alone the version that John Barrow collected.

On the issue of authenticity, much of the debate has centered on the question of whether "Molihua" and another tune called "Fresh Flower Song" (or "Fresh Flower Tune") actually belong to the same genre of "small song" (*xiaodiao*). As it was widely agreed that the melodic structures of the *xiaodiao* rely on simplicity and repetition, scholars in this debate ignore the melodic similarity of the two tunes and instead raise questions about minute details of textual difference, the choice of words, and their overall implication as a way to bolster their arguments.

Another thread of the debate is about whether these two songs are in fact variations of the same original tune. Some scholars argue that from 1940 on, this tune has been popular and widely used in regional narrative genres such as *Yangzhou qingqu* (plain singing from Yangzhou), *Suzhou pingtan* (narrative singing from Suzhou), *Nanjing Baiju* (Nanjing White Bureau), *Xuzhou qinshu* (*qin* and book narration from Xuzhou), *Yangju* (opera from Yangzhou), *Xiju* (Wuxi opera), and possibly a very localized musical theater called *Dahuagu* (striking the flower drum) (Li 2009). However, an earlier textual record presents conflicting evidence. The Ming dynasty writer Feng Menglong (1574–1646) edited an anthology of folksong lyrics that includes a song called "Guazhier" (Hanging Branches), and some scholars claim the lyrics in this version bear resemblance to the lyrics found in the current version of "Molihua," especially in the use of expressions such as "hands to pick a flower" and jasmine flowers to represent love or friendship. Following age-old literary tradition, the reference to lyrics is further explored. Another report mentions that the lyrics of "Molihua" resemble the words of a song that appeared in a Qing dynasty anthology of opera scripts, *Chuobaiqiu* (Stitching a Fur Coat). In volume 6, chapter 1, the song "Huagu" (Flower Drum) contains twelve verses, and the first three sentences contain words that are identical to one version of the current song. These studies not only verify the history of "Molihua," they also reaffirm the longevity of Han culture across time and space (Li 2009; Huang 2006; Xian 2012).

Perhaps the most interesting development regarding "Molihua" is the attempt to recast the meaning of the song. While most scholars agree that the original function of the tune is as a courting song and its meaning a metaphor for love, in recent years there has been a new interpretation of the lyrics. Curiously, some writers ascribe the meaning of the song to the recent PRC government's political anticorruption movement. In one newspaper article, the writer declares that this tune can be dated back to the beginning of the Ming dynasty and is closely related to the first emperor, Zhu Yuanzhang (1328–1398), and his high officials (Chen 2014). According to the author, this tune was purportedly created in a social gathering of a few high officials as a lament to the anxiety and atmosphere created by Emperor Zhu's way of ruling the nation. The article reports that when Emperor Zhu came to power, he was determined to consolidate his power by creating a regime free of corruption with strict rules and ruled by an iron fist, thus creating an atmosphere of fear among his officials. According to this account, it was during a court gathering that this song was created to express the officials' anxiety and as a reminder against corruption. The author corresponds the three kinds of flower in the lyrics to fame, greed, and power. He further suggests that the phonetic approximation of *moli* represents the expression "not to have greed." Although the author doesn't provide any evidence for his interpretation, it is intriguing to connect the timing of this publication to the current wave of anticorruption championed by the PRC government since the 2000s (Chen 2014; Wang 2014; Anonymous 2014).

Multifaceted "Molihua"

The above discussion provides four contexts for "Molihua" as it traveled through various cultural and political terrains. What the tune signifies in each case is heavily shaped by the unique social formation and cultural references of the time and place. Taken as a whole, the changing meaning of "Molihua" parallels the changing status of China in relationship to the outside world as China has transformed itself from being a player on the margins of European power and eventually into the center stage of a great nation. The amazing journey of "Molihua" from being an object of a Western exotic gaze to becoming a respected icon of the nation is a big leap. The tune itself has become the very substance through which this transformation is heard and realized. This speaks to the power of music as an agent for change as opposed to the pure aesthetic view that some modern-day composers and musicians continue to uphold. All contributors to this volume succinctly argue that music is about more than aesthetic enjoyment; it is entangled with its environment in complicated ways. As "Molihua" travels, its meaning is transformed, its modality is altered, and its tonality is modulated beyond its once delimited identity as a regional folksong. Puccini's adaptation of it in his opera provided the final push it took for it to attain global fame and set the course for its ensuing journey. The impact of the tune's newfound reputation is perhaps felt more strongly back in China than elsewhere. Recognition by powerful outsiders provided a much-needed validation for the nation to reconcile with its shameful defeat by Europeans in the geopolitical struggles on Chinese soil during the nineteenth and twentieth centuries. The worldwide acceptance of "Molihua" has turned into a national badge of honor for China to finally prove to the world that China is equal to other foreign powers through the strength of its culture. "Molihua" changed China as much as the world because of the song's flexible ability to capture, imagine, and project meaning (Radano and Olaniyan 2016).

Music has been carried from place to place and performed by itinerant musicians for centuries. In modern times, music's movement and traveling is further enhanced by mass communication: recording technology, social media, the internet, and digital mobile technology. These various channels allow music to flow across oceans, borders of nation-states, and chasms between cultural differences in great speed. When "Molihua" travels, it takes root in foreign soil with its identity altered and its intonations changed. Audiences hear it differently because the habits of listening indigenous to each place are anchored in the cultural practices and struggles of the place and time (Ochoa 2015).

In China, when "Molihua" is presented as the tune of the nation in various national and international state-sponsored events and performances, its meaning is channeled through its history and locality and its aurality is predetermined by the context. The sound of "Molihua" creates and is created by both the nation and locality. It is therefore not surprising to note that before the creation of the national anthem in the Republic era and for the PRC, "Molihua" was used in a meeting in Europe in the late nineteenth century by members of the Qing court because there is no national anthem for imperial China and the idea of a national anthem came with the emergence of the nation-state. It was only after the establishment of the Republic of China that China began to have its national anthem. The first Chinese anthem, "Three Principles of the People," was put in place in the late 1920s. Perhaps this is the reason that prompted composer Tan Dun to choose "Molihua" as the theme for his composition for the Olympic medal ceremonies. Tan remarked that since "Molihua" is such an iconic piece, it is almost a cultural symbol of China (Cui 2008). Thus, it is logical that he chose it as the basis of his composition.

This sentiment is not unique to Tan but to others as well. The linking of "Molihua" to China is most obvious in the promotional video of singer Song Zuying. Although Chinese audiences recognize it as a folksong, it has nevertheless been elevated to the level of a cultural icon of the nation, similar to the emergence of Peking opera as the opera of the nation. The channel that allows these transformations is complex. One thing that is certain is that the tune's ability to travel enables it to garner energy and tap into structures of feeling in various historical moments. In each context, it is changed and reborn as a new entity. Tracking traveling music requires paying close attention to the cultural environments, social expectations, values, histories, and racial politics of time and place (Gopinath and Stanyek 2014).

A main reason why "Molihua" was able to develop into a de facto national anthem is closely related to the formation of China as a modern nation-state. At the end of the nineteenth century, China embarked on its modernization project. The strategy was to introduce Western learning or *xixue*, institutions, and knowledge into China in order to bring China up to the level of foreign countries. According to this logic, to be modern required new approaches to culture, education, and the nation. Under the new thinking, music practice and performance underwent transformations. A national music curriculum was put in place, and a new national conservatory was established in 1927 in Shanghai. Western music was taught as part of the newly introduced school education system. Along with these new establishments were new music curricula, uniform performing techniques, new songs and pieces for schools, and an entirely new attitude toward performance. It was in this spirit that folksongs were arranged, standardized, and codified to be incorporated into classroom material (Liu 1992; Melvin and Cai 2004). The journey of "Molihua" to fame coincided with the nation's push to be modern. For a nation-state to be modern, it needed to have its own standardized music. "Molihua" fit the bill. This song was collected in children's songbooks and taught in schools. Its popularity also prompted the Shanghai record companies EMI and Pathe to record the song in the 1920s. As a song that stemmed from the folk tradition but was standardized and uniform, China's "Molihua" rode the waves of the social dynamics of the time to allow the nation to have its own modern music.

As we approach the latest journey of its travel, we return to the central question of why this humble folksong can have the power to incite group sentiment. There is no simple answer to this question. It is perhaps that this song is a simple song with a catchy melody and a uniform structure. Perhaps it is that this song is able to access a collective sentiment linking people to the nation. In my opinion, it is a combination of factors, and the most important is that it has been disseminated through schools, is alive and well among the general public, and is hugely popular in the West. Together, these factors created a snowball effect and circular process in consolidating its reputation to the point that "Molihua" can now stand as an icon of the successful new nation, and its melody is well known among audiences at home and worldwide. Its charm rests on its tacit power to speak the unspoken by giving voice to collective national memory and transcending the humiliations of the past.

The song's journey speaks to the power of music to narrate social and political orders. Music is an essential sign vehicle to impose and affirm cultural difference, social hierarchy, and political dominance. In following the changing meaning of "Molihua," we begin to track how music is circulated and consumed as it travels through specific logics of time, place, politics, and imagination. To understand traveling music as a process rather than a product, we need to focus on cultural frameworks that affect music's existence, creativity, and consumption rather than on the celebration of the global flow of music and commodities as a condition of a world cosmopolitan millennial culture. If Kenny G's "Going Home" can lead a totally new life in China, it is obvious that "Molihua" can continue its journey at home or elsewhere and live on forever in its multiple unrealized possibilities. Like waves, music churns and rumbles incessantly, creating new points of impact as it travels.

Notes

1. Kenny G (b. 1956 as Kenneth Gorelick), American saxophonist, was born and raised in Seattle. He is well known for his playing style and compositions. His sixth studio album, *Breathless* (1992), became the number one best-selling instrumental album ever, with more than 15 million copies sold worldwide and 12 million copies in the United States. He also secured a place in the *Guinness Book of World Records* for playing the longest note ever recorded on a saxophone. Besides many of his award-winning jazz-inspired albums and compositions, he has recorded Chinese songs such as "Jasmine" and "The Moon Represents My Heart," and his music is hugely popular in China and Asia.

2. John Denver (1943–1997) is an American folksinger whose career began in the 1960s. As a singer-songwriter, actor, activist, and humanitarian, Denver has written more than three hundred songs and has won twelve gold and four platinum albums with his signature songs such as "Take Me Home, Country Roads" and "Rocky Mountain High."

3. Céline Dion (b. 1968) is a Canadian singer raised in Quebec. She caught international attention when she sang at the Euro Song Contest in 1988 representing Switzerland. Among her award-winning songs, "My Heart Will Go On" was an international number one hit. She has won five Grammy Awards and remains the best-selling Canadian artist.

4. *Xixiangji* (Story of the Western Wing) is also translated as *Romance of the Western Chamber* (not to be confused with the famous novel *Dream of Red Chamber*). It is one of the most famous Chinese dramatic works written by the Yuan dynasty (1271–1368) playwright Wang Shifu (王實甫).

5. *Water Margin*, written in vernacular Chinese, has been considered one of the four great classical novels of Chinese literature. The author, Shi Nai'an (1296–1372), details the rise and fall of a group of bandits during the time of the Song dynasty in China.

References

Anonymous. 2014. 民歌《茉莉花》歌词本义喻反腐 (The Original Meaning of "Molihua" Is about Anticorruption). In Qingdao News. http://epaper.qingdaonews.com/html/lnshb/20141031/lnshb794170.html. Accessed September 15, 2015.

Appadurai, Arjun. 1996. *Modernity at Large: Cultural Dimensions of Globalization*. Minneapolis: University of Minnesota Press.

Barrow, John. [1804] 2010. *Travels in China: Containing Descriptions, Observations and Comparisons, Made and Collected in the Course of a Short Residence at the Imperial Palace of Yuen-Min-Yuen, and on a Subsequent Journey through the Country from Pekin to Canton*. Cambridge: Cambridge University Press.

Chen, Meng. 2014. "民歌《茉莉花》起源于明代 本意为反腐" (The Original Meaning of the Ming Dynasty Folksong "Molihua" Is about Anticorruption). 解放日报 (Liberation Daily), November 28, 2014. http://www.chinanews.com/cul/2014/11–28/6823834.shtml. Accessed January 20, 2016.

Cui, Xiaohuo. 2008. "Classical Piece Will Ring in Ears of Winners." In *China Daily*. Beijing. August 6. http://www.chinadaily.com.cn/olympics/2008-08/06/content_6907444.htm. Accessed November 29, 2016.

Gopinath, Sumanth, and Jason Stanyek, eds. 2014. *The Oxford Handbook of Mobile Music Studies*, vol. 1. New York: Oxford University Press.

Huang, Yi Nong. 2006. 中國民歌〈茉莉花〉的西傳與東歸 (The Dissemination of Molihua to the West and Its Return to the East). 文與哲 (Literature and Philosophy) 9, no. 12: 1–15.

Jiang, Mingdun. 1982. *Hanzhu Minge Gailun* (Overview of Han Chinese Folksong). Shanghai: Shanghai Wenyi Chubanshe (Shanghai Arts Publishing Company).

Levin, Dan. 2014. "China Says Goodbye in the Key of G: Kenny G." *New York Times*, May 10.

Li, Xilan. 2009. "《茉莉花》流传史" (The Dissemination of Molihua). http://www.5friend.cn/archives/419. Accessed June 6, 2016.

Liu, Ching-chih, ed. 1992. *History of New Music in China: A Critical Review 1885–1985*. Hong Kong: Hong Kong University Press.

Melvin, Sheila. 2016. "How China Influenced Western Classical Music." Caiixin Online. http://www.chinesethought.cn/en/detail.aspx?nid=114&pid=130&id=2359. Accessed December 9, 2016.

Melvin, Sheila, and Jindong Cai. 2004. *Rhapsody in Red: How Classical Music Became Chinese*. New York: Algora Publishing.

Ochoa, Ana Maria. 2015. *Aurality: Listening and Knowledge in Nineteenth-Century Colombia*. Durham, NC: Duke University Press.

Price, Monroe, and Daniel Dayan, eds. 2008. *Owning the Olympics: Narratives of the New China*. Ann Arbor: University of Michigan Press.

Radano, Ronald, and Tejumola Olaniyan, eds. 2016. *Audible Empire: Music, Global Politics, Critique*. Durham, NC: Duke University Press.

Rofel, Lisa. 2007. *Desiring China: Experiments in Neoliberalism, Sexuality, and Public Culture*. Durham, NC: Duke University Press.

Schweig, Meredith. 2013. "Chinese Music." In *Transmission/Tranformation: Sounding China in Enlightenment Europe* (online publication). Harvard University Department of Music. http://www.hcs.harvard.edu/soundingchina/Schweig.html.

Scocca, Tom. 2011. "Kenny G and Hu Jintao Make Protest Music: Tunisia's Choice of Revolutionary Symbols Confounds Chinese Censors." http://www.slate.com/blogs/scocca/2011/02/23/kenny_g_and_hu_jintao_make_protest_music_tunisia_s_choice_of_revolutionary_symbols_confounds_chinese_censors_video.html. Accessed December 3, 2016.

Tao, Yabing. 1994. *Zhongxi Yinyue Jiaoliu Shigao* (A History of Chinese-Western Musical Exchange). Beijing: Zhongguo Dabaike Quanshu Chubanshe (Chinese Enclyopedia Publishing Company).

Thrasher, Alan. 2008. *Sizhu Instrumental Music of South China: Ethos, Theory and Practice*. Leiden: Brill.

Turino, Thomas. 2000. *Nationalists, Cosmopolitans, and Popular Music in Zimbabwe*. Chicago: University of Chicago Press.

Wang, Xin. 2014. 茉莉谐音“没利”，是要看轻名利 扬州民歌《茉莉花》是明朝反腐神曲 “Molihua” Is the Same as Moli (without Profit), Is This Yangzhou Folksong an Anticorruption Song from the Ming Dynasty? Guangming Online. http://difang.gmw.cn/newspaper/2014-11/30/content_102399818.htm. Accessed January 3, 2016.

Xian, Ming. 2012. 六合民歌的前世今“声” (The Former Life of the Folksong from Liuhe and Its Current Sound). http://www.cflac.org.cn/ys/xwy/201210/t20121017_152727.html. Accessed April 25, 2014.

Ying, Zhen. 2008. “中国“第二国歌”《茉莉花》 惹来多少麻烦! (China's Second National Anthem: “Molihua” Attracts Troubles). http://www.sinovision.net/portal.php?mod=view&aid=51489. Accessed May 4, 2015.

Yu, Siuwah. 2004. “Two practices confused in one composition: Tan Dun's Symphony 1997: Heaven, Earth, Man.” In Locating East Asia in Western Art Music, edited by Yayoi Uno Everett and Frederick Lau. Middletown, CT: Wesleyan University Press, 57–71.

Zhongguo Yinyue Chubanshe Bianjibu (Editorial Board of the Dictionary of Chinese Music), ed. 1985. *Zhongguo Yinyue Cidian* (Dictionary of Chinese Music). Beijing: Renmin Yinyue Chubanshe Chubanibu (People's Publishing Company).

CHAPTER 5

Finding a Niche for the Avant-Garde Outside the Academy in the Early 2000s

A RADICAL MOMENT IN KOREA'S FUSION MUSIC

R. Anderson Sutton

CREATIVE impulses in music-making in the twenty-first century seem increasingly to involve mixture of musical sounds and concepts whose cultural origins are multiple and often clearly so. Indeed, cross-cultural combinations could be said to be the new normal, an inevitable result of the constant flows of peoples, commodities, ideas, and values. While such mobility is pervasive, in the realm of music and other forms of cultural expression the blend of commercial and creative impulses can work in ways that may be predictable and intended for enjoyment and consumption, but not always. The essays collected in this volume address but a sampling of the rich diversity of traveling musics and attendant discourses in Asia and the Pacific. Some represent intraregional flows, others multidirectional ones, and still others the intake and embrace of influences from afar, as in the Korean instances I address in this chapter. It is not musical sounds alone that have long been reaching Korea from the West, but the attendant discourses of aesthetics and notions of music as "art," establishing a firm hold for Western (art) music, and subsequently for some forms of Korean music and Western-Korean musical fusions as art.

What might have been seen as unauthentic, awkward, even unnatural blends and juxtapositions have now assumed a status as authentic, even (or especially) when the mixture has brought together a noncommercial, "traditional" music with the sounds and commercial apparatuses of popular music, evidenced in the already myriad instances of "world music" making. This growing phenomenon of musical mixture, often appearing under the rubric of "musical hybridity" or "fusion music" in scholarly musical studies and popular nomenclature, is widely documented and theorized by ethnomusicologists and cultural studies scholars (see Stokes 2004; Feld 2000; Frith 2000; Taylor 1997; among others). Alongside such terms as "world music" and the earlier "world beat," the term "fusion" (or its transliteration or translation) is often used by musicians and listeners. Most of the scholarship has focused on creative processes and musical products that involve popular music, but this is not the only realm in which musical fusions have been taking place. Among cosmopolitan musicians in many countries around the world, cultural borrowing and blending also permeate the realm of "art music"—a realm whose very existence has usually been shaped, in large part, by evolving responses to Western notions of art music, absolute music, and associated concepts.

My focus in this chapter is on a small number of musicians in South Korea whose approach to revitalizing what they and many others see as a stagnated "traditional" music culture has incorporated ideas and practices that have been labeled "radical" or "experimental" in the realm of Western art music of the twentieth century. These musicians have formed a kind of avant-garde niche outside the academic establishment—a niche neither permanent nor exclusive, with musicians moving into and away from it as their circumstances and musical proclivities change. I train my inquiry on the activities of these few musicians in the early 2000s, a moment in recent music history in Korea that, like all moments, has not stood frozen in time, but has been one of a complex array of cultural moments that has cast its influence on things that have come since.

These are cosmopolitan musicians, to be sure, trained in Korean music at prestigious formal educational institutions and highly knowledgeable of the sounds and ethos of Western art music. However fervent they have been in choosing unusual creative paths, none has proven to be a lifelong freelance avant-gardist, as each has responded to one or another pull in other directions, whether popular music, academic composing, performing, or some combination. Their following in the avant-garde realm has been small but enthusiastic, consisting primarily of younger persons, mostly in their twenties and thirties, with some knowledge of and interest in Korea's remarkable but little-appreciated indigenous, traditional music (usually referred to as *kugak*, i.e., "national music")—the very music these musicians have felt to be stagnant and unappealing to contemporary Koreans. Beside the well-established practices of jazz and pop combinations with Korean traditional music (known as *p'yujŏn*, i.e., "fusion," or as *p'yujŏn kugak*)[1] and the still largely academic genre of new composition for Korean instruments (*ch'angjak kugak*), these musicians, whose formal training has included practical and theoretical study of traditional Korean instrumental and vocal music as well as contemporary Western art music, have formed ensembles whose music explores beyond and between the boundaries of these very different musical traditions. These range from group improvisations reminiscent of the traditional Korean folk ensemble music *shinawi* and harmonized vocal music accompanied by instrumental music closely resembling that used for traditional court vocal music (*kagok*) to pieces employing Korean traditional instruments playing in styles informed by free jazz or electronically altered to obscure their traditional Korean sound, as well as pieces with recursive rhythmic and melodic patterns reminiscent of American minimalist composers Steve Reich and Terry Riley. I will focus on two groups and one musician who broke off from a third group in spring 2004 to explore new directions. The two groups are Sangsang, an instrumental trio mixing indigenous Korean styles with some aspects of Western contemporary art music and free jazz, and Chŏngga Akhoe, a vocal and instrumental group drawing on indigenous court instrumental and art song music. The individual musician is Koh JiYeon (Ko Chi-Yŏn),[2] former leader of the well-known *kayagŭm* (plucked zither) quartet Sagye, and who has been experimenting with electronically altering *kayagŭm* and human voice sounds.[3] Based on observations of concerts and rehearsals in 2003, 2004, and 2005, conversations with musicians and audience members then and over the next decade, as well as print coverage, I intend to provide an introduction to the aesthetics of the music and the underlying processes by which it has been created, and to interpret the music in relation to shifting notions of what constitutes "Korean music" and what constitutes its underlying value. In the process, I also caution against a too-facile mapping of Western art music concepts such as "avant-garde" and "experimental music" onto new Korean music, even when such music presents radical directions that seem to parallel those in Western art music.

Before turning to the individual cases, let me point out that the music under consideration is not widely known, nor is it viewed as a single genre or trend within the larger world of Korean music. In the emerging discourse among Korean critics and musicians, a number of terms are invoked, some borrowed directly from Western music discourse, and these deserve attention here before turning to the specific cases I intend to explore. The term "experimental music" (*shilhŏm ŭmak*) crops up frequently, but is problematic, since the same term has been used in Korea, as in the West (especially in the United States), to refer to the more daring and radical activities within the Western art music world, with focus most often directed toward the composers and musical process, represented most famously by John Cage. It is worth noting that neither edition of *The New Grove Dictionary of Music and Musicians* contains an entry for "experimental music," but a five-page entry appears under this heading in *The New Grove Dictionary of American Music*, in which author John Rockwell defines it as "a tradition of 20th-century musical practice (largely but not exclusively American), the fundamental characteristic of which is a continuing search for radically new modes of composition, music-making, and musical understanding" (Rockwell 1986, 91). Compared to "'conventional' contemporary music, the term is used for a bolder, more individualistic, eccentric, and less highly crafted kind of musical expression" (ibid.).[4]

In the realm of Korean fusion music, the first instance I know of the use of the term "experimental music" is on the cover of an album by a now-defunct percussion group, Durae-Pae Samulnori (Turae P'ae Samul Nori). The album uses the four traditional Korean percussion instruments of the *samulnori* genre—*changgo* (hourglass drum), *puk* (barrel drum), *kkwaenggwari* (small flat gong), and *ching* (medium-sized flat gong)—joining forces with free-rhythm atonal melodic playing on some tracks and heavily distorted rock guitar on others (Durae-Pae Samulnori n.d.). While the musicians that represent the focus of my inquiry in this chapter all agreed they were seeking to create music that sounded "fresh" and "new" and also "Korean," some rejected my initial attempt to call their music "experimental," as their intent was not simply to sound "new" at any cost. Other terms that frequently came up in discussing their music were *ch'angjak* (creative), *shin* (new), *chayu* (free), *hyŏndae* (contemporary), *p'ŭri* (from English "free"), *abang karŭdŭ* (from French/English "avant-garde"), and *chŏnwijŏk* (new and edgy; often glossed as "avant-garde"). Of these, *ch'angjak* (creative) has been used in conjunction with the word for indigenous Korean music (*kugak*) for many decades to refer to newly composed works for traditional Korean instruments. Less commonly, the same composer-focused works have been referred to as *shin kugak* (new traditional Korean music). The word *hyŏndae* is more often applied to Western and Western-inspired music, but is sometimes combined with the word *kugak* to refer to the more daring new music for Korean instruments. The English loan words *p'ŭri* and *abang karŭdŭ* have appeared more recently, and yet neither of these is widely accepted as a label for the kind of music I consider here. All of these words are applied in opposition to *chŏnt'ong* (traditional).

One may question the accuracy of applying the term "avant-garde" to the music under consideration here, but I believe it is appropriate. One often associates this term with bold originality, a quality that characterizes at least some of the work of these musicians and yet also presupposes an ongoing tradition, to which the avant-garde musician is contributing as she or he pushes ahead. It also has usually implied an oppositional stance to mainstream, bourgeois values, and in this sense as well, this music and the attitudes of those who make it can be identified as "avant-garde."[5] In the introduction to her insightful study of Pierre Boulez's IRCAM,[6] Georgina Born draws on the theoretical approaches of Bourdieu and Williams to the logic of the avant-garde, contrasting its emphasis on the accumulation of cultural capital to bourgeois art's economic capital. She notes the "'negative correlation between success and true artistic value'" (1995, 27, quoting Bourdieu 1981, 284) and the "avant-garde ideology as disdaining material luxury and abjuring economic interest" (Born 1995, 27). As will be seen below, especially in the discussion of Chŏngga Akhoe, whose members articulate explicitly a disdain for material luxury or economic "success," and in Koh JiYeon's choice to leave the highly successful Sagye ensemble, these musicians position themselves largely (although not in all cases) at the avant-garde end of the continuum between commercial/popular art and avant-garde/high art. Chŏngga Akhoe members also stress the importance of "dissent and opposition" (Born 1995, 27, after Williams 1981, 225)—not only artistic, but also political. Some of these musicians' careers, especially Kang Eunil's, support a more complex view: of musicians sometimes aiming for economic success through popular kinds of fusion music-making, and other times exploring new and unusual musical sounds that are likely to be appreciated by only a small elite. And even Chŏngga Akhoe members say they seek at least a modicum of "popularity," though they do not believe in commercially oriented aesthetic compromises.

I do not wish to impose a single label on what are at times contrasting approaches to music-making, but certain features tie them together. Beyond the experimental and avant-garde elements in their music and the underlying philosophical beliefs, they share a commitment to finding new ways of fusing older Korean practice with other musical styles. All of the musicians involved are performers, formally trained in traditional Korean music. Though in 2003–2004 Chŏngga Akhoe identified one member, Yi T'ae-Wŏn, as its "composer," he was also a performer with the group and composed with the others, in rehearsal, rather than sitting alone in a studio.[7] Music critic and scholar Lee So-Young (Yi So-Yŏng) has pointed out the collapsing of the (Western-inspired) division between composers and performers as one of the key identifying factors in Korea's burgeoning fusion (*p'yujŏn*) music, setting it apart from the established category *ch'angjak kugak*, in which composers write, almost always using Western staff notation, and others perform (Lee 2003). *Ch'angjak kugak* composer Hwang Byŏng-Ki (Hwang Pyŏng-Ki) is something of an exception in that he has written many works for *kayagŭm*, an instrument that he himself plays with great skill, but his pieces are published and clearly intended to be performed by others as well. Another feature of fusion music is, of course, its explicit basis in hybrid combinations, some of which blend and "fuse" while others merely juxtapose (see further Lee 1999, 2003, 2005; Howard 2006; Sutton 2003, 2011). Here I am not so much interested in how successful or seamless the blending of deeply Korean and other elements might seem, but rather in the processes of music-making and the ethos they strive to create, or re-create.

Sangsang: Free Music Group

In an article titled "Chŭlgŏun Kŭrim, Shinbihan Sangsang" (Enjoyable Kŭrim, Mysterious Sangsang), Korean music scholar and critic Yun Chung-Kang contrasts two small ensembles that appeared in a single concert devoted to fusion music in August 2003 (2004, 159–162). Kŭrim, which translates both as "picture" (i.e., drawing or painting) and as "the forest," presented a variety of fusion pieces, involving simple Western harmonies and an easy, clap-along beat. The ensemble consisted of synthesizer/keyboard, electric guitar, electric bass, a battery of Western and Korean percussion (two players), and four traditional Korean instruments: *kayagŭm*, *kŏmun'go* (six-string zither, played with stick), *taegŭm* (large transverse bamboo flute), and *haegŭm* (two-stringed fiddle). Founded in the 1980s, when other groups also began mixing pop and Korean traditional instruments and structures, Kŭrim became, as Yun notes, a "new age group" with a distinctive Korean sound (ibid., 159). But while Kŭrim's music was not conventional, presented refreshing new rhythms, and "stimulated the imagination" (ibid., 160), it was basically light and easy listening for the mostly younger-generation crowd. Sangsang, on the other hand, represented a stark contrast. Sangsang—literally translating as "imagination" (with secondary interpretations also possible, including "first/highest," "thinking of each other," and "always thinking")[8]—consisted of just three musicians, all women, highly trained in Korean traditional music, each an accomplished performer on one stringed instrument: Heo Yoon-Jeong (Hŏ Yun-Chŏng) on *kŏmun'go*, Kang Eunil (Kang Ŭn-Il) on *haegŭm*, and Yu Kyong-Hwa (Yu Kyŏng-Hwa) on *ch'ŏl hyŏn'gûm*, a steel-stringed, slide zither.[9] They were sometimes joined by one or two other soloists, and Yu Kyong-Hwa sometimes shifted to percussion instead of playing *ch'ŏl hyŏn'gŭm*.

On their website home page (www.kukak.com/artist/sangsang/english/indexmain.htm, no longer active), which they presented in three languages—Korean, English, and Japanese—they offered the following self-description in English: "The project group, who provides the new tunes of free-style music, will stimulate the endless imaginations of audience by the re-interpretation of the Korean traditional music as being unrestricted, direct, and improvisatory nature [*sic*]." Lee So-Young presented Sangsang in several concerts she organized, and also has written about them in reviews and scholarly articles and publications (see Lee 2003, 2005). She has described them in several instances as a "free music trio" (Koreanizing the English as *p'ŭri myujik t'ŭrio*; program notes to July and August 2003 concerts) and elsewhere as "avant-garde" (*abang karŭdŭ*; 2003, 224).[10] Yun identifies Sangsang as a "soloist ensemble" (*not* "new age group") and builds his short review around the contrasts between the two groups Sangsang and Kŭrim. Sangsang's music, he says, was serious/earnest (*chinjihan*) and tranquil (not bright and full of hope like Kŭrim's), "absolute" music (not "program music" like Kŭrim's), evoking a feeling of "gray" mystery (not "green" clarity like Kŭrim's), taking the listener to the realm of the surreal (not to a "cool refreshing forest" or park, like Kŭrim's).[11]

Indeed, the motivation behind Sangsang and the musical processes they used to create their music, is unusual—contrasting with those of most other Korean fusion music groups (see Sutton 2003, 2011; Lee 2003). Instead of organizing around an acknowledged group leader or director who composes or arranges the music, Sangsang had no "leader" and created its music largely through interactive improvisation in rehearsals and performance. These three women became aware through informal interaction and attending each other's solo concerts that their musical interests converged in certain ways. During one of several interviews I conducted with *kŏmun'go* player Heo Yoon-Jeong in August 2004, she told me that the main impetus behind their joining together was a mutual concern with the loss of spontaneity and improvisation in Korean music, despite their strong role in the non-court music (*minsok-ŭmak*) in earlier times. Not only were they discouraged by the (mostly Western-inspired) directions that academic *ch'angjak kugak* was taking, but also by the sharp decline in improvisation among players of traditional (*chŏnt'ong*) *kugak*. Heo pointed to the genre known as *sanjo*, the well-known practice of solo melodic instrument performing with hourglass drum (*changgo*) accompaniment that flourished in the nineteenth century and formed the basis for much Korean instrumental performance in the twentieth century. Because the music is technically challenging and exciting, she said, this music still draws a positive response from audiences today, but there are no new *sanjo*s being created; instead students (or "disciples") are expected to reproduce accurately the *sanjo*s that their teachers, or their teachers' teachers, standardized and had notated and recorded. Other than *sanjo*, there is very little repertory for the *kŏmun'go* except the few standard ensemble works of court music. Heo attempted to compose for *kŏmun'go* but was dissatisfied with the results. Writing, she said, made her produce dead, unnatural music, focusing on timbre and rhythmic patterns. Among the many *ch'angjak kugak* composers, she pointed out, very few actually have mastered traditional *kugak* instrumental performance. And even those with competence on one or two instruments will often write for other instruments, relatively unaware of those instruments' potential.

Beginning in January 2000, Heo Yoon-Jeong and Kang Eunil joined a weekly workshop on "free music," offered by jazz saxophonist Kang T'ae-Hwan. They met every Saturday afternoon for two months, each participant having to create his or her own piece or improvisation and perform it for Kang T'ae-Hwan. Solo pieces he would judge based on novelty/originality, beauty/appeal to the senses, and appropriate length. For group/small ensemble pieces he would also comment on the balance, ensemble "harmony" between players. They were encouraged to stand out individually (as in jazz solos) but not throughout the piece; parts taking merely accompanying roles were discouraged. A festival of solo and small group performances marked the end of the workshop and, in effect, the birth of Sangsang.

At first, their music was largely improvised and, naturally, different each time the same "item" was performed. They each were developing solo careers and met only occasionally as a group to rehearse and explore before a Sangsang concert. By summer 2000, these three musicians were appearing in concerts, such as the one Finchum-Sung describes, which was given at the P'an Art Hall on July 14, 2000, "as part of the Modern *Kugak* Guest Presentations Series (Hyŏndae kugak madang ch'och'ŏng yŏnju series)" (2002, 75). At that time, they were not identified officially as Sangsang but simply as the Free Music Trio. One after the other, each of the three musicians presented extensive solo performances before they appeared together in group improvisation, joined by a fourth player on *changgo*.

Of the three members, Kang Eunil has been the most fervent supporter of improvisation. Based on an interview conducted with Kang Eunil in July 2000, Finchum-Sung reports the following: "she said that, to her, 'free music' means music that comes from nature (a *kugak* aesthetic). She said that it cannot be contained within a musical framework, and, because of this, should not be composed or written down. It is music without boundaries. She considers 'free music' to fall within the realm of *kugak* because it celebrates the natural sounds and timbres of the instruments" (2002, 76). Finchum-Sung goes on to describe the sound of the instrumental techniques employed by Kang Eunil and Heo Yoon-Jeong at that concert: "The furious bowing and glissandos on the haegŭm, the pounding and aggressive plucking of the strings on the kŏmun'go reflected not the subtlety and restraint of what has come to characterize kugak, but, instead, gave into the aggression, daring, and speed of the 21st century South Korean temperament" (ibid.).

Though all three members were of very similar persuasion concerning freedom and improvisation early on, Yu and Heo have moved toward relatively greater fixity, albeit through group composition, lest the music become too "manneristic," Heo told me in an interview while she was in New York in early 2008. In a concert I attended in summer 2003, Sangsang performed an excerpt from a long piece titled "Yun-hŭi" (Transmigration of the Soul), which in its full version consists of five sections, each inspired by existing genres or pieces of Korean music: (1) royal ancestral shrine music (*chongmyo cherye-ak*); (2) court music (*chŏng-ak*, mixing instrumentally accompanied *kagok* vocal music and the Buddhist-based instrumental ensemble piece "Yŏngsan Hoesang"); (3)

a folk melody ("Menari") from the eastern region of Korea, whose scale is also shared with the court music of the previous item; (4) *sanjo* (the now standardized but formerly improvisational instrumental solo genre); and (5) shaman ritual music (*mu-ak*). The version I heard presented shortened versions of parts 2, 3, and 4. The musicians felt that all five of these genres shared a sufficient number of musical elements in common to make them combine well. Yet they saw their core inspiration—their "soul" (*chŏngshin*)—to be the group improvisational genre *shinawi*, which is closely related to (some would say the same as) shaman music. Indeed, *sanjo* rhythms and instrumental styles bear close relationship historically to shaman music. Thus, their performance reminded me, and no doubt other listeners, of traditional Korean shaman music, even though the percussion part involved timbres one would not normally hear in shaman music. Contributing to the feel of these genres was the addition of one *taegŭm* (transverse bamboo flute) player and a separate percussionist.

The second piece they performed contrasted markedly in style and texture but also relied heavily on improvisation, though more directly inspired by free jazz than by *shinawi*. Titled "Sangsang Chayu" (free imagination), the piece featured much more individualistic playing, from the often introspective and delicate forays of Yu Kyong-Hwa on the *ch'ŏl hyŏn'gŭm* to the frenetic fireworks display of Kang Eunil on *haegŭm* and forceful and relentless rhythms of Heo Yoon-Jeong on *kŏmun'go*.

However experimental Sangsang's music may have been, it must be noted that even in the early 2000s this was but one of several musical outlets for these performers. Each devoted considerable effort to her own solo career,[12] and Kang Eunil joined forces with numerous other musicians in various kinds of fusion ventures. After playing fusion music with other Korean musicians, such as the Shin Kwanwoong Jazz Trio (Shin Kwanung T'ûrio), in 2004 she released her first album, *Oraedoen Mirae/Ancient Futures*, consisting neither of traditional *kugak* nor of free improvisation, but instead mostly of a variety of harmonically based pieces fitting clearly the "New Age" category of Korean fusion music (see further Sutton 2003). The core musicians on this album and on her subsequent album *Mirae ŭi Kiŏk/Remembering the Future* (2007) constitute the now well-known fusion group known as Haegŭm Plus, which is still active in 2016 and aims at a wide domestic and international audience, playing an array of popular and New Age arrangements. Still, Kang Eunil's distinctive *haegŭm* technique is evident throughout, often representing a stark contrast in timbre and intensity to the harmonically predictable and dynamically more subdued accompanying ensemble. Others also note Kang's unique *haegŭm* sound, contrasting with other fusion *haegŭm* players, such as Jeong Soonyon (Chŏng Su-Nyŏn) and Kim Ae-Ra (see Yun 2004, 258–263).

A brief outline of their group activities as Sangsang appeared on their website and documented their appearances at numerous festivals (jazz, new music, free music, modern music, modern *kugak*) and other events. Sangsang performed at many of the more prestigious venues in Seoul, such as the Sejong Center, the National Kugak Center (formerly the Center for Korean Traditional Performing Arts) various art halls, universities, and festivals, but became inactive after 2007 as the three members pursued their own paths and careers.

Chŏngga Akhoe: New Korean Chamber and Vocal Ensemble

Taking rather different approaches in their new Korean music, the chamber and vocal ensemble Chŏngga Akhoe in the early 2000s was a group evolving in membership and in artistic direction. From early on, the group leader, Ch'ŏn Chae-Hyŏn, and composer, Yi T'ae-Wŏn, required of Chŏngga Akhoe members that they have no other major professional commitment in the music world. Musicians who were members of any of Korea's traditional music orchestras (which play *ch'angjak kugak*) or held full-time teaching positions were also excluded from membership. Ch'ŏn and Yi decided to limit membership to only those who could foreswear the financial benefits and aesthetic compromises required of formal academic or orchestral positions. This constraint severely limited membership, of course, as many talented musicians sympathetic to the aesthetic directions taken by Chŏngga Akhoe were simply unable to survive on the very meager earnings of the group, whose little-known music and aversion to commercial recordings made it wholly unthinkable as a viable profession, particularly for anyone with family to support. During the early 2000s (until 2005) only four musicians were officially "members," coming faithfully to rehearsals (at their own expense) and performing (often for little or no fee): Ch'ŏn Chae-Hyŏn (leader and *kŏmun'go* player), Yi Sŭng-Hŭi (*haegŭm* player), Yu Hong (*taegŭm* player), and Yi T'ae-Wŏn (composer and frequent vocalist, also *kŏmun'go* player).[13] Other parts, vocal and instrumental, were taken by "guests," who rehearsed with the group on an invitational basis and received no more or less recompense than members for concert presentations.

The group's self-image is articulated by Ch'ŏn Chae-Hyŏn and Yi T'ae-Wŏn in a book, *Kagok ŭi Saegim*, devoted to this unique group, consisting of interviews, articles by group members, as well as concert reviews and reissues of articles about the kinds of traditional vocal music (especially *kagok*) the group has long favored (Chŏngga Akhoe 2003). On the very first page of the preface, Yi T'ae-Wŏn asserts that Chŏngga Akhoe is not a representative *kugak* group, standing at some distance even from most other younger generation *kugak* musicians (ibid., 5). They are disenchanted with most academic *ch'angjak kugak*, finding it hopelessly dry and unable to touch the emotions. They stress their desire for "sharing and communication" (*nanum kwa sot'ong*). And while some of their major concerts drew criticism for failing to share or communicate well with more than a handful of sophisticated audience members, they did not reject wholesale the idea of popularity (*taejungsŏng*). But in contrast to many more popular fusion groups, who publicly profess to be seeking to popularize traditional Korean music but do so by offering hybrids that often consist basically of Western-style pop music simply decorated with traditional Korean instrumental timbres, Chŏngga Akhoe eschewed the use of pop music instruments (electric guitars, synthesizers, etc.) and offered its audiences music that was always strongly based in Korean traditional instrumental performance style, and sometimes vocal style as well (which is hardly ever emphasized in more popular fusion music), seeking to maintain a largely traditional artistic quality (*yesulsŏng*). Though the term *chŏngga* can be interpreted to mean "court" or "refined" (*chŏng*) "song" (*ga*), they clarify, through spelling with the appropriate Chinese character (情, and not 正), that they intend their group name to be interpreted by a different meaning of *chŏng*, namely "affection/love"—hence, "affection for song."

In contrast to Sangsang, whose driving concern was the reinfusing of Korean music with spontaneity and improvisation, Chŏngga Akhoe was more concerned about conveying the inherent beauty in the sounds of the little-appreciated small ensemble court music (both vocal and instrumental). During an interview with Ch'ŏn Chae-Hyŏn in August 2004, when I mentioned my interest in "experimental music" in Korea, he told me straightforwardly that Chŏngga Akhoe was not, in his mind, an experimental group at all. The term suggested to him the more radical experiments and disdain for tradition typical of late twentieth-century composers (in Korea as well as in the West, especially the United States). Their concerts often involve presentation of traditional works, only slightly modified from the versions they learned from their teachers. Yet in other works, they added harmonized vocal parts that, while not governed by the constraints of Western functional harmony or counterpoint, were nevertheless evocative of certain forms of Western choral music, even though the members devoted considerable effort in rehearsal to adhere to indigenous Korean scale structures in some pieces rather than always duplicating the Western equal-tempered intervals so prevalent in *ch'angjak kugak* and in the commercially popular fusion music.

When asked by Lee So-Young what the group's intentions were, members responded that their main purpose was to be different from other *kugak* musicians, from orchestra members, from pop fusion musicians, from music professors, and so forth. And when asked what they considered to be their specialty, they responded that they didn't want to have a specialty; they simply wanted to be pure and to communicate. They were concerned about social issues and wanted not only Korean music, as exemplified in their playing, but also Korean society to find a healthy (healthier) existence, eliminating pollution, poverty, corruption, commercialization. One member likened their artistic ideal to a musical equivalent of a modest restaurant whose décor is not luxurious but which serves organic food (no chemicals, no MSG).

In addition to performing traditional music and pieces inspired by traditional music, they also frequently enhanced their stage performances by projecting slide photographs or even by acting. In a performance I attended in July 2003, the group began with "Chŏ Komoge Sesun" ("New Sprout on That Old Tree"), for voices and traditional instruments, and then proceeded to a purely instrumental piece from their recent concert *Namu* (tree/wood). The opening sounded very similar to the restrained small-ensemble court music of previous centuries, but as slides of impoverished Korean countryside dwellers unfolded on a screen situated stage-left of the performers, the music gradually transformed to a texture of arpeggiated minor harmonies and unfamiliar melodies, the Korean feeling coming primarily from the instrumental timbres rather than indigenous rhythms or melodic material.

Chŏngga Akhoe's history of early public performances and media appearances includes a variety of venues and events, as given in their book (Chŏngga Akhoe 2003, 118–119) and on their website (www.freechal.com/jgah). Their concerts consisted mainly of invitations to small venues, such as art galleries, small halls, or schools. The sponsorship was various and included churches, private associations and societies, and even some broadcast media, both television and radio. Their major concerts, given only once a year, more or less, appear in this list as "regular concerts" and have been the major creative landmarks in the group's career, consisting of new works and new modes of presentation each time. From September 21 to 23, 2004, Chŏngga Akhoe held a "regular concert," involving collaboration with a Western string quartet, a singer of Korean dramatic-narrative (*p'ansori*), guest female singers, and actors. A piece titled "P'ung Nyŏn'ga 2004" (Bountiful Harvest Year Song 2004) was performed with projection of photographs of impoverished farmers whose lives, to paraphrase the publicity blurb on the internet, fester as if strewn with pesticides, despite an abundant harvest (www.freechal.com/jgah). The first piece consisted of an ancient song, "Sŏgyŏng Byŏlgok," dating from the Koryŏ dynasty period (918–1392) and known only in surviving notation, not part of the active repertory of *kugak* for centuries. Chŏngga Akhoe performed it as an arrangement for small Korean ensemble and Western string quartet, whose music, composed by Yi T'ae-Wŏn, was secondary to the more musically active and traditionally based Korean ensemble.

With these kinds of approaches to music, Chŏngga Akhoe managed with its few members and its many guests to present its own unique combination of political statements and musical explorations, always aiming for a powerful message, but subtly rendered with music strongly rooted in Korea's refined court music. As of 2016, Chŏngga Akhoe remains active, performing in Korea and in international festivals (primarily in Europe) and releasing new CD albums. Though former stringent requirements on membership have been relaxed, some of the original members have left, taking teaching jobs and starting families. However, Ch'ŏn Chae-Hyŏn remains as leader, working with Yi Hyang-Hŭi as artistic director (*yesul kamdok*), and their approach to music continues to stress experimental arrangements and combinations of the more esoteric forms of *kugak* with some stylistic features of avant-garde Western art music.

Koh JiYeon: Experimental Soloist

After several very successful years on the international concert circuit with the very obviously Western-inspired Sagye (Four Seasons) *kayagŭm* quartet, a group whose very name is taken from the Vivaldi composition they became famous for arranging and presenting in concert,[14] founding member Koh JiYeon broke away from the group in spring 2004 to pursue a solo career, turning to music with far less potential for wide public appeal. Her interest in going beyond the traditional *kugak* she had learned in her years of training, including majoring in *kayagŭm* performance at Korea's prestigious Seoul National University, led her to help form the Sagye quartet, which certainly went beyond Korean traditional conventions, not only in playing arrangements of Vivaldi and Bach, but also in creating an ensemble of four of the same instrument (cf. Western string quartet) rather than the usual Korean small ensembles, which seldom have more than one of each kind of instrument.

Growing wary of such indebtedness to the West, and despite a concert in December 2002 in which the group performed some original and unusual new works by *ch'angjak kugak* composers, Koh JiYeon developed a desire to push for even more radical directions by herself, recording and releasing an album (not widely available in stores well-stocked with other Korean fusion and *kugak* music)[15] of her own new musical experiments on the *kayagŭm*, with her voice, and defining input by sound technician and producer Byung-Jun (Byŏng-Chun). On the album, following her skillful rendition of a short version of the Kang T'ae-Hong (one of her teachers) school *kayagŭm sanjo*, she offers five short tracks containing "processed forms" (*kagong toen hyŏngt'ae*) of passages from the same *sanjo*. These have been so profoundly altered electronically (by Byung-Jun) that one can barely tell it is a *kayagŭm* producing the original sounds. In another piece, "Min Mulgogi" (Freshwater Fish), she offers snippets ("realtime processing and restructuring by Byung-Jun") from recorded interviews she herself conducted and recorded, asking the simple question "What is *kugak*?" In the final track, "Sarangŭn ŏdie?" (Where Could Love Be), she presents a simple, refreshing love song, composed by Kim Hwal-Sŏng (close friend of Yi T'ae-Wŏn and other Chŏngga Akhoe members).[16] The album is a true collage of different approaches to sound, from traditional Korean (*sanjo*) and Western-influenced song to truly experimental, electronically altered fragments.

Koh JiYeon performed with other groups, regularly providing accompaniment for internationally acclaimed Korean avant-garde dancer An Eun-Mi (An Ŭn-Mi) and forming a multimedia group, Koh JiYeon Kayagŭm Project, involving music for Korean and other (mostly Western) instruments. With this group she articulates her artistic aims as follows: (1) to achieve the creation of a complex art genre of *kugak* by combining traditional *kugak*, contemporary music, electronic music, dance, and visual/image; (2) based on traditional Korean culture, to make a place for stage art where an international audience can be gained; and (3) to achieve an active and creative blend of popular, innovative, and experimental performance. She has also performed with a number of art musicians from the West, such as the international performance network known as Fatzer-Project. Her December 2008 performance with this group was based on work by Heinrich von Kleist, conceived for Korean performers (dancers, actors, musicians) in collaboration with German artists, a work whose focus is on "music," where the function of music is not to provide background sound but actually to suggest a play as a "musical architecture" (Koh Jiyeon webpage).

When I spoke to Koh JiYeon in August 2004, shortly after she left Sagye, she was not sure of what she might do next in her "own" music. She seemed happy to be independent of the commercial demands of the Sagye group, even though she had told me in a July 2003 interview (before she left Sagye) that her most treasured moments were being on stage with her fellow Sagye members and performing for an appreciative audience. Since then she has ventured into music that will more often perplex an audience than bring hearty applause. And she certainly stands to find difficulties getting performance engagements or lucrative recording contracts. Nevertheless, she told me it felt "right" for her to be exploring this new direction—aesthetically and, perhaps, politically.

Clearly there is much that distinguishes the musical sound and the creative process employed by the members of Sangsang, the members of Chŏngga Akhoe, and Koh JiYeon. Yet all have worked to find a musical style and aesthetic philosophy sufficiently removed from the academic *ch'angjak kugak* and the commercial fusion music that to them represent inadequate attempts to solve the problem of what Korean music should be, what it *must* be to be vital in the postcolonial but socially stratified Korea of the twenty-first century. In both originality and rejection of conformity to commercial expectations, the music seems to conform to the defining principles of "avant-garde" as it developed in the West. And some of the kinds of original musical sounds they make would seem to justify describing it as "experimental." Yet the cultural world in contemporary Korea incorporates not only the modernist push for "the new," as in Western culture during the twentieth century, but additionally the constant presence of powerful aesthetic and philosophical ideas introduced from elsewhere, confronting and challenging indigenous ideas and practices. The sounds and the ideology originating from the West have not merely washed up on Korean shores, like gentle waves on a beach, but penetrated deeply and lastingly. One may be tempted to follow the wave metaphor to liken such penetration and lasting change to a tsunami (and some conservative musicians and listeners would likely concur), but I would urge us to understand these developments as more transformative than destructive, and not disastrous. After all, it is skilled, thinking musicians who are creating this music, not a random and uncontrollable geological event.

These musicians in their most radical creative ventures have been concerned not to accommodate their music to the heavily Westernized, media-saturated culture world of contemporary Korea, but to offer an alternative and to contest the current cultural and (overtly, in the case of Chŏngga Akhoe) social conditions. One can analyze their music in terms of its locus of influences, and certainly the West is present, lurking in the occasional triadic harmonies, arpeggiated ostinatos, even the English-derived rhetoric of "free music," "experimental music," and "avant-garde" itself. It is perhaps telling that musicians from both Chŏngga Akhoe and Sangsang performed not only in the same public concerts in summer 2003, but at a small gathering of anti-Iraq war protesters at a church in June 2004, organized by the music critic-scholar I mentioned earlier, Lee So-Young. To them, the yearning to keep hapless Korean soldiers from the dangerous quagmire created by American foreign policy folly is consistent with the rootedness of their music in Korean traditions. Just as they faced rather than turning away from the challenges of revitalizing Korean music, so have they engaged with the important political issues of the day.

When I began research in 2001 on Korea's fusion music, focusing primarily on the many examples of commercially oriented blends of *kugak* with pop and jazz, it seemed the guiding motivation was to accommodate, to compromise, to meet the public, largely unsympathetic to *kugak*, more or less on their own grounds, acceding to their need for triadic harmonies, bass guitar riffs, drum backbeats, rock and pop vocal styles, and so forth. Gradually I came to know these other young musicians whose vision was different and who, despite great divergence in the music they create, seemed driven by a set of common forces. "Experimental" or "avant-garde" music, of course, may disappear or become less marginal, more mainstream. It remains to be seen what place the music of Sangsang, Chŏngga Akhoe, and Koh JiYeon may hold into the future, but clearly in the early 2000s they were engaged in a dynamic struggle against entrenched attitudes and artistic trends, a struggle that yielded new music that even now can be said to succeed at being new, challenging, and clearly, if not quintessentially, Korean.

Looking back on their activities now more than a decade ago, it is already apparent that, while academic *ch'angjak kugak* and commercial fusion *kugak* (or *kugak* fusion) continue to be composed, performed, and consumed, younger musicians trained in traditional *kugak* are also resisting these more entrenched varieties of non-traditional *kugak*. Among these have been Byeol-ak (Pyŏl-ak), YIEN (Yen), and Ensemble Sinawi (Shinawi),[17] three groups each of whose music contrasts in sound and style with that of the others, much as Sangsang's and Chŏngga Akhwe's does. The groups sponsored by the Korean government's "21st Century Korean Music Project" (21 C Han'guk Ŭmak P'ŭrojekt'ŭ) form part of this cohort, though such groups rarely remain intact for long.[18] In fact, most performers are active in multiple settings, solo and ensemble, and some in multiple genres as well. While Kang Eunil was still active with Sangsang, for example, she also formed a more commercially oriented fusion group known as Haegŭm Plus, which remains active in 2016. Other members of Sangsang moved in different directions. Heo Yoon-Jeong leaned away from improvisation toward more fixed *ch'angjak kugak* compositions, but seeking and performing unusual new music, including fusion collaborations with foreign jazz and classical musicians in her Tori Ensemble. Chŏngga Akhoe is still active and gaining in listenership at home and at international festival engagements, and is less radical socially than it was in its early years. Koh JiYeon, after deep engagement with an experimental group known as Be Being in the years after her *Nuun Namu* album, has moved away from public musical performance.

Indeed, though the ethos of a noncommercial, avant-garde approach to music as "socially responsible" art with loftier purpose than commercial gain does indeed persist, the musicians who create and perform it are routinely involved with other activities, including musical ones, that do not fit this description. Do they risk being labeled hypocrites or sellouts? By and large, I don't think so. Idealistic musicians in their twenties and early thirties often do get married, have children, need to take care of aging parents, and need to make a living. Musicians and followers largely understand this. For even a few years devoted to this avant-garde edge of Korean music-making enables these and similar groups and individual musicians to carve out new realms of experience and inspires others to take the next steps. Therein lies a healthy future for *kugak*—selectively incorporating sounds and ideologies that have been making their way to Korea for more than a century.

Notes

I wish to express my gratitude for the support provided by the Korea Foundation and the University of Wisconsin–Madison Graduate School for the research on this project in the summers of 2003 and 2004, and by the Center for Korean Studies at the University of Hawaiʻi at Mānoa for follow-up research in 2015. I also wish to thank Dr. Lee So-Young, who facilitated my initial contacts with the musicians discussed in this chapter, and Dr. Moon Hyun (Mun Hyŏn) for an intensive series of private lessons in Korean classical vocal music during the summer of 2004.

1. Korean music critic and scholar Lee So-Young has problematized this terminology, suggesting that *p'yujŏn kugak* suggests a closed genre and repertory (i.e., as a subcategory of *kugak*), whereas *kugak p'yujŏn* suggests "fusion of Korean music with other kinds of music" and is therefore more appropriate (Lee 2003, 192).

2. Romanization of Korean uses the McCune-Reischauer system, except in instances when Korean individuals have chosen alternative Romanized spellings of their own names or for publication titles, in which case I provide the McCune-Reischauer equivalent in parentheses on first appearance.

3. The literature on new music in Korea has largely focused on the *ch'angjak kugak* composers and their music, though with a few important exceptions, notably Howard (2002, 2006) and Finchum-Sung (2002, 2012).

4. Tracing the movement back to Charles Ives, Rockwell lists John Cage, David Tudor, Christian Wolff, Morton Feldman, LaMonte Young, and minimalists Terry Riley, Steve Reich, Philip Glass, and Brian Eno, among others (Rockwell 1986).

5. In this regard, the recent hybrid music of Chinese-born composers identified by Lau as "avant-garde" and also as "new wave" would seem not to be purely or even mainly "avant-garde." (2004, esp. 36–39).

6. Institut de Recherche et de Coordination Acoustique/Musique, opened in 1977 with funding from the French government.

7. See Yi T'ae-wŏn's contributions in *Kagok ŭi Saegim* (Chŏngga Akhoe 2003) and his earlier book *Ttŏllim kwa Sallim* (2002).

8. As described to me in an interview with Heo Yoon-Jeong, August 11, 2004. See also Yun (2004, 161) for the four possible meanings of "Sangsang" identified by different *hanja* (Chinese characters).

9. The *ch'ŏl hyŏn'gŭm* is an unusual instrument, invented by the traditional comedian/tightrope worker Kim Yŏng-ch'ŏl around 1943 (Yun 2004, 164).

10. In fact, early on, before they took the name Sangsang, this group appeared in concerts as the "free music trio." See the description of a concert in July 2000 given below, based on Finchum-Sung's account (2002, 75–76).

11. Kŭrim's name is often given in both Korean phonetic alphabet (*han'gŭl*) as 그림 (with a primary meaning of "picture") and in a combination of English "the" and the Chinese character (*hanja*) for "forest" (林), which is pronounced either as "yim" or, after the particle *kŭ* (Korean for "that," "the"), as "rim."

12. Yun Chung-Kang's collection of essays includes a review of a 2002 solo *kŏmun'go* concert by Heo Yoon-Jeong (Yun 2004, 306–308), as well as reflections on Kang Eunil's solo and ensemble concert career (ibid., 253–257).

13. Yi T'ae-wŏn had to resign from full membership in the group when he married and subsequently took a teaching job to enable him to support himself and his wife.

14. Though Sagye recorded arrangements of other Western classical pieces, as well as versions of Korean folksongs with Western harmony, neither of their CDs (2001, [2004]) includes Vivaldi's famous concerto. The name Sagye can also translate as "four worlds," an interpretation presented on their website (www.sagye.com). Yun Chung-Kang discusses Sagye's ambitions to incorporate all kinds of music in their repertory, noting the "citified" renditions they give of Korean folksongs and the "Koreanized" renditions they give of Western classical pieces (Yun 2004, 233).

15. The album is titled *Nuun Namu/A Tree Lying Down: Koh JiYeon Gayageum Album, Vol. 1,* and lists a release date of December 2003, but became available commercially only in late 2004.

16. In addition to composing, Kim Hwal-Sŏng is author of a book on musical life in Korea (2002). He also composed and performed the vocal part for several songs on Sagye's second CD album (Sagye [2004]).

17. These three groups and the recent distaste for "fusion" music as overly commercial are discussed at length by Yeo Hyunjin (2013).

18. This impermanence is even implied in the word "project." On these *kugak* projects, see further Finchum-Sung 2012.

References

Born, Georgina. 1995. *Rationalizing Culture: IRCAM, Boulez, and the Institutionalization of the Musical Avant-Garde*. Berkeley: University of California Press.

Bourdieu, Pierre. 1981. "The Production of Belief: Contribution to an Economy of Symbolic Goods." *Media, Culture, and Society* 2, no. 3: 261–294.

Chŏngga Akhoe, eds. 2003. *Kagok ŭi Saegim* (Etched Contours of Traditional Art Song/ *Kagok*). Seoul: Minjok Ŭmak Yŏn'guhoe.

Feld, Steven. 2000. "A Sweet Lullaby for World Music." *Public Culture* 12: 145–171.

Finchum-Sung, Hilary V. 2002. "*Uri Saenghwal Ŭmak:* Music, Discourse, and Identity in South Korea." PhD diss., Indiana University.

———. 2012. "Designing a Fresh Tradition: Young Kugak and Sonic Imaginings for a Progressive Korea." *World of Music* (new series) 1: 121–144.

Frith, Simon. 2000. "The Discourse of World Music." In *Western Music and Its Others: Difference, Representation, and Appropriation in Music*, ed. Georgina Born and David Hesmondhalgh, 305–322. Berkeley: University of California Press.

Howard, Keith. 2002. "Korea: Contemporary Genres." In *The Garland Encyclopedia of World Music, Volume 7, East Asia: China, Japan, and Korea*, ed. Robert C. Provine, Yoshihiko Tokumaru, and J. Lawrence Witzleben, 951–974. New York: Routledge.

———. 2006. *Creating Korean Music: Tradition, Innovation, and the Discourse of Identity.* Perspectives on Korean Music, vol. 2. Aldershot, UK: Ashgate.

Kim, Hwal-Sŏng. 2002. *Ŭmak kwa Ilsang* (Music and Daily Life). Seoul: Minjok Ŭmak Yŏn'guhoe.

Lau, Frederick. 2004. "Fusion or Fission: The Paradox and Politics of Contemporary Chinese Avant-Garde Music." In *Locating East Asia in Western Art Music*, ed. Yayoi Uno Everett and Frederick Lau, 22–39. Middletown, CT: Wesleyan University Press.

Lee, So-Young (I So-yŏng). 1999. *Nanŭn Tarŭge Tŭnnŭnda* (I Listen Differently). Seoul: Yesol Publisher.

———. 2003. "Reading New Music in the Age of Fusion Culture: Focused on Korean Fusion Music/Pyujŏn Shidae ŭi Saeroun Ŭmak Ilkki: Kugak Pyujŏnŭl Chungshimŭro." *Tongyang Ŭmak* 25: 189–214 (English), 215–226 (Korean).

———. 2005. *Han'guk Ŭmak ŭi Naemyônhwadoen Orient'allijŭmŭl Nŏmŏsŏ* (Getting Past Korean Music's Internalized Orientalism). Seoul: Minsogwôn.

Rockwell, John. 1986. "Experimental Music." *The New Grove Dictionary of American Music*, vol. 2, ed. H. Wiley Hitchcock and Stanley Sadie, 91–95. London: Macmillan.

Stokes, Martin. 2004. "Music and the Global Order." *Annual Review of Anthropology* 33: 47–72.

Sutton, R. Anderson. 2003. "Innovation and Accessibility: Towards a Typology of Fusion Music in Korea." *Tongyang Ŭmak* 25: 227–250.

———. 2011. "'Fusion' and Questions of Korean Cultural Identity in Music." *Korean Studies* 35: 4–24.

Taylor, Timothy. 1997. *Global Pop: World Music, World Markets*. New York: Routledge.

Williams, Raymond. 1981. *Culture*. London: Fontana.

Yeo, Hyunjin. 2013. "Alternatives to 'Fusion': Contemporary Practices of *Gugak* and Their Aesthetics in Twenty-first Century South Korea." MA thesis, University of Wisconsin–Madison.

Yi, T'ae-Won. 2002. *Ttŏllim kwa Sallim* (Vibrations and Revival). Seoul: Minjok Ŭmak Yŏn'guhoe.

Yun Chung-Kang. 2004. *Kugagi Pakkwigo Itta* (Traditional Korean Music Is Changing). Seoul: Minsogwôn.

Websites (none still active as of 4/30/16)

Chŏngga Akhoe's website: www.freechal.com/jgah. Accessed September 23, 2004.

Koh JiYeon's website: www.kohjiyeon.com. Accessed December 14, 2008.

Minjok Ŭmak Yŏn'guhoe's website: www.minum.or.kr. Accessed September 23, 2004.

Sagye's website: www.sagye.com. Accessed November 27, 2004.

Sangsang's website: www.kukak.com/artist/sangsang. Accessed December 8, 2004.

Discography

21C Han'guk Ŭmak P'ŭrojektŭ: 2009 Promotion of Newly-Composed Korean Traditional Music. Seoul: Universal Music Korea/Gugak FM CD, DU8506.

Durae-Pae Samulnori. n.d. *Durae-Pae Samulnori Shilhŏm Ŭmak*. CD, Sori Madang SCD-0010.

Kang Eunil. 2004. *Oraedoen Mirae/Ancient Futures*. CD, YBM Seoul Records SRCD-1528.

Koh, Jiyeon. 2003. *Nuun Namu/A Tree Lying Down: Koh Jiyeon Gayageum Album Vol. 1*. CD, Mul/DreamBeat, DBKAD-0259.

Sagye. 2001. *Sagye: Kayagŭm Ensemble*. CD, Polimedia, DU 5722.

———. [2004]. *Kayagŭm Angsangbŭl Sagye, 2 Chip/Kayagum Ensemble Sagye, Part 2*. CD, EMI/Taegwang Record EKCD-0611.

CHAPTER 6

Singing Policemen, Dancing Firemen

ALLIANCE BUILDING AND INTERETHNIC REMASCULINIZATION IN POST–WORLD WAR II HAWAI'I

Kati Szego

Before the first interview question hovered in the air—before I could even hit Record—Donald Chang was gushing, telling me how much he loved the Honolulu Fire Department he had retired from in 1994. His gently rasping voice rattled with pride and affection. In its conviction, that moment echoed another I shared with "Rosey," a retired lieutenant of the Honolulu Police Department.[1] We were talking about public relations when, unexpectedly, he exhorted his commitment to fairness in policing. Only later would I fully appreciate these ardent expressions of loyalty to fellow workers and work.

My conversations with Chang and Rosey converged on the topic of choirs created by the Honolulu Fire and Police Departments in post–World War II Hawai'i: choirs that drew these men into sustained engagements with host Hawaiian cultural practices; choirs that spread, through distant and proximal travels, carefully calibrated images of their masculinity. When police and firemen established singing groups in 1952 and 1959, respectively, they were, in many respects, following the lead of many civic service agencies and businesses in Hawai'i—the Board of Water Supply and Young Laundry among them. Each enacted a practice of music-making in the American workplace that had been in operation since the early twentieth century (see Clark 1929).[2] Departing from this model, however, the police and fire departments cultivated choral singing to help soothe tensions that had emerged within and beyond Hawai'i's borders, stemming from its colonial history and multiethnic population. In 1952, Hawai'i was still a territory of the United States, a status imposed in 1898 following American-backed deposition of the Hawaiian monarchy. Following annexation, Hawai'i's *haole* (white)[3] political and economic elite petitioned for statehood several times, but were thwarted by continental Americans' fears of a nonwhite majority in the islands; that majority consisted largely of Hawaiians,[4] East Asians, and Filipinos. Then, in 1959, Hawai'i became the fiftieth state in the American union. In this sociopolitical milieu, the interethnic police and fire choral groups were strategically deployed by their respective chiefs to effect new public alliances.

I am indebted here to Beverley Diamond's theoretical revisioning of ethnomusicological studies in terms of alliances, that is, in terms of "music's capacity for defining relationships" (2006, 171). In this chapter I examine how the Honolulu police and fire departments used hybrid Hawaiian expressive practices—the products of century-long, transpacific traffic in song, dance, and dress—to forge new relationships with the citizenry of Hawai'i and continental Americans, respectively. I argue that the cultivation of alliances required nuanced modulations of masculinity. This chapter considers how, in the case of policemen, gentlemanly "soft power" displays of expressive culture were intended to relieve public anxieties about ethnically charged abuses of power within Hawai'i's borders (cf. Ray 1995; Dennis 2007).[5] In the wake of statehood, firemen used Hawaiian choral song and hula as invitations to continental Americans to think well of Hawai'i and its Indigenous and nonwhite settler populations.[6] Carefully inflecting hula movement, firemen performed a heteronormative masculinity that reinforced an American gender binary. This chapter also considers the interpersonal affinities generated by men's cultural labors. Singing and its attendant activities allowed policemen to rehearse an alternative sociability (Richards 2007)—one that minimized the importance of rank in their interactions with each other.

While administrative support for singing policemen lay in a bid to regain public trust, and the decision to put firemen on display was linked to American imperial designs, I am less concerned with the macropolitical outcomes of cultural praxis—which are hard to substantiate in any event—than I am with subjective resonances. Toward the end of this chapter, I pay attention to the effects/affects of musicking in the lives of Chang and Rosey, two Local non-Hawaiians. Chang's and Rosey's voices underscore Diamond's assertion that "alliances produce . . . identities" (2006, 171). Indeed, one reason for my attraction to alliance studies is its tactical move away from "identity," a construct that productively guided much ethnomusicological research for over a quarter century. My unease with "identity" comes down to this: I don't know how to characterize the complex subject positions of the Local men who populated the police and firemen's choruses; labels like "Hawaiian" and "Local" do some work in describing ethnic heritage and valual orientation, but even then, rather poorly. Add to that a historical remove of some sixty years, and I'm at a loss to ascribe identities to the policemen and firemen who sang and danced their way across the Hawaiian archipelago, the United States, even the world.

The mobilities I address in this chapter are sometimes as literal as those just mentioned, that is, the tours that police and firemen embarked upon as part of their chiefs' entourages, or the transport of genres across national, state, and cultural borders. More often they are figurative, indexical of men on the move. Here I have in mind the traversal of new cultural terrain: Local men singing songs in an incomprehensible language (Hawaiian), dancing a dance then commonly associated with women (hula), dressing themselves in unaccustomed garb. Even when they stayed at home, they were, in James Clifford's sense, travelers, "acquiring complex knowledges . . . and intercultural understandings" (Clifford 1997, 34). This was often as true for Hawaiian members of the police and firemen's choral groups as it was for non-Hawaiians. Hawaiian men certainly carved out their own gendered spaces (Walker 2011), but they felt the effects of American assimilation keenly, including the loss of language and ancestral cultural practices (Tengan 2008). As a function of mobility, participation in the police and fire department choral groups put non-Hawaiian Local men, together with their Local Hawaiian colleagues, in the role of Hawaiian culture bearers, which was both a sign and producer of commitment to an Indigenous modernity.

Choralism and Gender in Hawai'i

We might trace Hawai'i's singing men to an Indigenous expressive heritage grounded in chanted *mele* (poetry) (see Tatar 1982). Choral singing, though, has a shallower history in Hawai'i. Rooted in Christian hymnody—one of the most portable genres of the nineteenth century—it dates to 1820, the year of the first American Congregationalist mission to the islands. As Hawaiian churches proliferated in the wake of missionization, so did Hawaiian-language hymns (*hīmeni*). Over time a multiplex relationship developed between intoned *mele*, a logocentric and largely individual practice, and the part-singing favored by missionaries. Faced with an increasingly cosmopolitan array of cultural material in the nineteenth century, Hawaiians confected new syntheses from Euro-American hymnody, minstrelsy (Carr 2014), and Italian opera as well as other genres offered by touring companies or absorbed by Hawaiian seamen on their travels. In the process, Hawaiians generated a vast repertoire of secular Hawaiian-language songs, which they often rendered chorally. A vocality initially imposed, then, developed its own currency in Indigenous hands; even as specific genres of chanted *mele* were undermined by puritanical proscription, the poetic sensibilities—and even vocal techniques like falsetto—that infused *mele*, came to color Hawaiian choralism (Stillman 1987).

Musicking as a social enterprise followed a similar path. In the 1860s and

1870s, members of the Hawaiian royal family embraced the American glee club tradition, forming ensembles of singer–instrumentalists and composing Hawaiian-language songs (Liliʻuokalani [1898] 1985). Prince Leleiōhōkū led one of the most accomplished groups of male singers. Recalling its heyday, Curtis Iaukea wrote:

> In the interval between the King's visit to the United States in November of 1874 to his return in February of the following year, I was at the Prince's beck and call much of the time, especially of evenings when he felt free to make a friendly visit on one or two of his intimate friends . . . where the evening was spent in song till the "wee" hours of the morning.
>
> On those nightly errands and visits, the Prince usually took with him three or four of his boys forming the "Kawaihau Glee Club," of which I was a member. . . . It was at these rendezvous that the rendition of songs newly composed by either the Prince or his sister [the future Queen Liliʻuokalani] were heard for the first time, the latter having her own Glee Club as well as their brother King Kalakaua. . . .
>
> As a matter of fact those friendly and competitive renditions of Hawaiian songs and music formed an important theme in Hawaii's social life and intercourse. (Iaukea n.d.)

Whether the royal family's singing groups reflected grassroots trends or their practices trickled down to the general populace, the model for male singers was cast: alone, in duos/trios/quartets and still-larger ensembles, Hawaiian men sang vocally challenging songs that—nuanced with *kaona* (hidden meanings)—spoke poetically of land (*ʻāina*), sea (*kai*), divinity (*akua*), and love in its many guises (*aloha, hoʻoipoipo*). Still later in the nineteenth century, male singers found increasing validation through gender-exclusive high school glee clubs; these clubs were the nuclei for cultivating the Victorian American values of male closeness and camaraderie (Mook 2007) that resonated with Indigenous practices of gender segregation.[7]

By the mid-twentieth century, choruses were strongly associated with workplaces and rooted in the culture of the Hawaiian Civic Club Association, a network of Indigenous service organizations. Even Kalaupapa—a settlement on Molokaʻi for people afflicted with Hansen's disease—created its own choral group; it was conducted by one of the key choral music figures on Ōʻahu, Martha Hohu, who lent her directorial hand to the Honolulu Police Group for several years ("Artist in Profile" 1975). Of course, once it entered schools even earlier in the century, choral singing reached its most diverse population. Into the 1970s, choral singing held a central spot in Hawaiʻi's public and private schools, incorporating the offspring of Chinese, Japanese, Filipino, Portuguese, and other laborers who had been recruited for plantation work the previous century. It did so at the expense of other Indigenous arts such as chanted *mele* and *hula kahiko* (ancient hula). That may be why, as one of the most pervasive, public forms of collective musicking in Hawaiʻi for well over a century, choral singing hangs on by a tether today.[8] Though many sonic features of choralism persist, perhaps too much of Hawaiʻi's American colonial legacy was inscribed on choral bodies.

Utilizing a genre of music that traveled to Hawaiʻi on missionary waves—a genre ineluctably tied to the performance of virtuous civic life—this chapter provides two interlinked case studies of men's profession-based choral groups that endeavored to redress troubled relations at home and on the continental United States, and helped to reshape postwar masculinity in this multiethnic setting.

Honolulu Police Department

The Honolulu Police Department (HPD) inaugurated its all-male choral group in 1952; women were not included as they could not become officers until 1975. The choral group wasn't the policemen's first engagement with public music-making, but it was probably the most ambitious in that it gathered together forty-plus men from different units within the force (e.g., traffic, crime prevention) and included officers of different rank.[9] The impetus for its growth—rather than its genesis—was Daniel Liu, Honolulu's longest-serving police chief (1948–1969), whose mission was to modernize and restore public trust in the department. The HPD's troubles stretched back several decades. Honolulu residents' faith in the HPD was badly shaken in 1931 by its mismanagement of the Massie case, named for Thalia Massie, a white naval officer's wife who brought accusations of gang rape against five Local men of Hawaiian, Chinese, and Japanese descent. Though the trial ended in a hung jury, the fallout was tragic (see Stannard 2005): "Before a retrial could be convened, one of the accused—Joseph Kahahawai—was kidnapped and killed by a group that included Grace Fortescue (Thalia Massie's mother) and Thomas Massie (her husband) in January 1932. The Massie-Fortescue group was found guilty of manslaughter in May 1932. Under enormous federal and public pressure from the continent, Governor Lawrence Judd shortened the group's ten-year prison sentence to one day, fearing that Hawaii's status as a territory might be stripped in favor of a commission-form of government headed by the U.S. Navy" (Rosa 2001, 56 n. 4).

In the Territory of Hawaiʻi's ethnically stratified society, *haole*s had come out on top again, and this time they literally got away with murder, exposing painful divisions between *haole* and Local residents. "Local" is a broad designation for people that has terminological roots in the Massie case (Rosa 2014, 5). As a social phenomenon, "its historic origins [lie] in... the common working class background of Native Hawaiians and the immigrant plantation groups including Chinese, Filipinos, Japanese, Koreans, Okinawans, Portuguese and Puerto Ricans. Together these groups shared a collective subordinate social status in opposition to the dominant *haole* (white) planter and merchant oligarchy" (Okamura 1994, 162–163). "Local" is thus a relational category rooted in ethnicity, race, and class, and Localness is marked by particular modes of interaction and discourse, such as the use of Pidgin (Hawai'i Creole English).[10]

Prosecution of the Massie case revealed the HPD's corrupt white leadership and shoddy investigative practices.[11] Internally the HPD was in disarray, and Kahahawai's death confirmed what many Locals had long felt: that despite an ethnically diverse corps of police officers, the highest levels of the HPD were tainted by racial prejudice that did not favor them. At the close of World War II, the HPD was further "rocked by disclosure of graft in its vice squad," leading to its continental *haole* chief's premature departure (Ng 1999, 200). He was succeeded by two Local men, William Hoʻopai (1946–1948) and Daniel Liu. Racial tensions exacerbated by antagonism between Hawai'i's civilian and largely white military populations also weighed heavily on Liu as he worked to rehabilitate the HPD and modernize his force through officer training and community engagement (see "Human Relations and Law Enforcement in Honolulu, Hawaii" 1953).

Honolulu Police Choral Group

The Police Choral Group's genesis can be traced to a casual quartet of barbershoppers whose encounter with Drew Kaye, a Honolulu radio executive and pianist, gave rise to the idea of a larger ensemble ("Singing Policemen" 1954). Under Kaye's direction the police group made its public debut in Christmas 1952. Thrilled by the performance, Chief Liu vowed to support the singers' efforts. In terms of ethnic composition, the PCG reflected the department as a whole, as represented in the 1951 percentages listed in table 6.1 ("Human Relations" 1953, 14); that is, a majority were Local, i.e., of Hawaiian, East Asian, and mixed ethnic heritage, and a minority were *haole*.

Through Kaye's media connections the men sang live on radio and TV, issuing their own album of Christmas music in 1960 (Harpe 1960). After Kaye's return to the continental United States, the group continued briefly under "Papa" Panoke, followed by Martha Hohu and her accompanist daughter Leila Kiaha; another female conductor, Alvina Nye Kaulili, led the group for the longest period, until its demise in the early 1970s.

Rosey, of Filipino heritage, was one of the first to join the PCG in 1952 and

Table 6.1 Ethnic Composition of the Hawaii Police Department, 1951

Ethnic Group	*% of HPD*
Hawaiian and Part Hawaiian	39.4
Japanese	18.8
Chinese	7.9
Korean	3.9
Filipino	2.0
Other	4.2
Subtotal	*76.2*
Caucasian and Portuguese[12]	23.8

remained a member for more than ten years. He recalled that the PCG alone served as the public relations arm of the HPD, and claimed that singing improved community relations in a number of ways. From 1952 until the early 1970s (just after Liu's retirement), the PCG performed regularly at nursing homes and shopping centers, police conventions and governmental celebrations; its activities were closely monitored and supported by the establishment media. In 1959, for example, the *Honolulu Star-Bulletin* lauded the PCG's community engagement, noting that "the group has entertained generously, with special emphasis on the underprivileged. Many are familiar with its annual Christmas serenade tours through the city" ("A Fine Show for a Fine Cause" 1959). As Rosey told me, constant performing "elevated our self confidence in communicating with the public" (2002).[13] This was crucial for a corps that had previously had minimal training;[14] like many urban American police departments, the mid-twentieth century was a period of increasing professionalization for the HPD (Ray 1995, 566). Chief Liu must also have recognized in the PCG's earliest performance the "soft power" potential to mollify a disenchanted public.

Coined by political scientist Joseph Nye, "soft power," like its correlate "hard power," is a means to an end. Whereas hard power rests "on inducements and threats," soft power relies on indirect influence, on attracting others and shaping their preferences (Nye 2008, 29). Police often rely on hard or command power through intimidation and/or coercion, but as Nye points out, "even in the military, attraction plays an important role. As the former [U.S.] army chief of staff Eric Shinseki put it, 'You can certainly command without that sense of commitment [from others], but you cannot lead without it. And... command is a hollow experience, a vacuum often filled with mistrust and arrogance'" (ibid., 30). While soft power may be predicated on qualities such as personal magnetism, there are myriad values/objects/practices that can be deployed as soft power resources, including music and dance.[15] Of course "soft power" is hardly new to ethnomusicologists who have long understood the capacity of sound to affect human understandings and compel action, often with hegemonic force. Soft power may not be inherently virtuous, nor does its use guarantee benevolent outcomes, but its noncoercive, malleable qualities arguably allow for more contributive conduct and speaking across difference. My application of Nye's concept to relations that obtained between a local civic organization and the public it served departs from its extensive use in international studies, where the principal players are nation-states. This chapter contributes, instead, to budding interest in soft power as a riposte to hard power in smaller-scale social groups and institutions (e.g., Crewe 2011).

Chief Liu's administration provided logistical backing for the PCG. Arranging choristers' work schedules so they could convene rehearsals and performances required a kind of flexibility that could only be realized with approval from the very top. As was the custom in American workplaces, the HPD provided space and time for rehearsal, but no financial subsidy (see Clark 1929). The PCG earned money from its weekly shows at the Halekulani Hotel and from corporate sponsors, but lack of fixed income necessitated fundraising, which drew in extended family networks. The effort had soft power effects. Knocking on doors, selling *kalua* pork, Portuguese sausage, and sweetbread made policemen grateful for their neighbors' goodwill and put an obliged face on the HPD. Their most ambitious fundraiser was a *lūʻau* (feast) for four thousand people ("'Stars-a-Poppin' July 17" 1960) which put policemen in the roles of ticket sellers and food servers. All of these endeavors were necessary for the purchase of a piano, special uniforms, and off-island travel. Even when traveling as part of Liu's entourage, the PCG's travels were personally funded and deducted from annual vacation leave—points that Liu brought to public attention (Liu 1960). Recognition of choristers' self-sacrifice garnered great goodwill. When Honolulu residents read a news columnist's plea for clothing to keep the choristers warm during their sojourn in New York, Chicago, and Washington, DC, the police station was overrun with overcoats in just two days (Krauss 1960a, 1960b).

Not only did the PCG accompany Chief Liu to events like the 1960 Interpol conference, but they frequently used those destinations as departure points for more distant and much-coveted world travel. When their official singing duties ceased, a subset of the group continued performing for Hawaiʻi expats in places such as Norway, Singapore, and New Zealand.[16]

Fashion as Rhetorical "Technology"

It's hard to overstate the importance of dress to police authority. Recalling his 1934 recruitment to the HPD, Eugene Kennedy remarked that "the first thing is you'd go...have your uniforms made because without a uniform you were no good to them really" (Kennedy 1986, 1244). Recognizing the attired body as a locus of identification, the PCG used fashion as a "technology" (Yano 2003; de Lauretis 1987) to encode messages about gender, as well as ethnicity, class, place-based identity, and national allegiance. In her study of the contested development of the New York State Police in 1917, Gerda Ray notes how the chief focused on officers' appearance in winning public acceptance of his new force, attending "first to uniform design" (1995, 573). In New York, police "invoked elite definitions of masculine authority...to legitimate a controversial extension of the state's coercive power" (ibid., 566). Chief Liu's choral group, by contrast, used fashion rhetorically to temper policemen's hard power public personae.

As representatives of the department, the choral group wore different uniforms to portray different masculinities—each matched to song repertoire and occasion. Invitations from Hawai'i's military brass to sing the national anthem or hymns necessitated dark, form-fitting dress uniforms. Matching aloha shirts were appropriate for "lighter" Hawaiian material, including hulas, with sashes reserved for dancers. The open-neck, short-sleeved shirts, featuring relatively muted colors (compared with tourist kitsch) and tropical floral motifs, were recognizable as distinctively, geographically "Hawaiian" both at home and away. A "creolized garment" combining several sartorial traditions in its loose, comfortable cut (Filipino) and design motifs (Japanese, Chinese, Hawaiian), the aloha shirt was worn by men of every socioeconomic class and ethnicity by the 1950s (Arthur 2003, 10). In this way it came to signify Local culture. Initially regarded as casual wear, the shirt gained currency as a kind of business dress in the decade or so that the choral groups were active (ibid., 27). By spanning the formal and informal, aloha attire invited audiences to read the singers as ordinary, approachable island men: well put together but not uptight.

For Broadway musical numbers such as "Stouthearted Men" and classical Hawaiian fare such as "Sweet Lei Mamo," the choral group donned pale gray (and, later, maroon) dinner jackets adorned with pocket squares and police patches. Coupled with dark slacks, white shirts, and bow ties, the single-breasted, sack cut dinner jackets or "tuxedos," as they were called, stood out in my interviewees' memories, calling to mind civilian sophistication and constraint. Unlike the aloha shirts, there were probably few events in policemen's lives that called for this kind of attire, thus creating the "feeling of being dressed" (Ruggerone 2016). While bow ties and jackets were common for American popular music groups of the 1950s and 1960s, significantly for the PCG, they bore no markings of rank and their neutral color, freer cut, and elegance offset the impression of policing as blue-collar work, invoking images of cosmopolitan middle-class urbanity instead. Here costuming and music-making worked in tandem: rank-and-file policemen were often narrowly defined in terms of their coercive and physical power, but in orchestrating their image sonically and visually, they also played with class categories, defining themselves as sensitively refined and skilled (see Connell 2005, 55). For the middle-aged members of the PCG and its audiences, the dinner jackets may well have brought to mind Humphrey Bogart's romantic hero in *Casablanca* (1942). As an enduring visual icon of American wartime popular culture, Bogart's white-jacketed, bow-tied character drew together many desirable qualities: mental strength, moral rectitude, American patriotism, confident nonchalance, tough-guy sexual allure. Through the technology of fashion the PCG tried to humanize policemen's bodies, while still projecting an impression of discipline and corporate identity through uniformity. Sartorial choices summoned audiences to reimagine them, to see them as different kinds of men. Dinner jackets and aloha shirts offered instantly recognizable alternatives to policemen's regimental wear in ways that nationalized—that is, Americanized—and tied them to a particular place: Hawai'i.

Rehearsing Sociability

Strategic soft power moves like those noted above generated nonstrategic collateral alliances within the HPD. Because policemen worked individually in patrol cars, there was little shared physical, conversational space for developing fraternal bonds and friendships—the kind witnessed as commonplace on American TV cop shows. If anything, the lone police officer working his beat exacerbated the separations built into the HPD's steeply hierarchical organization. These working conditions often led to discomfort when policemen met in the corridors of police headquarters. Retired officer Clarence Kelley recalled how his morning salutations to a superior were habitually ignored (2004). There are few places where this kind of disregard wouldn't be taken as a sign of animus or snobbery, but in the HPD's Hawaiian-centric subculture, the contravention of customarily extended greeting routines was particularly egregious (see Fong 1994). By contrast, the PCG welcomed everyone, with the effect of flattening relations among choristers. As Rosey said, "Everybody, whether they sergeants, lieutenants—we're all the same level when we sing" (2002). No one was more surprised by the chorus's leveling effects than police brass, who were invited to the PCG's parties.

It would be shortsighted to think that simply singing together bred new cooperation among policemen (see Wiltermuth and Heath 2009; Pearce, Launay, and Dunbar 2015). Rehearsals offered a space for enacting modes of interaction associated with Hawaiian and Local lifeways. There men practiced an alternative kind of sociability (see Richards 2007) by participating in verbal routines associated with a Hawaiian "rhetoric of solidarity" (Boggs 1985).[17] As anthropologist Stephen Boggs observes, Hawaiians' playful teasing and contradiction of one another "are ways to relate in situations where unequals are striving to be equal" (ibid., 100). Choral members frequently inducted each other into these routines: "Hey, you forgot da words, eh?" one would taunt; "yeah, but you outta tune, uh?" the other would retort in jest (Rosey 2002). In this way shared singing experiences provided verbal grist for the solidarity mill. Postrehearsal gatherings at neighborhood eateries paved the way for "talking story" about singing, work, and family, extending and cementing a sense of amity among emergent equals (Boggs 1985, 91).

Relationships were more richly interwoven when the wives of PCG members started accompanying their husbands to rehearsals as casual observers. During Martha Hohu's tenure as director, the women were invited to form a separate "Hawaiian Group" and eventually merged with the PCG (Helen Kelley 2004). Friendships among the women also drew their husbands into new companionable configurations, which were then reinforced in multiple ways, including fundraising for expensive transoceanic travel.

Honolulu Fire Department

Like the HPD, the Honolulu Fire Department (HFD) performed a public service and faced real—perhaps even greater—dangers in its work. There was rarely, however, a punitive dimension to firemen's labors, making them more likeable. So the kind of public outreach that the HFD pursued through singing was never a matter of healing wounded community relations, and internally there was no significant interpersonal friction or managerial strife. Though I cannot cite numbers, my sense is that the ethnic makeup of the fire department resembled that of the police department, with more Hawaiians and fewer *haoles*. In the 1950s and 1960s, the HFD's organizational structure was only nominally hierarchical.[18] Familiarity was reinforced by first-name address and by the fact that firemen worked together on twenty-four-hour shifts, sleeping at the firehouse, cooking meals for each other, and sharing cleaning duties. Cohabiting and maintaining the firehouse created a domestic space characterized by comfortable relationships. Even off-duty the men sought each other's company and met regularly at Rosie's, a local Hawaiian bar (see also Thurnell-Read and Parker 2008).

Honolulu Fire Department Chorus

Choral singing in the Honolulu Fire Department followed a trajectory different from that in the HPD, though both departments relied on chiefs with a vested interest in singing. Like the police chief, the fire chief was (and is) a political appointee of the mayor of the City and County of Honolulu. In 1959, the year Hawai'i was granted statehood, Mayor Neal S. Blaisdell appointed his brother, William F. Blaisdell, to the top job.[19]

According to Donald S. M. Chang (2004), a founding member of the fire department chorus, Blaisdell was a "proud Hawaiian" who wanted to resurrect the tradition of a performing group within the HFD.[20] He asked Captain Isaac Harbottle, also Hawaiian, to form a choral group as well as a string combo that would develop a repertoire of Hawaiian songs. Once under way, the HFD choral group, like its police counterpart, was busiest at Christmastime and performed for seniors' homes, business openings, and the funerals of civil servants. Like singing policemen, the HFD depended on fundraising and gigs at Waikīkī hotels as well as business sponsorships to underwrite travel and uniforms. And like the policemen, they were darlings of media personalities who featured them on their live radio and TV shows.

But the HFD's choral project differed from the HPD's in its self-conscious desire to put a Hawaiian stamp on an American institution in a place that had just been fully incorporated into the American union. Whether supportive, ambivalent, resigned, or resistant to statehood (see Tengan 2008, 59), Hawaiians in positions of political power in 1959, like the Blaisdells, used their positions to co-opt Hawaiian cultural practices to show the rest of America what Hawai'i was *really* about.[21] Caught in the endlessly refracting consequences of the Massie case—William Blaisdell himself had been a juror in one of the trials (Rosa 2014, 97)—proponents of statehood in the late 1940s found that continental Americans' memories were still susceptible to racialized mainland media caricatures of the five male defendants as foreign "dark-skinned" brutes (Stannard 2005). Even in 1959, lingering suspicions about Hawai'i's Asian and Indigenous populations had made statehood a hard sell, especially among southern senators who continued to defend segregationist policies in the midst of a burgeoning civil rights movement (Saranillio 2010, 289).

Hawai'i's change of political status ushered in the need to entertain fire chiefs and other VIPs visiting from the continental United States, as well as new expectations to visit them abroad. A "big-hearted" "tough guy" (Chang 2004), Chief Blaisdell would have been sensitive to American apprehensions and, I argue, established the choral group to demonstrate Hawai'i's civility to continental holdouts on the subject of statehood. Blaisdell soon took his choral contingent to the regional fire chiefs' convention in San Francisco. Donning a similar array of clothing as the policemen, including white, shawl-collared dinner jackets and black bow ties, the firemen sang songs from their Hawaiian-centric repertoire (fig. 6.1). Carinthia Pua'a,[22] who was asked by Harbottle to direct the chorus (fig. 6.2), drew from a vast collection of TTBB arrangements

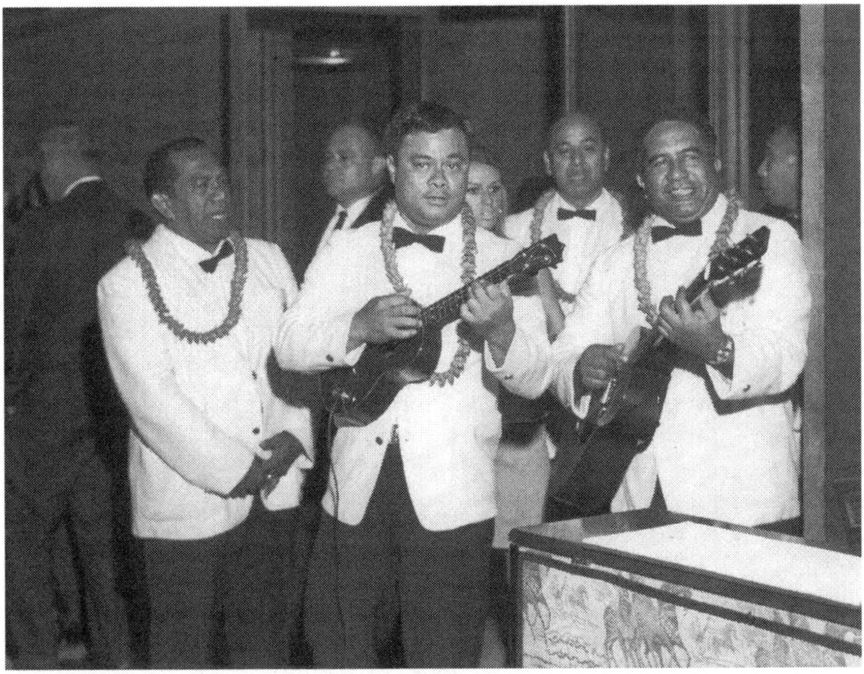

Figure 6.1 Some Honolulu Fire Department Chorus members in dinner jackets; Isaac Harbottle, far right. Courtesy of Carinthia Harbottle.

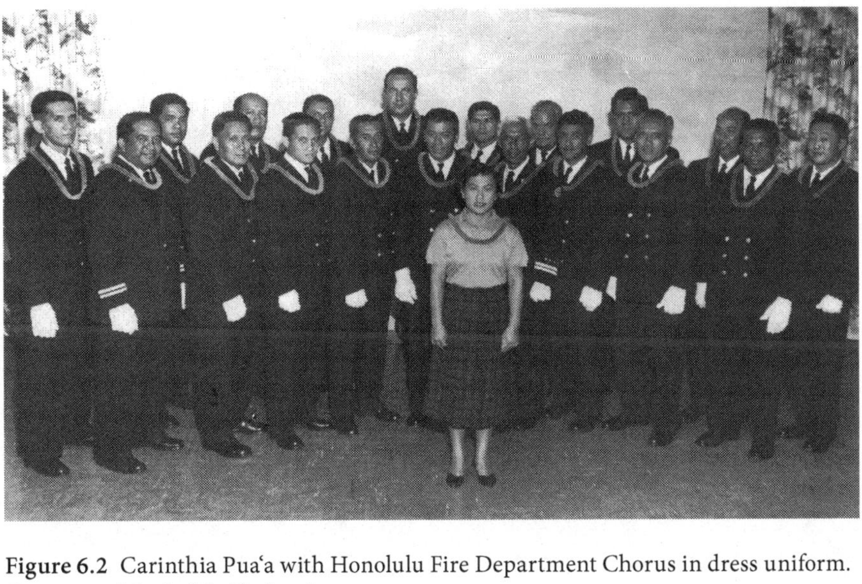

Figure 6.2 Carinthia Puaʻa with Honolulu Fire Department Chorus in dress uniform. Courtesy of Carinthia Harbottle.

that had been used at Kamehameha Schools, famous for their Hawaiian-language choral practices (Szego 1999).[23] She added her own arrangements of hula and *hapa haole* (Hawai'i-themed English) songs, Christmas tunes, and newly minted pieces celebrating statehood (Harbottle 2009). Harmonically and structurally, the arrangements would have been reassuringly familiar to American ears, as would the group's blended sound ideal. What marked the firemen as sonically Other was the use of string ensemble accompaniment ('ukulele, guitar, bass) and falsetto (a technique that hearkened to chanted *mele*) on hula songs, as well as the use of Hawaiian language. The sonorities afforded by a Hawaiian phonetic palette lent the choral groups a subtle yet distinct timbral signature (see Szego 2003). Singing in Hawaiian was de rigeur, even if language proficiency was a rarity among choristers and directors. Practically speaking, Hawaiian language was more frequently sung than spoken, and the firemen (as well as policemen) labored under the guidance of their female director to memorize texts phonetically, perfect pronunciation, and decipher the subtleties of Hawaiian poetic texts. The firemen thus performed "America" and "Hawai'i" simultaneously; while obeying the sonic conventions that allowed choral music to float effortlessly back across the Pacific, they also indexed Indigeneity and difference from mainstream America.

In San Francisco, the choral group won the hearts of the local fire chief and his men, who subsequently hosted them lavishly—chauffeuring them about town, providing sumptuous meals and free liquor (Chang 2004; Paiaina 2004). In effect, they were treated to the same kind of hospitality for which Hawaiians are duly famous (see Chun 2006; Fong 1994). These are the stories I heard from firemen: by drawing others to them, they converted aesthetic skill into social currency. For those raised in and around Hawaiian communities where most activity was "organized around intensifying affiliative ties" (Gallimore and Howard 1968, 10), the gestures of reciprocity they received from continental hosts were immensely satisfying and taken as indications of successful diplomatic engagement. Occasionally those connections lasted beyond initial encounters. Isaac Harbottle, for instance, developed a warm bond with one West Coast fire chief, and when that chief later experienced personal difficulties, he found refuge in Hawai'i and his friendship with Harbottle (Chang 2004; Harbottle 2009). For Hawai'i firemen, hard-won opportunities for travel could be translated into meaningful relationships that were in stark contrast to the entertainer–visitor roles that would increasingly trouble Hawai'i's tourist sphere—where even the most appreciative visitor audiences had little choice but to approach musicians and dancers as objects of consumption, and where artists rarely sidestepped the structures of capitalist exchange.[24] Off-island mobility also gave firemen (and policemen) a sense of world citizenry, of participating positively in global, cosmopolitan cultural circuits (see also Imada 2012).

It was the cultural resources that Hawaiians shared—especially music—that initially attracted Donald Chang (fire chief 1993–1994) to the choral group. Chang was with the choral group from its inception. As a young Local Chinese boy raised in a single-parent home and bound to a broad network of Hawaiian aunts, uncles, and cousins, Chang wanted desperately to belong, to be identified as Hawaiian, too. While scholars point to the stigma attached to Hawaiianness for most of the nineteenth and twentieth centuries (e.g., Osorio 2009), Chang's story suggests that there were non-Hawaiians attracted to Indigenous values and culture in more than a superficial way. Chang married a Hawaiian; he later celebrated achievements of the Hawaiian Renaissance, such as language revitalization, and fully supported his children's participation in it. In fact, in the early 1960s, when a renaissance was still beyond most people's imagination, the HFD's foray into Hawaiian cultural production helped fulfill Chang's youthful yearning. An integral part of that production was hula.

Hula

When director Carinthia Pua'a told the HFD chorus that they would add hula to their performance repertoire, she was initially met with squirmish reluctance. Chang recalled her insistence: "NO, no, no, no, dis isn't some sort of sissy thing. Ah, this is man hula, it's the *man*-type, it's the *mas*culine hula. *Not* the feminine hula" (Chang 2004). Chang's recollection, performed emphatically, speaks not only to movement style, which I address later, but to the American transformation of hula into a female art. For Isaac Harbottle and Pua'a, hula would have been an obvious performance choice in that it was already a stock component of cultural display aimed at tourists. However, most presentational conventions since the early twentieth century relegated women to the role of hula dancer and men to the roles of singer and instrumentalist (Imada 2012). In the 1950s and 1960s, male dancers headlining in Waikīkī were rather exceptional.[25] While they tended to be from prominent Hawaiian music/dance lineages, most Local men (Hawaiian and non-Hawaiian) were vulnerable to a Euro-American stance that regarded hula as soft and feminizing (Tengan 2008, 152–155).[26] A photo of the HFD dated 1937 (fig. 6.3) suggests that there were always some men outside of the entertainment industry who danced hula, but again, they were few.[27] Significantly for the fire department, Maiki Aiu, a *kumu hula* (hula teacher) once married to a fireman, was keen to revive male hula (Chong-Stannard 2002) and provided the choral group with instruction.[28]

Hula was and is gendered in many ways (Stillman 1996; Tengan 2008; Imada 2012). When I asked Carinthia Pua'a Harbottle what made the firemen's dancing "masculine," she identified their high energy and use of "straight" hands or fists in contrast to undulating wrists/hands/fingers (Harbottle 2009).

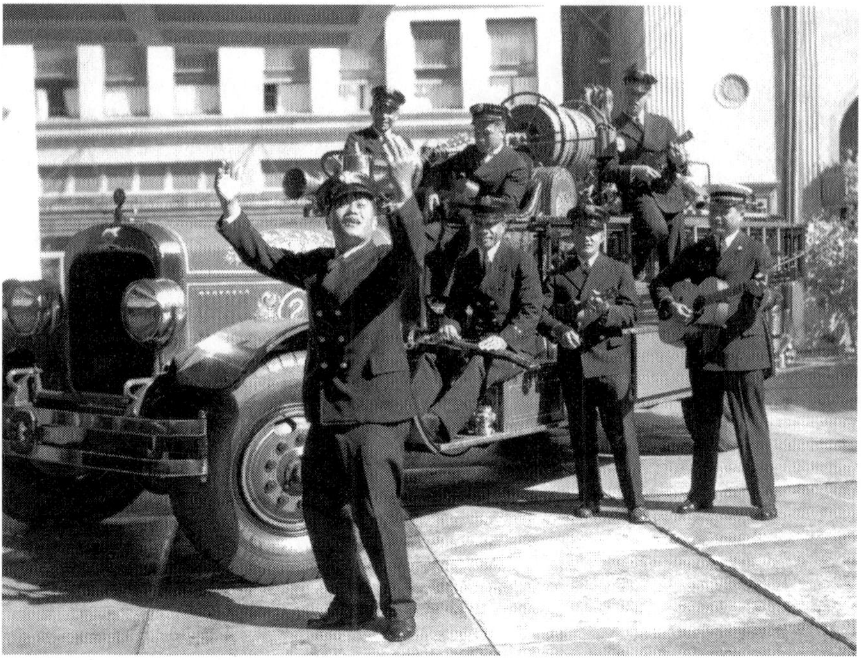

Figure 6.3 Honolulu Fire Department dancer, 1937. Courtesy of the Bishop Museum.

Milton Ī, Maiki Aiu's first male dancer, recalled that a hallmark of her style was very erect posture, and that men were further distinguished by movements generated "from the waist up"; there was little bend in the knee, thus limiting lateral hip motion (Ī 2012). "Masculine" hula was also defined by repertoire. In a representational genre like hula, choreography is conditioned by song words. The firemen learned *'auana* (modern) and *hapa haole* hula repertoires with texts depicting heteronormative Euro-American and traditional Hawaiian male activities. As examples, " 'Ālika" is a song that depicts the *Arctic*, a ship that sailed Hawaiian waters in the eighteenth century; references to the vessel's prow and rigging are veiled phallic allusions that can be made apparent through gesture. "Laupāhoehoe Hula" celebrates the muscular, broad-shouldered body of a cliff-climbing, canoe-paddling, poi-eating Hawaiian "boy." And the group's signature song, "Fireman's Hula" praises firefighters' speediness and skill, identifying them also as objects of desire. All are up-tempo dances that firemen happily "played to the audience" (Harbottle 2009).

Historically, Hawaiian culture supported a variety of gender categories and sexualities, including *māhū*, a cross-Polynesian term that evokes qualities of both genders (Ellingson and Oda 2008). *Māhū* is now commonly and colloquially glossed as transgendered, gay, or effeminate (see Robertson 1989; Xian and

Anbe 2001; Matzner 2001; Tengan 2008, 152; Imada 2012, 39). Traditionally, "men, including māhū, occupied the highest echelons of hula" (Imada 2012, 39), but over a century of American gender and sexual reeducation pressed male hula dancers to the margins of hula praxis and *māhū* to the margins of Hawai'i society. Burt Ramsay traces "trouble with the male dancer" in American culture to the nineteenth century. Speaking of ballet, he writes that the "ways that male dancers appeared on stage became a source of anxiety to bourgeois male spectators. To enjoy the spectacle of male dancing is to be interested in men. . . . The male ballet dancer came too close for comfort to the blurred and problematic line that separates . . . necessary and approved homosocial male bonding from forbidden homosexual sexuality" (Ramsay 1995, 27–28). The balletic antidote to this anxiety was to showcase dazzling athleticism (Hamera 2007, 123); the solution for the fire department was to encode heterosexuality in repertoire choice and choreography.[29] Maiki Aiu chose quick-stepping, often cheeky dances that presented the men as *kolohe* (mischievious, fun-loving), while choreographically she distinguished them as masculine through the use of closed movements: fingers drawn together or balled in a fist, hip movements limited in ambitus. Dance was as much a "technology of gender" (Yano 2003) as dress, and worked to disambiguate the men's sexual orientation while displaying their good humor and warm sensuality.

In addition to Maiki Aiu's kinesic and choreographic formulas, firefighters' initial qualms about dancing were probably offset by the presence of recognized dancers in their company, such as Clem Paiaina Sr., who danced within the family fold.[30] His son, Clem Paiaina Jr., told me that younger firemen like himself joined the chorus, knowing they would have to dance because they looked up to seniors who had distinguished themselves as men who could "eat smoke" (Paiaina 2004). If brave men could dance, so could they. Presumably choristers like Clem Jr. also found gratification in developing new kinds of mastery over their bodies and affirmation in their audiences' hearty reception (fig. 6.4).

It's tempting to view firemen's displays of Hawaiian culture to American audiences as acts of ideological surrender to imperialist forces, to the extent that they shored up the recent move to statehood. After all, tempering Americans' attitudes seems to have been Blaisdell's intent. The firemen's cultural work, as well as I can determine, shone the spotlight on Hawaiianness—constructed as timeless and compartmentalized—rather than on Hawai'i's historically intersecting cultures.[31] Did they then effect an ethnic "erasure" in the same way that female dancers working continental hula circuits in prior decades symbolically "cleansed" Hawai'i of much-feared Asians (Imada 2012, 185)? Undoubtedly. Presenting a modern Hawaiian monoculture that integrated an array of ethnic groups was more likely to advance Chief Blaisdell's goal of acceptance than, for example, the inclusion of Japanese songs, especially in the post–World War II era.

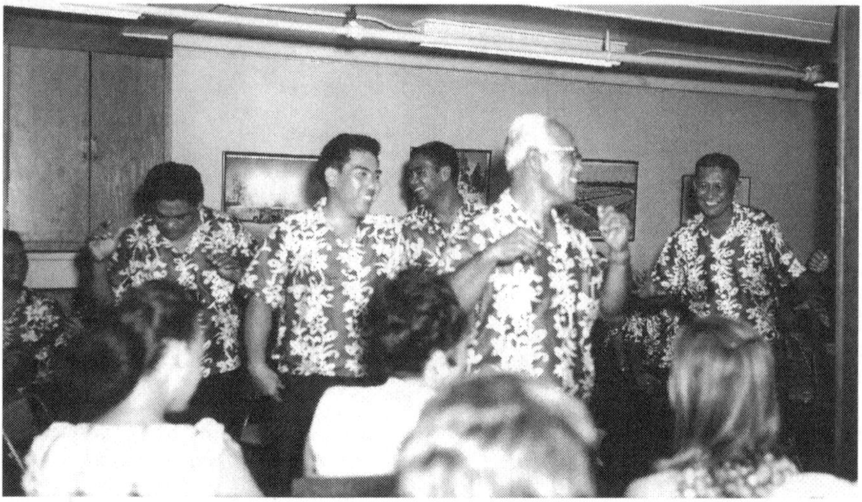

Figure 6.4 A lighthearted moment as Clem Paiaina Sr. leads other firemen in a hula, 1960s. Courtesy of Michelle Paiaina-Makua.

The challenge that firemen's hula presented to then-current and changing definitions of masculinity, however, muddies any narrative of absolute capitulation to American imperialism. We can ask whether the firemen's interethnic choral group performed acts of cultural obduration or reclamation even as Chief Blaisdell championed, and his men embraced or resisted, statehood. The contradiction that seems to inhere in this question is no contradiction at all, but is a prevailing condition of colonial cultural zones: performative acts can enable even as they constrain (Giddens 1984). Donald Chang, for example, overcame his reservations about dancing, with powerful effects: "It opened doors for me in something I was always wanting to be part of.... Bill Au, Bucky Yee—we're not Hawaiians, but we felt we were Hawaiians, you know.... Proud you know, you can dance the hula, you can sing Hawaiian song—where can you do that, you know? In a *fire* department? What fire department sing Hawaiian song and dance hulas?... But we were proud. We had great times" (Chang 2004). Chang was seeking identification and found it by assimilating himself to a small corner of the aesthetic worlds of Hawaiian-language song and dance. While his enculturation was hardly immersive, it required dedication and courage, especially when we consider that dancing hula with other men carried risk of censure.[32]

If Chang's desire to "be Hawaiian" was driven by personal predilection and familial circumstance, his attitude toward Hawaiian song and dance was more widely shared. The HPD's Rosey, born in Hawaiʻi to Filipino parents, took his sociogeographical position to mean that "this is part of your growing up and singing Hawaiian songs. Eh, you live in Hawai'i, you gotta learn how to do dis, do dat, and everything else make you a full person.... This is part of living here; you gotta do dat" (Rosey 2002). Of course, Rosey loved to sing, but for him Hawaiian cultural practices were also at the core of a sustainable Local society. Chang, on the other hand, seemed to regard Hawaiian song and dance as exceeding the possibilities he had encountered in 1960s Local circles. In both cases, the kinds of citizenship Rosey and Chang sought through voluntary enculturation articulate a process-based sense of place that, after Doreen Massey, is "constructed out of a particular constellation of social relations, meeting and weaving together at a particular locus" (Massey 1994, 154). As a Local Filipino and member of the police force in the post-Massie era, Rosey was well attuned to ethnic/racial tensions in Hawai'i. Embedded in his and Chang's statements about Hawaiian singing and dancing were feelings of affection and responsibility toward Hawai'i as a place that layered Indigenous with Asian settler experiences.

In the Police Choral Group, hula was a specialist activity with a strongly gendered division of labor. When the policemen and their wives combined forces, most of the women were expected to dance. However, only a few men, like James Wong and Herman Meyers, performed hula publicly, and usually as part of a smaller ensemble that accompanied Chief Liu to public events. James Wong and his wife also frequently performed hula as a couple (Kelley 2012). Within the larger group, husband-singer and wife-dancer divisions reinforced American gender norms, underscoring policemen's "compulsory" heteronormative masculinity (Yoon 2009).[33]

Even with a handful of dancers standing for the whole, the potential payoffs from men's hula were even higher in the PCG than in the fire department. For policemen, whose public interactions had been previously colored by hard power—that is, a strongly gendered threat of penalty, coercion, and perhaps even physical submission—dancing was a site where "masculinity [could be] reimagined without reinscribing [police] authority" (Giese 1998, 119).

Alliances Sought, Alliances Gained

In the 1950s, Honolulu police chief Liu ventured to replace the Local population's fear and mistrust of his force with respect, understanding that trust cannot be achieved through command. Policemen needed to make themselves friendly and attractive enough that Hawai'i's citizenry would want to help them achieve their shared objectives. Displays of song, and occasionally dance, by fashionably attired men (and later, their wives) were central to this project, and their active presence in Honolulu's charitable music scene put them on the same footing as other profession-based choral groups. Just how effective were the policemen in reshaping broad public perceptions? Nye himself concedes that "the gap between power measured as resources and power judged as the outcomes of behavior is not unique to soft power. It occurs with all forms of power" (Nye 2007, 391–392). Although the choral group did not outlive Chief Liu's enthusiasm for it, Rosey cited the appointment of the HPD's first community relations officer in January 1967 as recognition of the singers' public achievements (Rosey 2002).[34]

Chief Liu capitalized on the attractive potential of men's singing as part of his agenda to improve the department's daily functioning and transform its image; he had to neutralize if not reverse the effects of its miserably corrupt and coercive past, which had left Hawai'i's multiethnic fabric in tatters. The singing policemen I spoke with were genuinely invested in Liu's rehabilitative efforts. Rosey insisted that "all the police officers—dey cannot be on deah high horse all da time.... You got to treat everybody fairly, whether he lives in [working-class] Kalihi or live in the high, rich areas. Fairness is my ting" (Rosey 2002). I take his statement as testimony to the inversion of police–civilian relations that Liu was trying to effect. Policemen were very cognizant of public scrutiny, and some, like Clarence Kelley, tried to demonstrate that "besides being law and order, you...can be humble too" (C. Kelley 2004); humility is one of those Local values that can be indexed by group affiliation generally and choral singing specifically—that is, by not standing out or flaunting one's status and power. Kelley's statement also acknowledges the co-presence of "hard" and "soft" power in police work. Their entanglement, however, is noisier than Nye's critics would suggest (see note 34). Attitudinal changes toward police could only manifest if there were changes on the ground—that is, if Liu's modernization project had real consequences for police–civilian relations. To be sure, Honolulu's citizenry still had occasion to be angered by police action, but the HPD's retraining of its personnel in the Liu decades, in concert with public outreach, must have dampened cynicism about police incompetence and internal corruption, if not *haole* favoritism.

The Fire Department's forays into the cultural realm were motivated by Chief Blaisdell's parallel desires to welcome visiting American dignitaries and to network at national fire conventions and beyond—all on the heels of a battle for statehood that alerted him to continental Americans' racial suspicions. Firemen's success in overturning mainlanders' fear is just as difficult to gauge—as difficult as it is to locate this rather ill-defined group of resisters.[35] Nonetheless, firemen read enthusiastic reception for their presentations of cultural fare that combined the familiar (choral music) with the exotic (Hawaiian language, falsetto, hula) at events like the 1962 Seattle World's Fair, as well as friendships forged with fellow firemen on continental tours, as having negotiated difference artfully. Their narratives of transoceanic travel used tropes of exploring and sharing; firemen (and policemen) prided themselves in impressing a vision of Hawaiʻi—however circumscribed it may have been—on new audiences in new places. The process of justifying national belonging, however, did not seem to excite a great deal of national pride, at least none that emerged in our conversations. Even though statehood harnessed the fortunes of Hawaiians and Asian settler populations more tightly to the United States, what I heard were deeper identifications with Hawaiʻi, with fellow workers, or with individuals encountered on their travels.

As a part of their respective sociopolitical missions, each choral group had to manage its members' publicly projected masculinities. Tempering images of hard power, singing policemen made themselves legible as more complete human beings through displays of sonic unity, through fashionable civilian attire —playing visually with categories of class, national and cultural association— and through obedience to the directorial hands of Hawaiian women. The policemen I talked to all spoke with reverence about Martha Hohu and Alvina Kaulili especially, and submitted happily to their direction. Gendered interaction onstage increased as time went on. Husband–wife pairs populating the Police Choral Group pushed domestic roles onto the presentational stage by dividing aesthetic labor along predictable lines: women danced while men sang and played for them.[36] Firemen, on the other hand, disarmed their continental audiences by dancing in "unexpected places" (Deloria 2004)—that is, in place of women. The decision to put male dancers centerstage was joined to a tacit injunction to convey a heterosexual masculinity. Kinesically, the message that firemen gave off was clear: they were straight "men's men" (Harbottle 2009), not *māhū*, and thus acceptable partners in the American union. Their contained "masculine" style was also a corrective to the cartoonish mimicry that attached itself to "feminine" hula, that is, the flapping arms and hyperbolic hip circling that typified renditions by tourists and imitators generally.

The choice to put policemen and firemen on display and to convey them across the Pacific was not without precedent. I can only surmise that Chiefs Liu and Blaisdell modeled their own efforts at cultivating local and national alliances after those that were played out on the international stage during the Cold War. Musical diplomacy was exercised frequently in this period and the United States was both patron and recipient of such missions. For example, in the immediate aftermath of the Korean War (1950–1953)—a war increasingly disavowed by Americans—a South Korean children's choir launched a fundraising tour to the United States. The sight and sound of impeccably rehearsed and colorfully attired innocents, warbling against a backdrop of iconic American sites, spoke both to America's munificence during the war and a democratic, forward-looking Korea in its wake (Woo 2015). Also concurrent with Hawai‘i initiatives discussed in this chapter was the U.S. State Department's Cultural Presentations Program, which took jazz groups to newly independent African nations between 1957 and 1969. Eager to attract the most recent members of the United Nations to the democratic cause, but embarrassed by the grim state of internal race relations, the State Department funded tours by mixed-race bands—led largely by African American jazz greats—to symbolically counteract America's notoriety as a racist nation (Monson 2007, 126). In many ways, this action most closely resembled the work of the HFD chorus; while ethnic/racial distinctions among its constituent members were visible, their concerted efforts presented a simpler, reassuringly monocultural voice.

Following Olwage's analysis of black choralism in nineteenth-century South Africa, Hawaiian choralism might be understood as an enduring artifact of American missionization; in other words, the Honolulu fire and police departments' choral displays can be read as "exhibition[s] of discipline" (2004, 41) demonstrating the civilization of Hawaiian and Asian bodies in the ethnically charged pre- and post-statehood periods. Hawaiian choral singing's accompanying comportments—still, erect figures, symmetrically arranged; eyes dutifully trained on a conductor—performed an ethics of civil containment, as did homogeneously blended voices. As noted at the outset of this chapter, in fin-de-siècle Hawai‘i, singing expertly was a sign of skill and refinement, and singing together in close harmony was both an encouragement and sign of Hawaiian homosocial solidarity. Interpreting this mode of male expressive behavior as simply another triumph of American colonialism would be to ignore the ways that it continued to feed and be fed by a Hawaiian poetic sensibility, a timbral aesthetic afforded by Hawaiian language and occasional use of falsetto, and Hawaiian/Local modes of social enactment. Through hula, furthermore, firefighters presented new possibilities for Indigenous and Local expressions of masculinity, even as they sustained an American sexual ideology.

I have been cautious about making claims for the larger social consequences of expressive culture that required travel in the literal sense. Metaphorical travel, however, generated obvious alliances. Within the police department, the acquisition and practice of new musical skills effected changes in a troubled workspace. The PCG's inclusive subculture and shared musical goals allowed men to temporarily bracket distinctions in rank, and the shared social spaces of rehearsal, fundraising, and performance allowed Local policemen, regardless of ethnic heritage, to practice a Hawaiian rhetoric of solidarity and equality. Policemen's protracted face-to-face interactions also mellowed in the presence of the PCG's strong female conductors, spilling over into postrehearsal and postperformance life.

The Honolulu police and fire department choral groups were crucibles of interethnic contact. There, men—even Hawaiian men—submitted themselves to regimens of singing, dancing, and self-presentation that stretched their cultural knowledge and self-understandings. For a Local Chinese like Donald Chang, work and self were complexly intertwined such that his sense of belonging was transformed by the Hawaiian songs and hulas he learned through association with other firemen and tradition bearers like Maiki Aiu. Rosey's participation in the PCG was tied more practically to a sense of cultural stewardship, which he regarded as a Local imperative; work simply provided the conditions for exercising his responsibility. Significantly, the kinds of relation and subjectivity Chang and Rosey expressed were neither naïve expressions of cultural transcendence or fusion, nor were they iterations of a "discourse of aloha" (Pierce 2004) that trivialized Hawai'i as a multiethnic island utopia. Learning a broad repertoire of Hawaiian choral songs and hulas as Rosey and Chang did speaks to the role that non-Hawaiian Local men could play in sustaining and shaping modern modes of Hawaiian cultural praxis. They did this in collaboration with Hawaiian colleagues, and together extended the sonic/poetic, sartorial, and kinesic compass of Local masculinity in postwar Hawai'i.

Notes

I am indebted to Mandy Blake Bowers for her warm support and resourcefulness in helping me track down sources. I wish to thank Leon Chisholm, Rebecca Draisey-Collishaw, John Rosa, Harris M. Berger, and Beverley Diamond for their insightful comments on various drafts of this chapter; any inadequacies that remain are mine to bear. This chapter is dedicated to Ric Trimillos, superb scholar and generous mentor.

1. "Rosey" is the pseudonym chosen by my interviewee, a man of Filipino descent.

2. There is an enduring relationship between music and work stretching to the preindustrial era (see Korczynski 2003, 314). In early twentieth-century North America, music-making was promoted in the industrial workplace. Manufacturers supplied workers with rehearsal space, even musical instruments, in a bid to secure loyalty, boost productivity, and diminish labor dissatisfaction. Said one American steel company superintendent in 1923, "The men have become keenly interested in their bands, orchestras and choral societies which have become important factors in developing them as efficient workmen. Last year they refused to join the steel strike" (in Grabel 1923, 303). Workplace music-making penetrated civic organizations, too. The New York Police Department, for example, inaugurated its choral group in 1916.

3. *Haole* like "Local," also used in this chapter, is a complex term whose meaning has shifted over the past century. "By the early twentieth century the term was used mostly in reference to whites from the United States, either those who had become entrenched in the Territory of Hawai'i over generations or the newly arrived servicemen and their families" (Rosa 2014, 32).

4. In this chapter, Hawaiian is used as a marker of Indigeneity rather than residency (see

Kauanui 2008, xi); thus, it refers to people indigenous to the Hawaiian archipelago. Hawaiians may also be referred to as Native Hawaiians, Kanaka Maoli (real or true people), or Kanaka ʻŌiwi (bone people).

5. Dennis's study of an Australian police band reveals the kind of affective work that music can accomplish. Carefully trained to rein in emotional behavior during their civilian interactions, police came to be viewed as lacking humanity. Musical performances "serve[d] to reanimate…police officers by making the emotions lurking beneath 'impartial' police skins audibly evident to members of the public" (2007, 2).

6. I am sympathetic to Michael Gard's concern that by using the word "masculinity" exclusively in reference to men, I end up "rehearsing the very distinctions between sex and gender [that researchers have] sought to avoid" (2006, 30). As used here, "masculinity" refers to "qualities commonly associated with men" (ibid., 31); it is not natural to the category "men." Unfortunately, I find Gard's terminological solution, "symbolic masculinity," to be unwieldy.

7. While there were many ways of enacting manhood in Victorian America figured on race, ethnicity, class, age, religious and political ideology, among other things (Griffen 1990), a common element of white male experience that played itself out in Hawaiʻi (by virtue of *haole* socioeconomic dominance) was homosocial fraternization. Singing in ensembles, including barbershop quartets, was a leisure pursuit, along with sports and participation in fraternal orders, that encouraged male closeness and companionship.

8. The most visible remnant of a vibrant choral culture is the Kamehameha Schools Song Contest, televised live annually.

9. In the late 1940s, Detective Sterling Mossman led a police glee club consisting of a small group of accomplished singers and instrumentalists. It is not clear how long the glee club lasted, but Mossman's off-duty entertainment career blossomed. From 1952 to 1969 he performed at the Queen's Surf in Waikīkī. A musician, comedian and dancer, Mossman was known as the "hula cop" ("Detective by Day, Entertainer by Night" 1953).

10. As Okamura (1994) points out, even within this discursive domain there have been historic ethnic and class cleavages, for example, between Japanese and other Local groups. Ohnuma, citing Chris Leong, notes that "there is no single definition, that the term is…gradational and shifts meaning with the speaker and situation, and…that it is a marker of belonging that must be agreed upon by others.…'Local' is above all an 'attitude'" (2002, 277). Ohnuma thus explores the possibility that *haole*s can be Local too.

11. A primary target of criticism was the chief of detectives, John McIntosh, who had been a pro-British constable in the Boer War and in New Zealand's colonial battles against the Māori before landing in Hawaiʻi in 1921. At the HPD, McIntosh treated his lower-ranked Hawaiian, Asian, and mixed-ethnicity detectives with disdain and asserted himself as guardian of the *haole* elites who controlled Hawaiʻi's economic and political fortunes (Stannard 2005, 85–88).

12. This category is problematic. "Caucasian and Portuguese" were probably grouped together because Portuguese were less visibly different from the dominant (white) American business class than other groups in Hawaiʻi and enjoyed a slightly elevated status. In plantation culture, for example, Portuguese often assumed the position of *luna* (foreman).

13. All quotations from my interviews with policemen and firemen are verbatim transcriptions. Their locution, phonetics, and syntax are often indicative of the use of Hawaiʻi Creole English, colloquially known in Hawaiʻi as Pidgin.

14. Eugene Kennedy, who joined the HPD in 1934, talks about the cursory training given police officers during World War II (1986, 1248); he also remarks on the haphazard route to

promotion within the department based on personal affiliation with the police chief, rather than on experience and competence (ibid., 1246).

15. Nye attributes a good deal of the West's Cold War success to the dissemination of its cultural capital to Eastern Europe. Of the pre-*glasnost* era he observes that "rock-and-roll music played a part [in dissipating conflict] despite Soviet efforts to discourage it. As one of Gorbachev's aides later testified, 'The Beatles were our quiet way of rejecting 'the system' while conforming to most of its demands'" (2008, 49).

16. Clarence Kelley (2004) recalled that "we were in Frankfurt, Germany, in a Chinese restaurant, owned by a guy from Hawai'i who graduated from McKinley High School [in Honolulu], and his classmate was our assistant chief of police."

17. Boggs's 1985 research is based on Hawaiian children's discourse, but his analysis of verbal routines applies equally well to Hawaiian adults and even to many non-Hawaiian Local adults. Some children's routines are learned from adults, Boggs contends: "Contradicting is a natural response to perceived assertiveness. But the contradicting routine itself originates in a startlingly different manner. Children are inducted into this routine by parents and other adults as a means of playful teasing in which adult and child act as equals. In form, the routine thus originates in the rhetoric of equality, not in true conflict" (1985, 74).

18. Positions, in order of command, were fire chief, battalion chief, captain, and then a range of titles based on function, such as driver, hoser. In practice, there was little difference among them; when firemen responded to emergencies, it was always as a mixed unit.

19. During the territorial period, and in the years following statehood, Hawaiians and Locals were able to acquire a measure of power at city and county levels of jurisdiction. William F. Blaisdell's father had also served as fire chief.

20. Musical groups have long been associated with the HFD. My search in nineteenth-century Honolulu newspapers uncovered a number of amateur concerts in 1869 organized by Mechanic Engine Co. No. 2; the concerts were noted for featuring Hawaiian musicians and Hawaiian-language songs. Photographic records indicate the existence of another performing group in the 1930s (see fig. 6.3).

21. Neal S. Blaisdell was mayor of the City and County of Honolulu from 1955 to 1969. Blaisdell supported Hawaiian statehood, but his political identity was as complex as that of his territorial counterpart, Governor Quinn. "Quinn . . . acted more like a Democrat than a Republican, as did Honolulu's popular Republican mayor, part-Hawaiian former football coach Neal Blaisdell. . . . Quinn, obliged to work with Democratic majorities in the legislature, and Blaisdell, forced to govern with a Democratic-controlled Board of Supervisors, maintained their individual popularity by disassociating themselves from the Republican party" (Fuchs 1961, 332).

22. Carinthia Pua'a later married Isaac Harbottle; she is best known by her marital surname.

23. I often encountered the opinion that the police and fire choral groups were heavily populated with Kamehameha graduates, but there was wide representation from different schools, public schools especially. Men were comfortable taking part in a singing tradition they knew through school, church, or other institutions.

24. I initially read the policemen's and firemen's work as subverting and destabilizing touristic relations. However, in the early 1960s, when hula teachers like Maiki Aiu Lake were working in Waikīkī—that is, when Hawai'i was starting to ramp up tourism in earnest—employment in and engagement with the tourist sphere still had "a rather positive caché" (Puakea Nogelmeier in Chong-Stannard 2002).

25. I have in mind Mahi Beamer and Sterling Mossman, the "hula cop" (see note 9).

26. *Native Men Remade* (Tengan 2008), documents the journey of a group of middle-class, middle-aged men in their bid to reclaim an "authentic" Hawaiian masculinity through participation in a men's organization, Hale Mua. Hale Mua consists of Hawaiian men of mixed ethnic heritage—many with occupational roots in law enforcement, firefighting, and the military—who are dedicated to recovering Hawaiian men's health and restoring the *lāhui* (Hawaiian nation). Donning traditional *malo* (loincloths), they train in Indigenous martial arts (*lua*) and engage a range of ritual activities that include ceremonial food and *'awa* consumption, *mele oli* (chanting), and *ha'a,* a genre of ancient, sacred hula that shares a gestural vocabulary with Hawaiian martial arts. It is, in other words, considered more "masculine."

27. Singletary identifies Andy Kellikoa [*sic*] as a "fireman who belonged to the Fireman's Hula Troupe back in the 1930s" (2006, 10); it's possible that the dancer featured here is Keli'ikoa.

28. Maiki Aiu Lake became one of the driving forces of the hula renaissance in Hawai'i (Chong-Stannard 2002).

29. Bold athleticism would come later, in the 1970s, with the revival of *hula kahiko* (ancient hula).

30. Hawaiian music/dance scholar Amy K. Stillman (pers. comm., 2013) suggests that stigmatization of male dancers and *māhū* gradually increased following statehood, as American practices and values were more fully institutionalized.

31. There are still many questions here. I haven't been able to recuperate the MC scripts or stage banter that would have accompanied the HFD's (and HPD's) presentations. Did they, for example, invoke a "discourse of aloha" (Pierce 2004) featured in so many tourist shows of the late twentieth century? Surely the knife dancers that both choruses employed for foreign tours were attempts at exoticization. And while the men I spoke with were on board with Blaisdell's agenda, it's possible that others were not; they may have been willing to participate in monocultural presentations for the travel opportunities it afforded them.

32. Recent examinations of the Local in Hawai'i have led to critiques of Asian settler colonialism (e.g., Fujikane and Okamura 2008). Chang's engagement with the choral group in the statehood era is particularly susceptible to such interpretation. The question remains: in the face of Asian/self erasure, can we read his affinity for Hawaiian culture as appropriation, especially when he and other non-Hawaiians in the HFD's interculture were invited to make Hawaiian music and dance by fellow Hawaiian firemen?

33. So did female impersonation. Clarence Kelley recalled: "We had a couple of guys who did clown dancing. They were a big hit. They'd stuff balloons inside their T-shirts" (Kelley 2004). I'm reluctant to say much about hulas in drag without more information about when and for whom they were performed, whether they were reflexive parodies or burlesques. If parodic, policemen would have invited a gaze that made hula's colonial naturalization as female visible (cf. Yoon 2009). In either case, hyperbolically sexualized images of women point to the way that hula, under American influence, had been reconstructed as femininely erotic.

34. One critique leveled against Nye is that soft power is only meaningful where it is backed by hard power: "only states with a capable military, economic power and industrial strength can claim to exercise soft power effectively" (Liaropoulos 2011). Is this true at the level of regional or municipal politics? Is soft power's efficacy contingent on an ever-present threat of force?

35. There was a jittery band of "Dixiecrat" senators ("Race Bias Held Peril to Hawaii State Bill" 1950), but it's doubtful that firemen ever reached them.

36. This is an inversion of traditional functional responsibilities that resulted from Ha-

waiian language loss under colonial rule. In the text-centered world of Hawaiian aesthetics, hula movement and gesture is considered an accompaniment to intoned *mele*.

References

Arthur, Linda B. 2003. "The Aloha Shirt and Ethnicity in Hawai'i." *Textile: The Journal of Cloth and Culture* 4, no. 1: 8–34.

"Artist in Profile." 1975. *Ha'ilono Mele* 1, no. 1: 3–4.

Boggs, Stephen T. 1985. *Speaking, Relating, and Learning: A Study of Hawaiian Children at Home and at School.* Norwood, NJ: Ablex.

Carr, James Revell. 2014. *Hawaiian Music in Motion: Mariners, Missionaries, and Minstrels.* Urbana: University of Illinois Press.

Chong-Stannard, Joy, dir. 2002. *Maiki Aiu Lake.* DVD 56:17. PBS Hawai'i.

Chun, Malcolm Nāea. 2006. *Welina: Traditional and Contemporary Ways of Welcome and Hospitality.* Honolulu: Curriculum Research and Development Group, University of Hawai'i.

Clark, Kenneth S. 1929. *Music in Industry.* New York: National Bureau for the Advancement of Music.

Clifford, James. 1997. "Traveling Cultures." *Routes: Travel and Translation in the Late Twentieth Century*, 17–46. Cambridge, MA: Harvard University Press.

Connell, R. W. 2005. *Masculinities.* 2nd ed. Berkeley: University of California Press.

Crewe, Ben. 2011. "Soft Power in Prison: Implications for Staff–Prisoner Relationships, Liberty and Legitmacy." *European Journal of Criminology* 8: 455–468.

de Lauretis, Teresa. 1987. *Technologies of Gender: Essays on Theory, Film, and Fiction.* Bloomington: University of Indiana Press.

Deloria, Philip. 2004. *Indians in Unexpected Places.* Lawrence: University Press of Kansas.

Dennis, Simone. 2007. *Police Beat: The Emotional Power of Music in Police Work.* Youngstown, NY: Cambria Press.

"Detective by Day, Entertainer by Night." 1953. *Honolulu Advertiser*, December 13.

Diamond, Beverley. 2007. "Music of Modern Indigeneity: From Identity to Alliance Studies." *European Meetings in Ethnomusicology.* John Blacking Distinguished Lecture for 2006. 12: 169–190.

Ellingson, Lyndall, and Carol Odo. 2008. "HIV Risk Behaviors among Mahuwahine (Native Hawaiian Transgender Women)." *AIDS Education and Prevention* 20, no. 6: 558–569.

"A Fine Show for a Fine Cause." 1959. *Honolulu Star-Bulletin*, June 1.

Fong, Randie Kamuela. 1994. "Ho'okipa: A History of Hawaiian Greeting Practices and Hospitality." MA thesis, University of Hawai'i at Mānoa.

Fuchs, Lawrence H. 1961. *Hawaii Pono: A Social History.* New York: Harcourt Brace and World.

Fujikane, Candace, and Jonathan Y. Okamura, eds. 2008. *Asian Settler Colonialism: From Local Governance to the Habits of Everyday Life in Hawai'i.* Honolulu: University of Hawai'i Press.

Gallimore, Ronald, and Alan Howard. 1968. "The Hawaiian Life Style: Some Qualitative

Considerations." In *Studies in a Hawaiian Community: Na Makamaka o Nanakuli*, ed. Ronald Gallimore and Alan Howard, 10–16. Honolulu: Bernice P. Bishop Museum.

Gard, Michael. 2006. *Men Who Dance: Aesthetics, Athletics, and the Arts of Masculinity.* New York: Peter Lang.

Giddens, Anthony. 1984. *The Constitution of Society: Outline of the Theory of Structuration*. Cambridge: Polity Press.

Giese, Julie. 1998. "Comic Disruption in the Work of Maxine Hong Kingston." In *Performing Gender and Comedy: Theories, Texts and Contexts*, ed. Shannon Hengen, 111–128. Amsterdam: Gordon and Breach.

Grabel, Virgil. 1923. "How American Industries Are Utilizing Music." *Etude Magazine for Music* 41: 303, 351.

Griffen, Clyde. 1990. "Reconstructing Masculinity from the Evangelical Revival to the Waning of Progressivism: A Speculative Synthesis." In *Meanings for Manhood: Construction of Masculinity in Victorian America*, ed. Mark C. Carnes and Clyde Griffen, 183–204. Chicago: University of Chicago Press.

Hamera, Judith. 2007. *Dancing Communities: Performance, Difference and Connection in the Global City*. London: Palgrave Macmillan.

Harpe, Shideler. 1960. "Backstage." *Honolulu Advertiser*, December 8.

"Human Relations and Law Enforcement in Honolulu, Hawaii." 1953. Honolulu: World Brotherhood, Hawaiʻi Chapter.

Iaukea, Curtis P. n.d. "Interlude of My Life with the Prince while He Was Regent." Curtis P. Iaukea Collection, Hawaiʻi State Archives, M-70.

Imada, Adria L. 2012. *Aloha America: Hula Circuits through the U.S. Empire*. Durham, NC: Duke University Press.

Kauanui, J. Kēhaulani. 2008. *Hawaiian Blood: Colonialism and the Politics of Sovereignty and Indigeneity*. Durham, NC: Duke University Press.

Kennedy, Eugene. 1986. Interviewed by Warren Nishimoto and Michi Kodama-Nishimoto. In *Waikīkī, 1900–1985: Oral Histories*, vols. 1–3, 1234–1255. Honolulu: Center for Oral History, Social Science Research Institute, University of Hawaiʻi at Mānoa.

Korczynski, Marek. 2003. "Music at Work: Towards a Historical Overview." *Folk Music Journal* 8, no. 3: 314–334.

Krauss, Bob. 1960a. "In One Ear." *Honolulu Advertiser*, September 14.

———. 1960b. "In One Ear." *Honolulu Advertiser*, September 16.

Liaropoulos, Andrew. 2011. "Being Hard on Soft Power." http://www.rieas.gr/researchareas/2014-07-30-08-58-27/transatlantic-studies/1519-being-hard-on-soft-power. Accessed May 2, 2017.

Liliʻuokalani. [1898] 1985. *Hawaii's Story by Hawaii's Queen*. Rutland, VT: Charles E. Tuttle.

Liu, Dan. 1960. "Policemen's Holiday." *Honolulu Advertiser*, September 24.

Massey, Doreen. 1994. *Space, Place, and Gender*. Minneapolis: University of Minnesota Press.

Matzner, Andrew, ed. 2001. *ʻO Au No Keia: Voices from Hawaiʻi's Mahu and Transgender Communities*. n.p.: Xlibris Corporation.

Monson, Ingrid. 2007. "Africa, the Cold War, and Diaspora at Home." *Freedom Sounds: Civil Rights Call Out to Jazz and Africa*, 107–151. Oxford: Oxford University Press.

Mook, Richard. 2007. "White Masculinity in Barbershop Quartet Singing." *Journal of the Society for American Music* 1, no. 4: 453–483.
Ng, Franklin. 1999. "Daniel S. C. Liu." In *Distinguished Asian Americans: A Biographical Dictionary*, ed. Stephen Fugita, Hyung-Chan S. Kim, and Dorothy C. L. Cordova, 200–201. Westport, CT: Greenwood.
Nye, Joseph S. 2007. "The Place of Soft Power in State-Based Conflict Management." In *Leashing the Dogs of War: Conflict Management in a Divided World*, ed. Chester A. Crocker, Fen Osler Hampson, and Pamela R. Aall, 389–400. Washington, DC: United States Institute of Peace.
———. 2008. *The Powers to Lead*. Oxford: Oxford University Press.
Ohnuma, Keiko. 2002. "Local *Haole*—A Contradiction in Terms? The Dilemma of Being White, Born and Raised in Hawai'i." *Cultural Values* 6, no. 3: 273–285.
Okamura, Jon. 1994. "Why There Are No Asian Americans in Hawai'i: The Continuing Significance of Local Identity." *Social Process in Hawaii* 35: 161–178.
Olwage, Grant. 2004. "Discipline and Choralism: The Birth of Musical Colonialism." In *Music, Power, and Politics*, ed. Annie J. Randall, 25–46. New York: Routledge.
Osorio, Jon Kamakawiwo'ole. 2009. "On Race, Blood Quantum and Ancestry." http://hehawaiiau.honadvblogs.com. Accessed November 24, 2009.
Pearce, Eilune, Jacques Launay, and Robin I. M. Dunbar. 2015. "The Ice-Breaker Effect: Singing Mediates Fast Social Bonding." *Royal Society Open Science* 2: 1–9.
Pierce, Lori. 2004. "'The Whites Have Created Modern Honolulu': Ethnicity, Racial Stratification, and the Discourse of Aloha." In *Racial Thinking in the United States: Uncompleted Independence*, ed. P. R. Spickard and G. R. Daniel, 124–54. Notre Dame, IN: Notre Dame University Press.
"Race Bias Held Peril to Hawaii State Bill." 1950. *New York Times*, July 22.
Ramsay, Burt. 1995. *The Male Dancer: Bodies, Spectacle, Sexualities*. London: Routledge.
Ray, Gerda W. 1995. "From Cossack to Trooper: Manliness, Police Reform, and the State." *Journal of Social History* 28, no. 3: 565–586.
Richards, Paul. 2007. "The Emotions at War: A Musicological Approach to Understanding Atrocity in Sierra Leone." In *Public Emotions*, ed. Perri 6, C. Squire, S. Radstone, and A. Treacher, 62–84. Basingstoke: Palgrave-Macmillan.
Robertson, Carol E. 1989. "Māhū of Hawai'i." *Feminist Studies* 15, no. 2: 313–326.
Rosa, John. 2001. "'The Coming of the Neo-Hawaiian American Race': Nationalism and Metaphors of the Melting Pot in Popular Accounts of Mixed-Race Individuals." In *The Sum of Our Parts: Mixed Heritage Asian Americans*, ed. Teresa Williams-León and Cynthia L. Nakashima, 49–56. Philadelphia: Temple University Press.
———. 2014. *Local Story: The Massie-Kahahawai Case and the Culture of History*. Honolulu: University of Hawai'i Press.
Ruggerone, Lucia. 2016. "The Feeling of Being Dressed: Affect Studies and the Clothed Body." *Fashion Theory* 20, no. 5. doi:10.1080/1362704X.2016.1253302.
Saranillio, Dean Itsuji. 2010. "Colliding Histories: Hawai'i Statehood at the Intersection of Asians 'Ineligible to Citizenship' and Hawaiians 'Unfit for Self-Government,'" *Journal of Asian American Studies* 13, no. 3: 283–309.
"Singing Policemen." 1954. *The Hawaii Weekly*, July 11, 3.
Singletary, Milly. 2006. *Hilo Hattie: A Legend in Our Time*. Honolulu: Mutual.

Stannard, David E. 2005. *Honor Killing: How the Infamous "Massie Affair" Transformed Hawai'i*. New York: Viking.
"Stars-a-Poppin July 17." 1960. *Honolulu Star-Bulletin*, July 6.
Stillman, Amy K. 1987. "Published Hawaiian Songbooks." *MLA Notes* 44: 221–239.
———. 1996. "Hawaiian Hula Competitions: Event, Repertoire, Performance, Tradition." *Journal of American Folklore* 109, no. 434: 1–24.
Szego, C. K. 1999. "Musical Meaning-Making in an Intercultural Environment: The Case of Kamehameha Schools." PhD diss., University of Washington.
———. 2003. "Singing Hawaiian and the Aesthetics of (In)Comprehensibility." In *Global Pop, Local Language*, ed. Harris M. Berger and Michael Thomas Carroll, 291–328. Jackson: University of Mississippi Press.
Tatar, Elizabeth. 1982. *Nineteenth Century Hawaiian Chant*. Honolulu: Bishop Museum Press.
Tengan, Ty P. Kāwika. 2008. *Native Men Remade: Gender and Nation in Contemporary Hawai'i*. Durham, NC: Duke University Press.
Thurnell-Read, Thomas, and Andrew Parker. 2008. "Men, Masculinities and Firefighting: Occupational Identity, Shop-Floor Culture, and Organisational Change." *Emotion, Space and Society* 1: 127–134.
Walker, Isaiah Helekunihi. 2011. *Waves of Resistance: Surfing and History in Twentieth-Century Hawai'i*. Honolulu: University of Hawai'i Press.
Wiltermuth, Scott S., and Chip Heath. 2009. "Synchrony and Cooperation." *Psychological Science* 20, no. 1: 1–5.
Woo, Susie. 2015. "Imagining Kin: Cold War Sentimentalism and the Korean Children's Choir." *American Quarterly* 67, no. 1: 25–53.
Xian, Kathryn, and Brent Anbe, dirs. 2001. *Ke Kūlana He Māhū: Remembering a Sense of Place*. VHS, 67 minutes. Zang Pictures.
Yano, Christine R. 2003. "The Burning of Men: Masculinities and the Nation in Japanese Popular Song." In *Men and Masculinities in Contemporary Japan: Dislocating the Salaryman doxa*, ed. James E. Roberson and Nobue Suzuki, 77–90. London: Routledge Curzon.
Yoon, Paul J. 2009. "Asian Masculinities and Parodic Possibility in Odaiko Solos and Filmic Representations." *Asian Music* 40, no. 1: 100–130.

Interviews and Telephone Conversations

Chang, Donald S. M. July 15, 2004, Aiea, HI.
Harbottle, Carinthia (Pua'a). June 27, 2003, Honolulu.
———. December 11, 2009, Honolulu.
Ī, Milton. July 14, 2012, Honolulu.
Kelley, Clarence. 2012. Honolulu.
Kelley, Clarence, and Helen Kelley. August 12, 2004, Kahalu'u, HI.
Na'auao, Roland. July 27, 2003. Honolulu.
Paiaina, Clem, Jr. July 6, 2012, Honolulu.
Paiaina, Clem, Jr., and Eugene "Bucky" Yee. July 13, 2004, Honolulu.
"Rosey." October 30, 2002, Honolulu.

CHAPTER 7

Kenny Endo and a Dream

FROM INTERZONES TO SOLIDARITIES

Deborah Wong

THIS essay is my attempt to think about a piece—or really a series of improvisations over many years—that perform what it can mean to think like an ally. Critical improvisation studies is driven by a progressive politics of intercorporeal commitment, but in this case, the piece I aim to understand is about a drum that is rarely on stage, and when it is, it is an entirely different drum played by someone who would not normally play a drum like that anyway and who plays a rhythm from somewhere else—nearby and related, but from somewhere else. In one instance, she is a musician from Hong Kong in a Pacific U.S. *taiko* group playing Tahitian rhythms on a *djembe* that is a symbol for a Hawaiian *pahu*. This is the most indirect performance of allyship I have encountered in a long time, but its obliqueness is intentional. I attempt to listen closely to a piece that is really a string of performances over more than twenty years. What I think I know about it, or have tried to learn about it, is the result of the composer's concise, sedimented answers to my many questions and his near absence of grand assertions. All the same, I am certain this series of performances addressing a dream about a drum addresses, over and over again, coalitional hope. It offers a model for what it can mean to be a (musical) ally.

Laura Pulido writes, "Activists must dream in order to develop a vision of the kind of world they would like to live in. [. . .] Although a vision is no guarantee of successfully remaking the world, it is a necessary first step" (Pulido 2006, 238). Kenny Endo, the musician in question, dreams musically; he does not use words to make an ideal space. He does not demand or expect intercorporeal presence. Instead, he reflects *through music* on a dream about a drum, and those improvised reflections, which are always new and unique to that moment, are a series of reiterated promises to be an ally: to acknowledge native sovereignty and thus to enact a set of rights that never arrive but are worth imagining. This essay is my effort to understand how some intercultural improvisation offers utopian visions for ideal relationships even when it takes place in an environment of precarity and deep damage.

Endo wrote "Yume no Pahu" in 1992 and first recorded it in 1994, for his album *Eternal Energy.* In his 1994 liner notes, Endo wrote that the piece was "dedicated to the indigenous people of Hawai'i in support of their struggle to control their land, their culture, their destiny"[1] and that the piece "was inspired by hula master and pahu drum maker Cioci," who had a dream about a strange and beautiful *pahu*, or Hawaiian ritual drum. *Yume no* means "dream" in Japanese, so the title of the work is in two languages and refers to Cioci's dream. The piece thus embodies an Asian Pacific encounter that was conceived by a non-Hawaiian Japanese American musician and is specific, respectful, and informed. Endo based one section of the piece (the intro and outtake) on the Hawaiian *mele* "Ua Nani 'O Nu'uanu"[2] and structured the internal section around a twenty-five-beat Tahitian rhythm recast by Endo as a twenty-four-beat rhythm on which the performers base their solos. Yet the dream of a drum that is at the heart of the piece is not literally "in" the piece; rather, it is the basis for a respectful reflection.

Improvisation studies has focused on a set of interrelated questions about intercultural encounter, including: How is respect performed, enacted, or imagined? Is subject identity located in sound, in bodies, or in material objects? Does identity presuppose presence? Is presence overemphasized in improvisation studies? What key metaphors make audible or visible improvised efforts to connect across difference? Improvisation studies helps me think about transpacific exchange and intercultural encounter in ways that push against the expected problems. Too often, intercultural musical efforts are critically disappointing—either appropriative and colonial, or one-off and superficial. Yet scholars in improvisation studies have offered exciting and inspiring theoretical models suggesting—sometimes in beautifully progressive, anticipatory, and utopian terms—that the improvisative encounter across difference can model better social relationships. If the encounter is driven by an ethics of respect and is based on a real knowledge of history and a committed ability to listen, then much is possible. The improviser and indeed the listener can shape the political terms for the present moment and for the future even as they potentially rechannel and reclaim the damages of colonialism.[3] This utopianism is critically aware, not celebratory. Gaye Theresa Johnson's critical concept of spatial entitlement makes visible the creation of "new collectivities" based on "new and imaginative uses of technology, creativity, and spaces" (Johnson 2013, x). Such spaces create the possibility for new kinds of coalitional relationships and new forms of belonging. As Johnson puts it, "Spatial entitlement requires an alternative understanding and construction of the meaning of citizenship" (Johnson 2013, xi). The spaces created by music and performance may be ephemeral but powerful.

This essay celebrates Ric Trimillos's influences on Asia Pacific music scholarship as well as Kenny Endo's fortieth anniversary year as a *taiko* player. A third-generation Japanese American from Los Angeles, Endo has lived in Honolulu for decades, and his school, the Taiko Center of the Pacific, represents a vibrant mixture of North American and Japanese post–World War II drumming practices (*kumi-daiko*, or *taiko*) as well as a uniquely Hawaiian intercultural meeting ground of Asian musics and ideas. Inspired by Ric Trimillos's effort to notice "decolonizable" spaces (Trimillos 2008), I ask how improvised musical effort in a colonized place opens up new possibilities. Rather than romanticize what happens, I consider how such efforts are limited and I focus on how it becomes our responsibility as thinkers, listeners, and allies to read as much political possibility into such musical experiments as possible. Rather than sit back and identify shortcomings, failures, and missed signals with expert precision, I call for a kind of committed interpretation that takes the effort further. These are the terms for coalitional politics: doing real work across difference means we must be ready to do more than just call out what's wrong or missing. The freedom of having nothing at stake is the ultimate privilege.

The musics of the transpacific triangulate Asia, the Indigenous, and the "Americas," showing how settler colonialisms are multiple and ongoing, without end. The resulting musics offer compelling histories of encounter upon encounter, difference piled upon difference, and the extant terminologies and taxonomies are never innocent even as they interrogate the terms for survival under the imperial gaze. Coalitional improvisation offers a set of strategies and tactics for decolonization. As Randy Shaw explains, "The great value of coalitions lies in their ability to propel to success groups who could not prevail on their own. ... Forming coalitions with groups you may oppose on other issues requires the highest level of tactical expertise" (Shaw 1996, 83–84). Improvisation does not imply or promise perfect agreement but it can activate connections and (always incomplete and imperfect) understandings if based on a willingness to listen, and listening is a crucial form of expertise. Further, improvisation emerges from, creates, and activates tactics in real time.

The improvisation I address here is a Japanese American acknowledgment of Hawaiian sovereign rights. In the Hawaiian context of Indigenous and immigrant Asian relationships, citizenship is multiple and troubled, yet Asian Americans rarely concede that they are implicated in settler colonialism. Haunani-Kay Trask has identified the ascendance of the Asian immigrant success narrative at the expense of Native Hawaiian rights in no uncertain terms (Trask 2000). Candace Fujikane argues that Asians in Hawai'i often claim minoritarian solidarity without adequately acknowledging that their successes rely on the settler colonial state. She asserts that it is politically necessary in Hawai'i to "identify Asians as settlers in order to bring about a shift in political consciousness, to identify the problems posed by Asian settler ideologies and practices that reflect their desires for a place in the settler state" (Fujikane 2008, 36). Any progressive effort to stand as allies to Indigenous Hawaiians must begin with a recognition that the settler state demands complicity in profound and sweeping ways. Her co-edited book *Asian Settler Colonialism: From Local Governance to the Habits of Everyday Life in Hawai'i* (Fujikane and Okamura 2008) is performatively organized to make this visible: "The structure of the book reflects the structure of colonialism in Hawai'i [...]. 'Native' comes first; 'Settler' follows it and supports it from behind" (Fujikane 2008, 30). That book offers examples of what can it mean to support Native Hawaiian rights "from behind," and of course it is also replete with the histories of opportunism, showing how the tropes of U.S. democracy and Hawai'i as the ideal multicultural and multiracial state are key mechanisms for disabling Hawaiian sovereign rights. Similarly, Judy Rohrer shows how long slow processes that indigenize non-Hawaiians as "Local" are an established form of settler racial logic in Hawai'i (Rohrer 2016). Dean Saranillio argues that Asian settler colonialism in Hawai'i "is obviously distinct from White settler colonialism" because it relies on a form of "settler innocence" based in narratives emphasizing immigrant triumphs over obstacles (Saranillio 2013, 281).

Kenny Endo's efforts to support Native Hawaiian rights "from behind" are thus striking and important, especially because they are musicked. Ethnomusicologists are good at parsing particular musical works, musicking individuals, and events. We open up the object ethnographically and show how its meanings reflect and construct the complexities of time and place. These disciplinary patterns are real strengths even if they are sometimes undervalued by our sister disciplines as technical rather than critical skills. This essay can be read in two ways, first, as an example of one ethnomusicologist's effort to unpack a particular musical piece, but more deeply, I hope the essay can be read in the other direction, as an example of how my search through improvisation studies for ideal social models led me to want to understand this piece. "Yume no Pahu" fascinates me because it emerged from a place and a set of circumstances that kept surprising me the more I learned, and because it offers the means to acknowledge how critical improvisation studies sometimes retreats to the liberal humanist hope that the intercorporeal encounter is the solution, or that the body is stable enough to offer the basis for change, or that we can trust the relationship between music and subjectivity to model a better way.

Hawai'i's importance as an intercultural paradise is embedded in "the Pacific as a space of exploration, exploitation, and expansion," as Viet Nguyen and Janet Hoskins put it. They argue for the "transpacific" as an emergent critical rubric that acknowledges how area studies, economic development, and imperial reach are interconstitutive (Nguyen and Hoskins 2014, 3).[4] Before the term "transpacific" was coined to activate new economic and political relationships, the "Pacific Rim" dominated academic and economic thinking precisely because it addressed specific needs during the new neoliberalism of the 1980s–1990s. Chris Connery wrote, "Pacific Rim Discourse is an imagining of U.S. multinational capitalism in an era when the 'socialist' bloc still existed, and it is the socialist bloc that is the principle discursive and strategic Other" (Connery 1994, 31–32). Late Cold War needs led to the neoliberal construct of the Pac Rim under Reagan, which was in turn predated by the "Pacific" and the "Asian Pacific," both of which Arif Dirlik famously revealed as Euro-American constructs, each prompted by specific imperial needs at different points in time (Dirlik 1992, 64–65). As Nguyen and Hoskins warn, each successive construct literally creates ideological regions needed by the nations dominant at any given moment and "encourages a reenvisioning of U.S. history" that obscures as much as it reveals (Nguyen and Hoskins 2014, 8).

Kenny Endo and *Taiko* in Hawai'i

My interest in this particular *taiko* piece emerges from these issues and from the tensions between the Pacific places and regions constructed to serve late capitalist expansion. *Taiko* has a long history in Hawai'i but is not 'from' there, though it is embedded in Japanese immigrant communities. *Taiko* is a post–World War II invention that is both traditional and intercultural. It is very old in certain ways, but the contemporary form that now has a global presence is the result of postwar cultural anxieties in Japan. Shawn Bender has explained how and why Daihachi Oguchi, a Japanese jazz drummer, turned to the *taiko* stored at his neighborhood temple in the 1950s; he is now regarded as the creator of *kumi-daiko* (Bender 2012). *Kumi-daiko* put down roots in Japan in the 1950s–1960s as musicians drew extensively from a range of traditional regional festival percussion traditions but constantly restaged and reimagined them. After Seiichi Tanaka, an immigrant Japanese martial arts teacher, offered the first *taiko* classes in the San Francisco Taiko Dojo in the late 1960s, *kumi-daiko* took root in Japanese American and Asian American communities in North America, followed by rapid and widespread interest by (mostly) Euro-descended participants in Western Europe and Australia, and Japanese immigrant communities in Peru and Brazil. It is not my purpose here to trace the reasons *taiko* groups were established in different parts of the world between the 1970s and the present, but it is worth noting that *taiko* became a global phenomenon around the year 2000, when new groups began to appear with startling frequency and intensity with more and more white participants. In Hawai'i, *taiko* was first played by Japanese immigrants at the turn of the last century, but the *kumi-daiko* movement came later, after it had taken hold on the U.S. mainland.[5] To the best of my knowledge, the chronology goes something like this:[6]

Year established	*Name of group*
1984	Hawaii Matsuri Taiko
1988	Kona Daifukuji Taiko youth group
1989	Taishoji Taiko
1994	Taiko Center of the Pacific
1996	Maui Taiko
1999	Zenshin Daiko
2005	Somei Taiko

In sum, *taiko* is spectacularly well established in Hawai'i, which is not surprising given the large and long-lived Japanese communities on the islands.

Improvised solos are a standard practice in *kumi-daiko* (Wong 2016), as is intercultural experimentation. New pieces are constantly written for *kumi-daiko* almost entirely by the musicians themselves, whether composed by individuals or by ensemble members working together collaboratively, and often have sections for improvisation. New compositions far outnumber "traditional" repertoire, and traditional pieces are constantly rearranged. Each group is proud to have its own unique repertoire as well as pieces learned from external guest teachers. Kenny Endo's creative output is not at all unusual but is very highly regarded and admired. He has written many original pieces for *taiko* and will no doubt write many more.

Kenny Endo was born in East Los Angeles in 1953 and is Sansei. He attended UCLA and was swept up in the Asian American cultural movement. In 1975 he joined Kinnara Taiko at Senshin Buddhist Temple in Los Angeles, an important and foundational *kumi-daiko* group that was (and is) Buddhist and radically egalitarian, placing a strong emphasis on improvisation. By 1978, Endo had graduated from college and he went north to learn from Seiichi Tanaka in San Francisco Taiko Dojo. In 1980, Endo went to Japan in search of traditional music and, as his website bio states, "he embarked on a decade-long odyssey in his ancestral Japan."[7] He studied *kumi-daiko* with Daihachi Oguchi, the jazz drummer mentioned above; he became a member of Oedo Sukeroku, one of the best *kumi-daiko* groups in Japan; and he immersed himself in *hogaku*, the "classical" Japanese music used in kabuki, eventually earning a *natori*, or a professional stage name with a place in the teacher's lineage. He and his wife Chizuko had two sons in Japan; they moved to Hawai'i and created the Taiko Center of the Pacific in Honolulu in 1994. After teaching *taiko* at the TCP for some years and establishing his own professional performing ensemble,

Endo decided to get an MA in ethnomusicology from the famous graduate program at the University of Hawaiʻi at Mānoa. He took classes and eventually wrote a thesis about "Yodân Uchi," one of Oedo Sukeroku's signature pieces involving several performers moving back and forth between the several drums (Endo 1999; Pachter 2015a). Over the years, he has recorded nine albums, received numerous commissions, and earned a global reputation as one of the outstanding *taiko* players of his generation.

Endo is known for both his rootedness in traditional practice and his willingness to experiment in decidedly contemporary ways. As I have written elsewhere, he is both a traditionalist and an innovator (Wong 2004, 225–227). A commitment to tradition marks his work, though his own compositions are often boldly contemporary. As Ben Pachter writes, "This mixture of influences would become a defining characteristic of his concerts and his compositions," and was markedly so from the early years of his career (Pachter 2015b). Endo's ideas and approach to creating new work for *kumi-daiko* have a strong and intentional base in traditional standards and training. He has said many times that he believes in rigorous traditional training before venturing out into original work. In my periodic conversations with Endo over the last fifteen years, he has maintained consistent positions on these matters (Wong 2004, 205, 213, 225–227). During 2015–2016, he marked his fortieth anniversary as a *taiko* player with a world tour, and although he gave slightly different concerts in different cities, he emphasized his "contemporary ensemble" featuring *taiko*, vibes, drums, ʻukulele, flute, *koto* or *guzheng*, electric guitar, and *shamisen*, featuring guest artists from Japan and the United States. He has collaborated extensively with musicians from far outside the *taiko* world, including jazz and pop, different world music traditions (Balinese gamelan, Indian music, etc.), and more. As Judy Mitoma writes, "He combines his training with Japanese masters with his own love of world music. His work is informed by a network of collaborators from Hawaiʻi, Cuba, China, Korea, Africa, Brazil, Indonesia and American Jazz. Concerts by Kenny Endo provide a wide palette of sound" (2016). Kenny Endo's work is important, stirring, and beautifully crafted. He is a traditionalist innovator with roots in California, Asian America, Japan, and Hawaiʻi. He has negotiated the shifting Pacific Rim and transpacific potential of musical styles, concert venues, and musicians' networks. Many of his musical works involve intricate expansions of material from elsewhere, both improvised and carefully calculated and choreographed. Daniel Fischlin, Ajay Heble, and George Lipsitz have written about what it can mean to take such aesthetic and political risks: "Improvisation is an art that requires doing work in the world, work that makes a difference, that requires reaching across genders and generations to expand space and time, cultivating creative capabilities to prepare for confrontations that may never come" (Fischlin, Heble, and Lipsitz

2013, 186–187). I address one of his many original compositions with a focus on his strategic position in Hawaiʻi, a home he chose because he can easily travel to Japan and draw on Asian artists visiting the islands. I turn to this particular piece to ask what's at stake and what's at risk, what struggles haunt the piece, and for what confrontations does it help us prepare.

Two Performances of "Yume no Pahu"

I now compare two performances of "Yume no Pahu," one from 2012 and the other from 2015. These are only two out of many, many times Endo has performed the piece with different collaborators over many years, but it offers a window on Endo's logics for supporting Native Hawaiian sovereignty specifically and perhaps intercultural expansion more generally.

I have long admired Joseph S. C. Lam's reading of "Yume no Pahu." He included a vivid description of Endo's original 1992 recording in his much-quoted article on what Asian American music is and is not. In his effort to drill down on the very terms for Asian American expression, Lam compares five pieces of music, including Endo's "Yume no Pahu." Lam describes "Yume no Pahu" as "a work that challenges conceptual and geographic boundaries of Asian America" even while enacting the "inherent tensions and regional diversity" of Asian American expression (Lam 1999, 52, 51). Placing the permanently hybrid Japanese modernity of *taiko* in conversation with the indigeneity of Hawaiian and Tahitian musical sounds creates several counterpolitics all at once that speak back to exoticism. The Asian Pacific that Lam refers to as "panethnic" (Lam 1999, 51) was how diasporic Asians and Pacific Islanders articulated shared experiences of discrimination and containment, resulting in the "Asian American" as a political identity in the 1960s and then, in the 1990s, in the more expansive rubric of the "API" or Asian Pacific Islander. These new ethnic categories were intentionally connective: they articulated how interethnic rubrics could reveal and address systemic inequities. As Laura Pulido writes, "oppressed people of color may favor nationalism as a political basis for mobilization" for real reasons (Pulido 2006, 231). Multiracial activism emerges across different collectivities in response to specific needs. She reminds us that "All people of color are not the same, but they do have certain things in common, and those commonalities can often serve as the basis for shared mobilization" (Pulido 2006, 234).

Endo's arrangement and rearrangement of "Yume no Pahu" over twenty years' time suggests that he continues to unpack the ideas and principles built into it. Its loose assemblage of musical ideas coalesce around Hawaiian emplacedness yet are mostly expressed through instruments and timbres that are specifically Japanese and reimagined through Japanese American, Japanese, white American, Hawaiian, and Pacific Islander musicians. The piece always features extended improvised solos that showcase the idiomatic skills, knowledge, and training of the individual musicians. The piece is not performed "by" the musicians; rather, Endo assembles musical ideas through which the musicians constitute relationships. The result is new with each performance, and the listener is invited to consider the relationship between the travels of *kumi-daiko* and its encounter with Hawaiian musical and cultural politics. Endo's attention to the place he has made his home is not based in any commonsensical politics of the intercorporeal. He does not stage the piece with "Hawaiian" performers or instruments as stand-ins for entire histories. Instead, "Yume no Pahu" makes *taiko* into a space for a coalition politics focused on Hawaiian self-determination while also creating an open-ended framework for individual musicians' subjectivities.

Even though "Yume no Pahu" has been performed by Endo in strikingly different configurations—from very small, e.g., Endo plus one other musician, to very large, with numerous performers—certain elements are constant. One is Endo himself: I do not know of any rendition of the piece that did not feature Endo as a performer. The piece is always performed in an ABCBA structure, with the C section focused on improvised solos. The other elements Endo deploys in most performances of "Yume no Pahu" are as follows: a free meter intro with an atmospheric and even mysterious feeling; the *mele* melody "Ua Nani ʻO Nuʻuanu," accompanied by Endo playing a simple rhythmic pattern on a *chudaiko* with his hands; the C section based on a fast twenty-four-beat Tahitian rhythmic pattern, leading to open-ended solos based on that rhythmic structure and ending with a long solo by Endo; a return to the *mele*, but usually stated only briefly; a return to the free-meter intro, creating the sense that the performance emerges out of and then returns to a mysterious ritual time-space.

I turn to two performances from 2012 and 2015, available on YouTube. One is small, with only three performers, and the other has nine. Endo was very familiar with all his chosen performers and in some cases had already collaborated extensively with them over many years. The two performances are different in size and instrumentation but identical in structure. They allow us to see how Endo's structures for improvisation create a politics of both presence and absence.

The 2012 performance of the piece featured only three musicians: Kenny Endo; Jeff Peterson, a slack key guitar player with multigenerational family roots in Hawaiʻi; and Riley Lee, a *hapa haole* (Chinese) *shakuhachi* player. Peterson and Lee had worked together many times at that point, but they met Endo when all three were part of a week-long residency in which each artist offered intensive workshops in their specialty. The three of them performed at the University of Hawai'i's Orvis Auditorium, archived on YouTube.[8] They subsequently recorded it again for their album *Island Breeze* (2014). On stage, Endo had a smaller version of his trademark multi-*taiko* set-up: two *chudaiko*, an *odaiko*, and a small table with an assortment of drumsticks, chimes, and small rattles. Peterson sat stage left with an acoustic guitar and a music stand. Lee perched on a stool between Endo and Peterson holding his *shakuhachi*. This version was just over six minutes long and featured improvised solos by Peterson on guitar and Endo on *taiko*; Lee played the *mele* on *shakuchi* at the beginning and end but took no solo. The performance opened with Endo playing slow free-meter patterns on the *odaiko* while the *shakuhachi* and guitar played floating trills and long sustained pitches for thirty seconds or so. Endo almost always begins and ends "Yume no Pahu" by playing spare riffs on the *odaiko* with a pair of very long, thin, lightweight drumsticks called *take*. In this performance, Endo marked the end of the introductory A section by moving over to the *chudaiko* and playing it—atypically—with his hands while Lee and Peterson played the *mele* melody on *shakuhachi* and guitar. This performance was a showcase for Peterson and Endo, who each took long improvised solos. After Endo established the twenty-four-beat Tahitian patterns by himself, he dropped down and kept playing the pattern quietly while Peterson swept in with an extended two-minute solo, first strumming loud thick chords, then throwing in single-string melodic fragments, then breaking out into figuration, then moving into little melodic hemiola patterns, and then back to big loud full-fingered chords, all while maintaining the twenty-four-beat pattern and evoking flamenco by strumming emphatically with all the fingers on his right hand and occasionally slapping the face of the guitar. As he jammed through his final iteration of the pattern, he signaled Endo with a smile and nod, and Endo went straight into his own elaborate solo, immediately pushing the tempo just a little while going into a long filled-in syncopated passage on a set of two *chudaiko* (medium and small) and a *shime*.[9] Endo is well known for his multi-*taiko* solo setup, which is arranged so he can stand in place and easily reach his *odaiko*, two *chudaiko*, three fan drums, a *shime*, a *ko-tsuzumi*, and a small table with rattles, several sets of drumsticks, and a set of orchestral hanging chimes. This long minute—which seems longer because it is so fast, intricate, and rhythmically complex—is breathtaking. He finally shouts a *kakegoe*, "Hey!," signaling the other musicians, and plays the beginning of the pattern on the *chudaiko* rim, clearly marking the beginning of the twenty-four-beat pattern. He plays it twice through, and at the beginning of the third time, Peterson catches it and joins in, strumming the pattern. Going straight into the B section, Lee plays the first four measures of the *mele*, blowing loudly and breathily, and then—clearly prearranged—all three musicians return to the A section: Lee plays long sustained pitches, crescendoing and decrescendoing as Peterson plays tremolos and Endo goes back to slow quarter notes on the *odaiko*. Lee and Peterson fade away, and Endo pauses before striking the *odaiko* twice more, *don don*—and the piece is over.

The performance of "Yume no Pahu" in *TEN TEN*, Kenny Endo's fortieth anniversary celebration concert in Honolulu on October 10, 2015, was seven and a half minutes long and featured nine musicians: Kenny Endo (multiple *taiko*), Kaoru Watanabe (conch shell, *fue*/bamboo flutes, multiple *taiko*), Hiromitsu Agatsuma (Tsugaru *shamisen*), Jeff Peterson (Hawaiian slack key guitar), Yi-chieh Lai (*guzheng*), Yeeman Mui on *djembe* (*pahu*), and three members of the Kenny Endo Taiko Ensemble (Eric Chang, Patrick Oiye, and Chizuko Endo) on *chudaiko*, conch shell, and shakers.[10] The A section features long blown calls on conch shells that establish a space of respect, followed in the B section by straightforward, prearranged statements of the *mele* melody on Japanese flute, *guzheng*, and slack key guitar. The internal C section is set over the fast Tahitian rhythmic pattern and features four improvised solos (Tsugaru *shamisen*, slack key guitar, *guzheng*, and *taiko*). The B section returns with the *mele* melody played again, followed by the conch shells and percussive riffs in the brief closing A section.

This performance opens and ends with long sustained calls on three conch shell horns called *horagai*, deeply associated in Japan with Buddhism,[11] while Endo strikes the *odaiko* with long thin *bachi* and Chizuko Endo uses a small rattle to create an unmetered shimmer on top. Endo's use of a loose *oroshi* pattern (slow deliberate beats that gradually accelerate and then taper off into silence) evokes how *odaiko* are played in Shinto contexts. The overall effect is of a solemn ritual frame, with Kaoru Watanabe, Eric Chang, and Patrick Oiye blowing long notes on the three conch shells: the conch shell pitches are about a minor third apart but the musicians only loosely coordinate their breath rhythm, and it feels as if the pitch is less relevant than the sense of suspended time. After thirty seconds, there is a brief pause while the musicians move to other instruments and then the B section begins as Endo and Oiye play a simple pattern on the *chudaiko* uncharacteristically with their hands: playing with the hands is unmistakable homage to Native Hawaiian drum practices since *taiko* are always played with *bachi* (wooden drumsticks) whereas most Hawaiian drums are played with the hands. The *mele* melody then begins, played in unison on *yokobue* (Japanese transverse flute) and *guzheng* with supporting chordal figuration on the electric guitar...yet that simple statement, "the *mele* melody begins," requires a great deal of unpacking, as I will address below. Endo adapted the *mele* melody for *yokobue*, and its shape is simple, gentle, and symmetrical: fourteen four-beat measures, 4 + 4 + 2 + 2 + 2 measures, then back to the beginning, 4 + 4, and a gentle unresolved hanging pause. Watanabe put down his *yokobue* and he and Endo both picked up their *bachi* and went straight into a fast, complicated twenty-four-beat Tahitian rhythmic pattern on *shime* and the *chudaiko* rim. The overall effect is brightly percussive, dramatic, lively, and very different from the two preceding sections. They are quickly joined by Hiromitsu Agatsuma on Tsugaru *shamisen* and Yeeman Mui on *djembe*. The *shamisen* part is characteristically fast, filled in, and thrilling; Mui is in the back row playing the *djembe* with her hands. They all play the pattern in unison four times, with the freeze-frame silences creating brief exciting spaces, and then go straight into the extended C section featuring solo improvisations while playing the Tahitian pattern quietly underneath: *shamisen*, then electric guitar, then *guzheng*, then Endo on multiple *taiko*. The solos are structured not around the *mele* melodic material but rather around the twenty-four-beat Tahitian pattern. Everyone then plays that pattern four more times, with a focus on the *taiko* parts, and by now they have sped up a little and the syncopated complexity of the pattern is exhilarating. Finally, everyone breaks, subsides, falls away, flutters, and Watanabe again plays the first two measures of the *mele* on *yokobue*. It is a return to the B section, but now it is unmetered and floating; it suggests the *mele* rather than repeats it, and it is over in a moment. Endo goes back to the *odaiko* and plays a stately, low-key *don don don don don-don-don* phrase while the conch shell horns are blown, and the piece subsides and ends.

Again, these are only two performances out of many over many years, but in my view, Endo has created a simple structure that allows the featured musicians defined roles as well as considerable freedom during their solos. The sections for free improvisation are structured not on a set of chords or changes—as is typical in jazz—but instead on a Tahitian rhythmic pattern, and not a simple one. The aesthetics of the piece thus reflect a certain upending of the tradition of solo improvisation for melodic instruments while actually staying squarely within the *kumi-daiko* tradition of improvised solos, wherein the musician has a certain number of measures to play with rhythm. In this case, melodic instruments, whether Chinese or Japanese (*guzheng*, Tsugaru *shamisen*) or hybrid Western/Hawaiian (slack key guitar) are dropped into the space of *kumi-daiko* practices.

An Absent *Pahu* and a *Mele* without Words

The piece is a *taiko* player's reflection on a ritual specialist's dream about a sacred drum, and the rhythms played by any of the musicians—including on a *pahu* sometimes played by a member of Endo's ensemble—are not Hawaiian but Tahitian. Endo's deployment of the materials is not in a one-to-one framework but is rather allusive. Yet it is not at arm's length, either: Endo knows John Cioci Dalire, who is a noted beekeeper, woodworker, and *pahu* maker.[12] In the early 1990s, Endo was introduced to Dalire by his hula teacher (*kumu hula*) Vicky Holt Takamine and went to see his *pahu*. Dalire told Endo about the dream and Endo eventually purchased the dream *pahu* for the Drum Museum in Tokyo at the Miyamoto Unosuke Shoten in 1992, to which he has close connections. Endo notes that Dalire's former wife, the late Aloha Dalire, was considered one of the greatest hula teachers and dancers in modern times, and his association with the Dalire family now extends across some decades. All three of Aloha Dalire's daughters have won the Merrie Monarch solo contest,[13] and Endo collaborated with the second daughter, Kapua Dalire, on "Yume no Pahu" when they performed it at a convention in 2015 where they were joined by Kapua's husband Tigilau Moe, an expert Tahitian drummer, three of his drummers, two of Kapua's dancers, Kenny, and his wife, Chizuko Endo. In that thrilling rendition of "Yume no Pahu," all the connections were direct: the corporeal connection to the dream drum (Cioci's actual family members) and Tahitian drummers played the Tahitian rhythms.[14] As Endo wrote to me, "Working with Çioci's daughter was a great experience not only because she's a great hula artist but because her father inspired Yume no Pahu."[15] In other performances over the years, Endo has played the piece with entirely different musicians, most of whom have had no direct association with the piece's origins. Its many iterations thus offer different but connected narratives about the Asian Pacific.

Although "Yume no Pahu" is unquestionably a *taiko* piece, the politics and poetics of Pacific Island encounters inform it. Jared Mackley-Crump argues that Indigenous festivals in New Zealand that bring many different Pacific ethnicities together are not about staged authenticity but rather offer "cultural collisions," "cultural mélange," and side-by-side vibrancy that perform presence (Mackley-Crump 2015, 195–202). Endo came to consciousness as a young Asian American and Japanese American in Southern California, and he absorbed the ethics of Hawaiian cultural rights as a graduate student in the ethnomusicology program at the University of Hawai'i. In his liner notes, Endo wrote, "In 1974, [hula master and *pahu* drum maker Cioci] had a dream that he was playing a pahu (Hawaiian drum) and chanting in a clearing in the forest. Not a typical pahu, this drum was shaped like a bowl and supported by four figures holding it by their legs and four holding it with their hands. After Cioci awoke he constructed a drum exactly like that in his dream." The chanting in Cioci's dream suggests a *mele pahu* and a channel of Indigenous knowledge that we can only guess at—the conjoined ritual knowledge in chant, drumming, and hula is powerful. It is not literally part of Endo's piece but rather offers a layer of unarticulated foundational meaning under it. A *djembe*—not the *pahu* of Cioci's dream—is played by *taiko* musicians during some of Endo's performances of this piece, but the rhythms are Tahitian rather than Hawaiian.

Any *pahu* is heavily imbued with the spiritual force of *mana* because its traditional performance contexts were largely *mele* for *akua* (gods) and *ali'i* (chiefs). Endo's decision to include its sounds but not the drum itself and not its ritual rhythmic patterns is considered.[16] With arrays of generic "world percussion" now commonplace in many kinds of music, one can almost expect to see and hear drums from anywhere played in culturally inappropriate ways, but in this case, Endo disassociated the *pahu* from its ritual drum patterns in a tactically respectful way. The actual deployment of the *djembe-pahu* in "Yume no Pahu" enacts a transpacific logic of both avoidance and connection. In two performances in 2015, the *djembe-pahu* was played but in completely different ways. In the 2015 performance in Honolulu, the *djembe* was played by Yeeman Mui, an immigrant from Hong Kong and a core member of Endo's professional ensemble. In another, Tahitian musicians and dancers related to the Dalires by marriage played the *pahu* and performed the dance choreographies that are inherently part of the Tahitian rhythms that were being played on the Hawaiian drum. As Endo told me in an email, "When the Tahitian drummers came into the piece, it took off in another direction which was both authentic and creative."[17] Clearly, Endo was not only pleased by that but had created a structure that allowed and invited it: Endo's word choice—"it took off in another direction"—suggests and approves the Tahitian performers' assertive agency. Brendan Hokowhitu argues that concepts like tradition and authenticity are a colonial legacy that haunt Indigenous studies and can close down the political possibility of the contemporary Indigenous body by placing it in an eternal past (Hokowhitu 2011). Endo both activates and respectfully avoids the presumption of replicating that body.

If the *pahu* is a key Hawaiian performative in Endo's hands, his use of the *mele inoa* "Ua Nani 'O Nu'uanu" is another. Endo transforms this piece into pure melody, and the performance of that melody is the cornerstone of the ABCBA structure of "Yume no Pahu." *Mele* were and are chanted but over time, some *mele* (including some *mele hula*) have been set to melodies. Beamer notes that this sometimes makes the message of a *mele* more accessible to listeners (Beamer 2001, 8), and Keola Donaghy confirmed that this is simply part of the life of these performatives, viewed as yet another way to maintain them.[18] "Ua Nani 'O Nu'uanu" is a *mele inoa* and its lyrics are as follows:[19]

Ua nani 'o Nu'uanu	Beautiful is Nu'uanu
I ka lau o ke kāwelu	With the *kāwelu* grass
Ua hālāwai aku lā	There one always meets
Me ka makani nui	With the strong wind
E 'i'ini ana ka mana'o	One looks forward
E 'ike 'iā Kahuwailana	To seeing Kahuwailana

'O ko'u hoa no ia	My friend is there
'O ka ua Ki'owao	The rain named Ki'owao
Ua pono nō kāua	It is good for us
Ho'okohu ana ia ka mana'o	Pleasing to the mind
Ha'ina mai ka inoa	To honor the name of
'O kalani 'Iolani	King Kamehameha IV 'Iolani

The extent to which anyone is expected to understand the *mele inoa* on which "Yume no Pahu" is based raises the question of what is understood, what should be understood, and how much cannot be understood. In Endo's rendition, the lyrics to "Ua Nani 'O Nu'uanu" are never sung, though some listeners might instantly associate the melody with the *mele*'s words and place associations. As Kati Szego puts it, "Working at the level of sign, singing Hawaiian *mele* [is] emblematic of being Hawaiian," indexing Indigenous poetic values in ways that can create possible selves and potential futures (Szego 2003, 320). The aesthetics of incomprehensibility can have powerful cultural effects. For some listeners, "Ua Nani 'O Nu'uanu" might carry its multiple histories with it, from "ancient" chant to Eddie Kamae's song setting of the *mele* to Endo's wordless melody. In "Yume no Pahu," the *mele inoa* becomes pure melody blown through a Japanese *yokobue* by a Japanese American musician, or through a *shakuhachi* by a *hapa haole* American. As Keola Donaghy put it to me, "It also further removes it from the *kaona* (hidden meaning), making it an almost complete abstraction from the original intent of the *mele* and its expression for those who don't know the words."[20] Endo's transformation of a *mele* into a melody is neither unique nor unusual in Hawai'i, but it suggests how deeply political the compositional process is at heart.

As Keola Donaghy writes, specific places are metaphorically, historically, and aesthetically foundational to how *mele* are composed and experienced, and place-names and allusive descriptions of landmarks in that place are evidence of key Hawaiian poetics. The specific kind of grass, a particular strong wind, and a place-specific kind of rain all are at play in "Ua Nani 'O Nu'uanu." As is characteristic for most *mele*, the lyrics for "Ua Nani 'O Nu'uanu" evoke specific places, in this case places associated with King Kamehameha IV. On the eastern end of O'ahu, Nu'uanu is a place with deep significance to Hawaiian history in several ways. The Battle of Nu'uanu Cliffs in 1795 was the last major battle fought by King Kamehameha I, leading to the unification of the Hawaiian Islands. Several nineteenth-century *ali'i*, including King Kamehameha III and Queen Emma, had summer palaces in the Nu'uanu Valley.[21] Versions of "Ua Nani 'O Nu'uanu" are easily found on the internet at the time of this writing, including chanted versions in hula performance and many renditions of Eddie Kamae's setting of the *mele* from the early 1960s,[22] recorded by any number of other artists and groups.[23] The evocation of place-names, wind, and rain probably continue to speak to some contemporary listeners in the ways they are supposed to. Whether heard, unheard, understood, or not, comprehending the emplaced logics of "Ua Nani ʻO Nuʻuanu" would contribute to a knowledgeable listener's experience of "Yume no Pahu." To an unknowledgeable listener, it is simply a melody. Place, knowledge, and Indigenous practice are all implied but never presented directly.

Intercultural Improvisation as Coalition Formation

Coalitions often begin with a decision to stand in solidarity or to stand beside as an ally. The praxis of intentional and productive political encounter is tricky, but its complexities are precisely the reason they're worth the attempt. They are always a counternarrative to the more visible and audible work of colonial appropriation, especially in music, where appropriation is usually normalized as the erotic exotic.[24] Certainly, some may perform allyship without actually showing up or operationalizing real support. Intercultural interaction is always about hybridity and newness but may also create the conditions for new ally relationships. The open-ended history of Kenny Endo's "Yume no Pahu" invites a triangulated relationship between Hawaiian, Japanese American, and Japanese musicians. Their locations and positions are not straightforward, nor are they meant to be. Cioci Dalire's daughter married a Tahitian. When Endo laid a Tahitian rhythm on the idea of a Hawaiian drum, I believe he did so knowing what should not be played on it in the absence of the appropriate Hawaiian culture bearers. But I also think Endo has internalized his own transpacific, inter-Indigenous currents and byways.

A bigger question is the matter of one-to-one correspondence: a *taiko* musician plays a *djembe* that is a stand-in for the *pahu*. Endo once played while the dreamer's daughter danced. Sometimes when Endo is in Tokyo, he plays the dreamer's *pahu*. Some versions of the piece are full of allusive, improvised shapeshifting. I believe Endo has quietly cultivated a strategy of distance and even avoidance in order to enact respect to his Hawaiian interlocutors. He has worked out replacements and stand-ins: the *pahu* is a *djembe*. By methodically *not* featuring or playing a *pahu*, let alone the *pahu*, he has worked out a praxis of respect that offers an ethics of intercultural dialogue. He made the radical decision not to include the Hawaiian Other. He outlined, evoked, referenced, and embedded the Indigenous. The vibrant absence at the center of (most performances of) the piece offers a model for respect that may be a unique contribution from the interzone of colonized Hawaiʻi, where Asians must make daily decisions about their participation in settler logics.

Through musical praxis rather than words, Endo came up against the problem of representation and what Ajay Heble calls "the limits of multiplicity" (Heble 2000b, 29). Although the tactic of including many voices and multiple sounds can lead to a "dehierarchization" of authority, it can also result in the opposite. The act of inclusion is a beginning but not in itself a game changer. Endo has taken on the long game. He assembles and reassembles elements that outline the Indigenous presence without presuming to inhabit it. He sidesteps narratives that posit a romantically vanishing Indigenous but instead evokes Native rights by speaking with, never for. At the same time, I must acknowledge the limits of any such work. Face to face coalitions addressing Hawaiian sovereign rights in direct ways are also urgently important to the Hawaiian political landscape. Endo has sometimes performed the piece with the Dalire family, activating an embodied, person-to-person history and alliance, but in the broadest sense the greater Hawaiian community probably is not aware of this piece, nor does that appear to be Endo's deepest purpose.

As musicians, scholars, and allies, I hope we can help instantiate that radical shift from encounter, contact, influence, borrowing, and so on, to more intentionally politicized metaphors focused on the ideals that drive coalitions, alliances, and arkestras. How can one perform solidarity without overrunning the promise or the assumptions of what it means to compose a piece of music? Prophetic and emergent third spaces are both fragile and powerful. Interzones can become solidarities; partnerships can become alliances, coalitions, and pacts. The resulting encounters offer decolonizable moments, and placing them within the framework of improvisation ensures that they will be repeated, reexplored, and reimagined.

Notes

I thank Kenny Endo for generously allowing me to write about his work and for taking the time to help me understand it better. I could not have written this essay without Keola Donaghy's help as a cultural expert and collegial interlocutor: he offered essential background on *mele* at exactly the right moment, and generously read and corrected a draft of this essay. Participants in the conference "Improvisation as Intercultural Contact and Dialogue," held at Memorial University of Newfoundland and co-sponsored by the Research Centre for Music, Media and Place and the Intercultural Institute for Critical Studies in Improvisation, offered useful feedback, especially Ellen Waterman, Jason Stanyek, and Dylan Robinson. Joseph Lam's work led to my fascination with "Yume no Pahu," so I thank him for opening the way with such good questions. Talking about intercultural musics and utopian experiments over several years with my doctoral students Dhiren Panikker and Elizabeth Stela McDonald shaped my thinking in this essay quite directly, and my colleague Liz Przybylski offered generous and productive feedback. Last but not least, Ric led the way: thank you for opening up decolonizable spaces for so many Asian, Pacific Islander, and Asian American scholars and artists.

1. Liner notes (Endo 1994).

2. Keola Donaghy told me that the melody is based on more than just "Ua Nani 'O Nu'uanu." In an email to me, he wrote that he had heard part of the melody "in several *mele hula ku'i*, including 'Hāna Chant,'" and that he was reminded of yet another *mele* but could not quite place it (pers. comm., August 29, 2016).

3. Notable and important examples include Fischlin and Heble (2004); Fischlin, Heble, and Lipsitz (2013); Heble (2000a); Heble and Fischlin (2003); Heble and Wallace (2013); Caines and Heble (2015).

4. The Trans-Pacific Partnership (TPP) was signed on February 4, 2016, after seven years of negotiation, creating a trade agreement between twelve countries (Brunei, Chile, New Zealand, Singapore, Australia, Canada, Japan, Malaysia, Vietnam, Mexico, Peru, and the United States).

5. I do not address Okinawan dance and percussion groups, which have their own deep history in Hawai'i (Sutton 1980).

6. I apologize for any mistakes and for groups missing; this is certainly a partial list.

7. http://www.kennyendo.com/about. Accessed June 17, 2016.

8. This performance is on YouTube, https://youtu.be/Jqk7kpgPf_8. Accessed August 17, 2016.

9. Out of sight in the YouTube video, just behind his two *chudaiko*.

10. This performance is on YouTube, https://youtu.be/iedHUC4SHL8. Accessed August 17, 2016.

11. Susan Asai writes, "In Buddhism, the sound of the *taiko* and a conch shell trumpet are believed to embody the sound of spiritual enlightenment itself" (Asai 1999, 120). Conch shell trumpets are generally blown only at the beginning and end of ritual and (by extension) musical pieces, to create a ritual frame. That is, in my experience, they are never played in the middle of pieces or along with other instruments, and in North America are mostly used by explicitly Buddhist *kumi-daiko* groups like Kinnara Taiko.

12. A newspaper article offers additional evidence that Dalire has dreamt of a *pahu* on at least one other occasion. An announcement for a woodworking exhibit in 2006 carries a photograph of a *pahu* with the following caption: "'Pahu Aumakua' by expert *pahu* maker Cioci Delire [*sic*], is a gift made specifically for Oprah Winfrey. Delire saw the talk show host grant a Waianae boy's wish to sing on television and felt compelled to thank her for the kindness. 'He reminded me of myself when I was young,' Delire says. The artist's yearlong attempts to get the pahu to Winfrey have been unsuccessful, and he says if he fails to deliver it to her, the pahu will be burned. 'It's an aumakua pahu, which means it's meant only for her,' Delire explains. The animals that adorn the lower portion of the drum—owl, lizard, turtle and shark—came to Delire in a dream, and he considers them Winfrey's aumakua" (Oshiro 2006).

13. The Merrie Monarch is a weeklong annual festival now regarded as one of the most prestigious and authoritative hula competitions in the world. It was founded in 1963 and is a rich venue for cultural heritage preservation as well as change in performance practice.

14. My thanks to Kenny Endo for sharing his private video footage, which redirected my understanding of the piece in productive ways.

15. Personal email communication, June 23, 2016.

16. As Keola Donaghy explained it to me, "*Hula pahu* are a specific genre: they are through composed, not strophic, performed with *pahu*, and general of a sacred nature. 'Ua Nani 'o Nu'uanu' is a *mele hula ku'i*. So [Endo is] actually using the *pahu* outside of the genre of music in which it would normally be performed." Personal email communication, August 29, 2016.

17. Personal email communication, June 23, 2016.

18. Personal communication from Keola Donaghy, June 16, 2016, with my thanks.

19. Taken from http://www.bethsnotesplus.com/2015/10/ua-nani-o-nuuanu.html, accessed on June 22, 2016.

20. Personal email communication, August 29, 2016.

21. The locale possibly described in "Ua Nani ʻO Nuʻuanu" is the area around the palace that served as a summer retreat for King Kamehameha IV, Queen Emma, and their son, Prince Albert Edward from 1857 to 1885. It is now a historic landmark known as "Queen Emma Summer Palace," or Hānaiakamalama (The Southern Cross).

22. One website cites his wife, Myrna Kamae, stating that "Eddie Kamae put the music to this chant but hasn't taken credit for it except on his own album that came out in 1964" (http://www.huapala.org/U/Ua_Nani_O_Nuuanu.html). I do not know to which album she refers.

23. The MELE Project/Hawaiian Music Archive Collection website, for instance, lists five other renditions of "Ua Nani ʻO Nuʻuanu" (http://ulukau.org/mele/mele.html), and another two versions are sold on Amazon.com. Eddie Kamae's liner notes indicate that the *mele* honors King Kamehameha IV's summer home (Sutherland 2008).

24. As Susan McClary wrote, "Nineteenth-century Europeans habitually projected onto racial Others the erotic qualities they denied themselves. The racial Other became a favorite 'feminine' zone within the narratives of European colonizers; and depending on the circumstances of the narrative, the Other was viewed with desire, envy, contempt, or fear" (McClary 2002, 63).

References

Asai, Susan Miyo. 1999. *Nōmai Dance Drama: A Surviving Spirit of Medieval Japan*. Westport, CT: Greenwood Publishing Group.

Beamer, Nona. 2001. *Nā Mele Hula: A Collection of Hawaiian Hula Chants*. Vol. 2. Ed. Mauliola Cook and S. Kaliko Beamer Trapp. Laʻie, HI: Brigham Young University (Institute for Polynesian Studies).

Bender, Shawn. 2012. *Taiko Boom: Japanese Drumming in Place and Motion*. Berkeley: University of California Press.

Caines, Rebecca, and Ajay Heble, eds. 2015. *The Improvisation Studies Reader: Spontaneous Acts*. London: Routledge.

Connery, Christopher L. 1994. "Pacific Rim Discourse: The U.S. Global Imaginary in the Late Cold War Years." *Boundary 2* 21, no. 1: 30–56. doi:10.2307/303396.

Dirlik, Arif. 1992. "The Asia-Pacific Idea: Reality and Representation in the Invention of a Regional Structure." *Journal of World History* 3, no. 1: 55–79.

Endo, Kenny. 1994. *Eternal Energy: Featuring the Kenny Endo Taiko Ensemble of Tokyo*. Audio CD. Bindu.

———. 1999. "Yodan Uchi: A Contemporary Composition for Taiko." MA thesis, University of Hawaiʻi at Mānoa.

Fischlin, Daniel, and Ajay Heble, eds. 2004. *The Other Side of Nowhere: Jazz, Improvisation, and Communities in Dialogue*. Music/Culture. Middletown, CT: Wesleyan University Press.

Fischlin, Daniel, Ajay Heble, and George Lipsitz. 2013. *The Fierce Urgency of Now: Improvisation, Rights, and the Ethics of Co-Creation*. Improvisation, Community, and Social Practice. Durham, NC: Duke University Press.

Fujikane, Candace. 2008. "Introduction: Asian Settler Colonialism in the U.S. Colony of Hawai'i." In *Asian Settler Colonialism: From Local Governance to the Habits of Everyday Life in Hawai'i*, ed. Candace Fujikane and Jonathan Y. Okamura, 1–42. Honolulu: University of Hawai'i Press.

Fujikane, Candace, and Jonathan Y. Okamura, eds. 2008. *Asian Settler Colonialism: From Local Governance to the Habits of Everyday Life in Hawai'i*. Honolulu: University of Hawai'i Press.

Heble, Ajay. 2000a. *Landing on the Wrong Note: Jazz, Dissonance, and Critical Practice*. London: Routledge.

———. 2000b. "Sounds of Change: Dissonance, History, and Cultural Listening." *Essays on Canadian Writing*, no. 71: 26–36.

Heble, Ajay, and Daniel Fischlin. 2003. *Rebel Musics: Human Rights, Resistant Sounds, and the Politics of Music Making*. Montreal: Black Rose Books.

Heble, Ajay, and Rob Wallace, eds. 2013. *People Get Ready: The Future of Jazz Is Now!* Durham, NC: Duke University Press.

Hokowhitu, Brendan. 2011. "Indigenous Existentialism and the Body." *Cultural Studies Review* 15, no. 2: 101. doi:http://dx.doi.org/10.5130/csr.v15i2.2040.

Johnson, Gaye Theresa. 2013. *Spaces of Conflict, Sounds of Solidarity: Music, Race, and Spatial Entitlement in Los Angeles*. Berkeley: University of California Press.

Lam, Joseph S. C. 1999. "Embracing 'Asian American Music' as an Heuristic Device." *Journal of Asian American Studies* 2, no. 1: 29–60.

Mackley-Crump, Jared. 2015. *The Pacific Festivals of Aotearoa New Zealand: Negotiating Place and Identity in a New Homeland*. Honolulu: University of Hawai'i Press.

McClary, Susan. 2002. *Feminine Endings: Music, Gender, and Sexuality*. 2nd ed. Minneapolis: University of Minnesota Press.

Mitoma, Judy. 2016. "Kenny Endo—A Lifetime Journey for a Boy from East LA." *Aratani World Series*. February 23. http://www.festivalofsacredmusic.org/kenny-endo-a-lifetime-journey-for-a-boy-from-east-la.

Nguyen, Viet Thanh, and Janet Hoskins. 2014. "Introduction: Transpacific Studies: Critical Perspectives on an Emerging Field." In *Transpacific Studies: Framing an Emerging Field*, ed. Viet Thanh Nguyen and Janet Hoskins, 1–38. Honolulu: University of Hawai'i Press.

Oshiro, Joleen. 2006. "Spirit of the Wood." *Honolulu Star-Bulletin*, July 9. http://archives.starbulletin.com/2006/07/09/features/story03.html.

Pachter, Benjamin. 2015a. "Nidan Uchi/Yodan Uchi." *TaikoSource*. September 3. http://taikosource.com/articles/nidan-uchiyodan-uchi.

———. 2015b. "Symmetrical Soundscapes." *TaikoSource*. October 28. http://taikosource.com/articles/symmetrical-soundscapes.

Pulido, Laura. 2006. *Black, Brown, Yellow, and Left: Radical Activism in Los Angeles*. Berkeley: University of California Press.

Rohrer, Judy. 2016. *Staking Claim: Settler Colonialism and Racialization in Hawai'i*. Tucson: University of Arizona Press.

Saranillio, Dean Itsuji. 2013. "Why Asian Settler Colonialism Matters: A Thought Piece on Critiques, Debates, and Indigenous Difference." *Settler Colonial Studies* 3, no. 3-04: 280–294. doi:10.1080/2201473X.2013.810697.

Shaw, Randy. 1996. *The Activist's Handbook: A Primer for the 1990s and Beyond*. Berkeley: University of California Press.

Sutherland, Susan Kang. 2008. "Favorite Son." *MidWeek*, February 6. http://archives.midweek.com/content/story/midweek_coverstory/favorite_son.

Sutton, R. Anderson. 1980. "Drumming in Okinawan Classical Music: A Catalogue of Gestures." *Dance Research Journal* 13, no. 1: 17–28.

Szego, C. Kati. 2003. "Singing Hawaiian and the Aesthetics of (In)comprehensibility." In *Global Pop, Local Language*, ed. Michael Thomas Carroll and Harris M Berger, 291–328. Jackson: University Press of Mississippi.

Trask, Haunani-Kay. 2000. "Settlers of Color and 'Immigrant' Hegemony: 'Locals' in Hawai'i." *Amerasia Journal* 26, no. 2: 1–24. doi:10.17953/amer.26.2.b31642r221215k7k.

Trimillos, Ricardo D. 2008. "Histories, Resistances, and Reconciliations in a Decolonizable Space: The Philippine Delegation to the 1998 Smithsonian Folklife Festival." *Journal of American Folklore* 121, no. 479: 60–79. doi:10.2307/20487587.

Wong, Deborah. 2004. *Speak It Louder: Asian Americans Making Music*. New York: Routledge.

———. 2016. "Faster and Louder: Heterosexist Improvisation in North American Taiko." In *Sounding the Body: Improvisation, Representation, and Subjectivity*, ed. Gillian Siddall and Ellen Waterman, 265–282. Durham, NC: Duke University Press.

Multimedia Sources

1965. *This is Eddie Kamae and The Sons of Hawaii*. LP. Hula Records H513.

1994. *Eternal Energy: Kenny Endo Taiko Ensemble*. Tokyo: Drum Museum.

2011. "Ua Nani 'O Nu'uanu." From the album *Ekahi*, by the Abrigo 'Ohana. CD. Abrigo 'Ohana LLC.

2013. "Ua Nani 'O Nu'uanu" (The Beauty of Nu'uanu)." From the album *Hawaii: Traditional Hula*, by the Halau Hula Ka No'eau (Hawai'i Arts Ensemble). CD. ARC.

2014. *Island Breeze: Kenny Endo, Riley Lee, Jeff Peterson*. CD Baby.

2015. Footage of "Yume no Pahu" shot at *Kenny Endo Ensemble—40th Anniversary Tour!*, November 21, 2015, Soka Performing Arts Center, Aliso Viejo, CA. Featuring Kenny Endo, Kaoru Watanabe, Chizuko Endo, Abe Lagrimas, Jr., and Shoko Hikage. https://vimeo.com/154704085, accessed on August 17, 2016.

2015. Footage of "Yume no Pahu" shot at the *TEN TEN Kenny Endo's 40th Anniversary Celebration Concert*, October 10, 2015, Hawaii Theatre, Honolulu, HI. Featuring Kenny Endo, Kaoru Watanabe (*fue*/bamboo flutes, *taiko*), Hiromitsu Agatsuma (Tsugaru *shamisen*), Jeff Peterson (Hawaiian Slack Key Guitarist), Yi-chieh Lai (*guzheng*), and members of the Kenny Endo Taiko Ensemble (Chizuko Endo, Yeeman Mui, Eric Chang, and Patrick Oiye). https://www.youtube.com/watch?v=iedHUC4SHL8&list=PLzsAw4c6dc9CfrQVzyvzv3sneQ6uIC9HZ&index=6. Accessed August 17, 2016.

CHAPTER 8

Performing Paradise

HAWAIIAN 'UKULELE IN JAPANESE SETTINGS

Christine R. Yano

On July 28, 2012, in the port city of Yokohama, 2,134 amateur musicians in Japan set a Guinness World Record by comprising the largest ʻukulele ensemble in the world in a performance at the annual Ukulele Picnic. The event at which the ensemble performed has been held annually since 1999, the brainchild of Japanese rock star–cum–ʻukulele aficionado Sekiguchi Kazuyuki (originally a bassist with the popular rock band Southern All Stars). Sekiguchi has become a vortex of ʻukulele promotion in Japan. He matched his Ukulele Picnic in Yokohama with an annual Ukulele Picnic in Honolulu since 2009, attracting not only performers from Hawaiʻi, Japan, and other Asian countries, but also scores of ʻukulele fans from Japan who arrive by the busloads on package tours (Ukulele Picnic in Hawaiʻi n.d.). In addition to the Ukulele Picnics, since 1996 he has been operating the Poepoe Hawaiian Culture Center, a school offering instruction in ʻukulele, hula, and other Hawaiian cultural arts, with locations in Tokyo, Nagoya, and (in 2012) Honolulu. Sekiguchi also spearheads Ukulele Foundation of Hawaiʻi, a nonprofit organization incorporated in 2007 and dedicated to establishing a ʻukulele museum in Hawaiʻi (Ukulele Foundation of Hawaiʻi n.d.). In interview, he encapsulates his dedication to the ʻukulele and its Hawaiian birthplace in an understated manner, saying, "It's very relaxing, comforting and soothing... When I play the ukulele, I never feel depressed" (Mark 2011).

Meanwhile, Yoko Matsuda, a Tokyo-based writer and editor who teaches ʻukulele, explains in greater detail: "For many Japanese, Hawaiʻi is a heavenly place. Especially if you're living in a big city like Tokyo, where summer is humid, winter is windy and cold, your room is small and dark, the sky is narrow and you always have to be concerned about people around you, Hawaiʻi represents everything you don't have" (Boehm 2011). In short, Hawaiʻi represents a utopic paradise of "everything you don't have," and, by extension, the ʻukulele serves as its iconic sound.

Or take the pronouncement of major Japanese ʻukulele maker and purveyor Kiwaya Musical Instruments Co., Ltd. on their website: "The original sound of ukulele makes you feel relaxed and brings you pleasure and excitement... Our policy [slogan] is 'offering happiness through the ukulele' and we're sure of it coming true!" (Kiwaya Musical Instruments Co., Ltd.). The slogan "offering happiness through the ukulele" is part of all e-mail messages from the company in their electronic signature. Clearly, connecting ʻukulele with happiness is part of what is for sale at Kiwaya.

This chapter takes these three examples as a window upon Japanese attitudes toward the ʻukulele (and Hawaiʻi) configured as paradisical objects of yearning and utopian desire. This is desire in the form of what I call a "plucked paradise"—a form of music-making upon a stringed instrument, as well as the image of a flower being harvested for one's use. Plucking a string produces a relatively delicate sound that decays quickly; plucking a flower is a small act of aesthetic appropriation. Both of these reference a paradise that is temporal, sensual, and aestheticized. This "plucked paradise" of desire fuels yearly gatherings of thousands at Sekiguchi's ʻukulele picnics in Yokohama and Honolulu. It is desire that has resulted in the founding of the Nihon Ukulele Association in 1959, with a current membership of more than two hundred, about half of whom meet monthly for lessons, lectures, and performances. It is desire that has made inroads into quality instrument making, especially with top-notch Japanese-made ʻukuleles sold globally through the internet and in music shops.

This research asks: What kinds of meanings do participants give to the ʻukulele and its music in Japan? How do infrastructural components facilitate the development of ʻukulele culture in Japan? By analyzing multiple dimensions involved in the creation of that "plucked paradise," I bring to bear the tensions, conflicts, and creative forces that shape the interaction. Although I do not claim that there is only one mode of regard upon the ʻukulele in Japan, my ongoing fieldwork and archival research point to widespread connections made between the instrument and notions of paradise, in the past and present. In this chapter I first discuss general aspects of the ʻukulele as an instrument and musical culture that have enabled its circulation globally. Then I focus on the historical background of ʻukulele in Japan, bringing to bear the changing context for its reception. And finally, I conclude with comments regarding that "plucked paradise" and its constituent parts that form a culture of transnational circulation.

The ʻukulele presents an important case study in making waves, considering images of paradise and their circulation. In Japan, the ongoing connection between ʻukulele and Hawaiʻi—including the centrality of paradise in each—remains in spite of the fact that much of the popular ʻukulele repertoire is not

Hawaiian music. In short, even when performing non-Hawaiian tunes, the ʻukulele retains its Hawai'i-based image as an idyllic sound associated variously with simplicity, happiness, naïvete, and sometimes nostalgia. To a certain extent, this holds true elsewhere. As I discuss later, the sometimes deliberate disconnect between the instrument and a particular music genre (i.e. Hawaiian music, with some musical groups explicitly stating, "We perform on ʻukulele anything but Hawaiian music") is part of the characteristic in-betweenness of the ʻukulele in its many performance settings. Categorical statements about the ʻukulele demonstrate not only the strength of the ongoing connection between the instrument and the image of Hawaiʻi in contemporary Japan, but also the desire by some artists to break that link. This study focuses on the relationship between the image of the instrument (rather than a musical genre) and its physical and sonic materiality.

In her work on the global consumption of tango, Marta Savigliano proposes a "political economy of passion," suggesting that high emotion—perhaps unavailable in daily life or pre-existing expressive forms—is what tango offers global patrons (1995). This research follows Savigliano's insights in examining the widespread popularity of ʻukulele in Japan, both historically and ethnographically. I suggest that a "political economy of paradise"—utopic visions of happiness through idyllic escape and even healing—may infuse consumption of things Hawaiian in Japan, including the ʻukulele. I thus propose a "political economy of paradise" and its infrastructural contexts, analyzing the meanings and practices with which Japanese engage in the ʻukulele.

This political economy of paradise, however, is not a static structure, but one that is undergoing constant change as part of the processes of transnational and domestic circulation. David Novak's rejoinder about circulation is important here: "circulation is not just movement and exchange, but performance and process. Its forms do not simply progress from one place, person, or sociocultural context to another. Circulation is a nexus of cultural production that defines the things, places, and practices within its loops" (2013, 17–18). Although Novak writes about the avant-garde genre Japanoise with its intense feedback loops, his approach to circulation is important for our thinking about ʻukulele in Japan as not mere replication (an instrument or body of music traveling from one place to another), but generative (the instrument or body of music shaped by the processes and responses of mobility). What results is an evolving music culture whose feedback mechanisms of histories, cultures, intermediaries, socioeconomies, and politics can be seen and heard in process. What is being performed by any one snapshot of ʻukulele in Japan through time and space is its very circulation, its mobility. That circulation traverses in macro tracks transnationally, as well as micro tracks domestically, with locally touring groups and mixings of genres in Japan.

'Ukulele as Instrument of Transnational Circulation

Before focusing specifically on Japan, let us consider the ʻukulele itself as an instrument that lends a certain practical and aesthetic flexibility to its own circulation. Here I suggest a case study of global transmission and theorize factors that may be considered conducive to the transnational circulation of musics and instruments. These form the infrastructure and preconditions for that circulation during particular historical periods of popularity. The story of the ʻukulele and its global circulation (including Japan) takes place within the context of American vectors of power initially tied to immigration and labor markets, making a place such as Hawaiʻi subject to historic waves of migrant workers, from Asia and as far away as Madeira (Portuguese archipelago in North Atlantic Ocean), and layers of cultural influence. These related forces also took geographic margins such as Hawaiʻi and placed them on public display through promotional technologies spanning the late nineteenth to twenty-first centuries: world expositions (in the United States, 1890s–1980s), Tin Pan Alley recorded music (1910s–1920s), Hollywood films (1920s–1960s), and overseas tourism (elite tourism in 1930s; mass tourism from 1960s on) (Hosokawa 1994). The ʻukulele is thus an instrument of circulation in terms of its arrival in Hawaiʻi, as well as its development as a representative icon of Pacific exotica and the symbolic travel inherent through global displays. These form a necessary backdrop to the movement of ʻukulele to Japan.

That movement was enabled by the instrument's flexibility. From its inception as a small, portable stringed instrument developed and introduced by Portuguese immigrants to Hawaiʻi in 1879, the ʻukulele quickly found a place in a range of music performances. Its adoption in Hawaiʻi came quickly in part because of the virtuosity and enthusiasm of its Portuguese musicians, in part because of its promotion by Hawaiian royalty, notably King David Kalākaua (1836–1891), dubbed "The Merrie Monarch." for whom the ʻukulele was a favorite (Berger 2012, 833). Kalākaua took the ʻukulele with him on his around the world tour of 1881, which included Japan, thus introducing Japanese to ʻukulele in a most prestigious context (Kobayashi n.d., 8). Here was an instrument performed by royalty from distant Pacific islands. The introduction of the ʻukulele to Japan by way of the Hawaiian monarch had only a few ripples of effect. The much larger ripple came in 1915, when the ʻukulele was performed as part of the Hawaiian ensemble at the Panama Pacific International Exposition in San Francisco. The sensation of the exposition came from the sounds emanating from the Hawaiian Pavilion, where a quintet of stringed instruments initiated a craze for things Hawaiian (or at least the version of Hawaiian sold to exposition patrons), and especially the ʻukulele.

A 1915 advertisement for the San Francisco music house Sherman Clay and Co. described the ʻukulele as follows: "The Hawaiian ukulele is the one musical instrument which anybody can learn to play. It is inexpensive. It is easily carried about. It is melodious—it has a charm all its own. It is a welcome addition to any social gathering... It affords great pleasure to old and young" (Tranquada and King 2012, 97). The century-old advertisement encapsulates many of the qualities that hold true today, including among fans in Japan that the ʻukulele is easy to play, inexpensive, portable, melodious, conducive to sociality, and pleasurable for young and old.

The ʻukulele garners an air of accessibility through the ease of performing, at least at a rudimentary level ("anyone can play"). For one, many Western songs (especially within popular and folk genres; here I also include "Hawaiian" acculturated songs developed with Western instruments and chordal structure) may be played with only three chords, most commonly C, F, G7. The lure is simple: learn three chords and a beginner can perform a long list of songs. This holds true for other strummed instruments, such as guitar, but ʻukulele has the advantage of being physically less difficult to play. Its strings are lighter and the instrument is smaller, making those three chords easier to perform.

Furthermore, as the advertisement quoted above indicates, the ʻukulele is cheap. The price of the instrument both limits and enables particular associated effects. A low price can suggest broad, rather than selective, availability, making the ʻukulele an instrument of the masses. Rather than an elite base of consumption and performance, the ʻukulele represents an instrument for all—children as well as adults, females as well as males, rich and not so rich. It also suggests that the paradisical imaging of the ʻukulele and its associations with Hawaiʻi may be broadly accessible. Even if travel to Hawaiʻi may be economically prohibitive (or, in the case of Japan, legally restricted in the postwar years until 1964), one may "travel" sonically through the ʻukulele. Here is where the concept of paradise intensifies as forbidden fruit dangling by way of films and is made accessible to everyday Japanese through the sound of the ʻukulele. The paradise that ʻukulele represents may be made with greater impact when one not only hears the sounds but also involves oneself bodily and emotionally through playing. Thus, the "cheapness" of the ʻukulele in combination with the ease of performance enhance the possibility of an accessible paradise found.

Furthermore, the ʻukulele represents the practicality of paradise found in its portability. Lightweight and compact, the instrument can become a companion. This suggests a particular kind of intimacy developed between instrument and owner, between paradise and its beholder. The ʻukulele's portability has also made it a common souvenir of travelers to Hawaiʻi. Like many souvenirs, the ʻukulele may have been stored with other dust collectors and eventually discarded by its recipient. However, in some cases, the souvenir ʻukulele has sparked the imaginations of those at home, who have gone on to play the instrument as a South Seas novelty or even an instrumental accompaniment to popular songs.

The very sound of the ʻukulele may be described in the 1915 advertisement as "melodious," but that does not quite capture the frequent connections between sonic imagery and affect. The size of the instrument and thinness of the nylon strings produce a light sound. In fact, it is this very lightness that may be characterized as an aesthetic linked to Japanese manufacturers. As Kiwaya Musical Instruments Co., Ltd. indicates on their website, "Kiwaya Ukuleles [the only Japanese-made ʻukuleles available for sale in the United States] are built as light as possible for tone and projection. Our craftsmen pay close attention to details such as intonation, action, playability and cosmetic appearance" (Takumi Ukulele Company; note that Takumi and Kiwaya are names used for different branches of the same company). The characteristic "melodious" effect, then, of the Japanese-made ʻukulele has particular resonance for a light, clear tone, which may be favored not only by Japanese consumers but also by other musicians who prefer that sound for certain kinds of songs. (Indeed, ʻukulele aficionados may collect a number of instruments, each for their particular resonance, which may match different genres or songs.) The fact that Kiwaya ʻukuleles may be exported to the United States (including Hawaiʻi), sold in stores and online, demonstrates the many arcs of mobility available to the "melodious" ʻukulele.

The sociality of the instrument and appeal to young and old are aspects of the ʻukulele characteristic of its global circulation, including that of Japan. Indeed, ʻukuleles join other musical instruments in enlivening social gatherings, especially with participatory music-making. The fact that the ʻukulele is easy to play encourages broad participation. Furthermore, the association of ʻukulele with paradisical elements such as relaxation, escape, pleasure, and fun enhance the social aspects of the instrument. That broad participation in the ʻukulele includes young and old, male and female—not unlike the Guinness World Record performance in 2013 that I describe at the beginning of this chapter. With four strings, open tuning, and an openness to take on all comers, the ʻukulele thus performs its own access and adaptability in Japan, as elsewhere.

The ʻukulele's repertoire includes a broad range of musics: not only hula accompaniment and "Hawaiian" songs (typically acculturated music with Hawaiʻi-based themes), but popular music, including period novelty songs from America's late nineteenth- and early twentieth-century popular music assembly line of production, Tin Pan Alley. The early twentieth-century association of ʻukulele with the American entertainment industry through novelty songs and later Hollywood films reflects an important development of Hawaiʻi as a tourist destination. Actual travel to Hawai'i was prohibitively expensive for any but the rich; instead, Hawai'i became the stuff of media-fed dreams: exotic, tropical, playful. Hawai'i—and the small string instrument that became its sonic icon—represented paradisical escape from everyday life. These images and sounds originated in Hawai'i, but elaborated, developed, and circulated by way of American media in the early twentieth century to other countries, including Japan. Any examination of the 'ukulele in Japan must thus be placed within the context of early American-led globalization of paradisical images, sounds, narratives, and tourism. The 'ukulele represented the perfect instrument of mobility.

Part of what enabled that mobility to Japan and elsewhere was the instrument's size. The ease with which one could carry it from place to place enabled its travel. But it was more than physical size that enhanced the 'ukulele's circulation. It was also symbolic size. In other words, the 'ukulele was viewed as a small, informal instrument, suited to a range of musical skills and people. Like the harmonica and jaw harp, it was an instrument *of* travel—portable, flexible in its repertoire, relatively simple to play in its physical and sonic materiality. In short, it was an "instrument lite" in its accessibility. If paradise needed a musical instrument, then the 'ukulele fit the bill in terms of its strumming portability and approachability.

The 'ukulele, however, is more than the easily accessible musical instrument of children and adults alike. Part of its in-betweenness lies in the degree to which at its uppermost reach, the 'ukulele has been subject to virtuosic performance or, more specifically, virtuoso performers who have used the instrument to display their (and the instrument's) range by overcoming the limitations of a simple instrument to perform the most complex musical feats. The virtuosic aspect of the 'ukulele rests in solo performance, bravado displays of speed and agility that have been part of its development from the early days in Hawai'i and elsewhere. Performing against the grain of the "simplicity" of the instrument built up through a twentieth-century history of novelty songs, children's instruction, and even the prominent development of plastic instruments sold for low prices at drug stores and toy departments in the United States in the 1950s, solo performers have worked hard to legitimize the instrument as "more than a toy" (Tranquada and King 2012, 142). The very in-betweenness that virtuoso performances on the 'ukulele display is itself part of the novelty act, akin to that of a child or subhuman animal producing "art" through smearing paint on canvas.

The fact that 'ukuleles became common souvenirs bought and sold in Hawai'i as part of the development of the tourist industry in the 1940s and 1950s further cemented the grain against which virtuoso performances were heard. In other words, the 'ukulele's very connections to paradise and tourism provided the fodder for its denigration as merely a plaything. Legitimizing the "plaything" meant extending its repertoire to bravado pieces such as American composer John Philip Sousa's famous march "Stars and Stripes Forever," normally performed by a marching band. ʻUkulele virtuosity itself became the spectacle of accomplishment for both player and instrument—an entire marching band reduced to four rapidly strummed strings.

Japanese Americans as Conduit for ʻUkulele in Japan

The conditions and characteristics of mobility discussed above provide important conditions for transnational circulation of the ʻukulele in various parts of the world, including Japan. But what makes the Japanese consumption of ʻukulele distinctive is the country's particular history of contract immigration to Hawaiʻi beginning in 1885 and subsequent link to music of Hawaiʻi through Japanese American performers. Although King David Kalākaua may have introduced the instrument to the Japanese public in 1881, it took a few decades before the ʻukulele had an impact in Japan. Imported popular music in Japan in the Taishō Era (1912–1926) followed the trends of the United States—that is, jazz and Tin Pan Alley, which included the rise of the ʻukulele and Hawaiian novelty songs (e.g. "Yaaka Hula Hickey Dula—Hawaiian Love Song," 1916), Broadway shows (e.g., *Hello Honolulu*, *My Honolulu Girl*, *The Ukulele Girl*, 1916–1919). Later in the 1930s, Hollywood movies provided images of Hawaiʻi globally (*Waikiki Wedding*, 1937, with Bing Crosby singing Harry Owens's "Sweet Leilani," which triggered a wave of popularity of Hawaiian or Hawaiian-themed music; *Hawaiian Buckaroo*, 1938; *Hawaii Calls*, 1938; *Honolulu*, 1939; *Hawaiian Nights*, 1939; *Moonlight in Hawaii*, 1941), although because of the rising tide of ultranationalism and war, these had less impact in Japan than previously. In general, the context of the early impact of the ʻukulele in Japan included American media output that imaged Hawaiʻi as a site of escapism and romance, especially as these sounds and images held global sway during the time periods of their popularity. However, the context in Japan also included more direct connections to Hawaiʻi through ongoing family ties with immigrants and their offspring, including travel and sometimes reverse emigration.

The fact that Japanese Americans in Hawaiʻi in the 1920s played ʻukulele is not surprising. In fact, children and adults of various ethnicities learned the instrument, often informally. With persons of Japanese ancestry constituting 43 percent of the population in Hawaiʻi, one could easily predict that a fair number of ʻukulele musicians might be among them. In short, ʻukulele was not a strictly "Hawaiian" instrument, reserved for Hawaiian music or for those of Hawaiian blood. Rather, it was considered a common instrument, cheaper than a piano or even a guitar, accessible to a broad range of people. Furthermore, the music played on the ʻukulele included Hawaiian music, but also other musics such as American popular songs. In Hawaiʻi, as elsewhere, the ʻukulele was not a restricted instrument by status or ritual, nor one confined to a single genre. Instead, its versatility—always against the backdrop of its companionate accessibility—made the instrument a ready avenue of musical expression, including that of Japanese Americans.

In fact, the history of ʻukulele as a social trend in Japan can be uniquely seen as a series of introductions, facilitations, and circulations primarily by and through Japanese Americans. Although influential ʻukulele musicians in Japan have not been exclusively Japanese American (with the notable historical exceptions of father and son Ernest Kaai Sr. and Jr. of Hawaiian ethnicity, who performed Hawaiian music and jazz in Japan, and issued the first Japanese instruction book on ʻukulele, *Ukulele no Hikikata* (How to Play the Ukulele) in 1927, the place of those with ancestral connections has been significant and long-lasting. Because of their varying ties, Japanese American ʻukulele performance has been a bridge between several strands of circulation: (1) ʻukulele by way of the United States, (2) ʻukulele by way of Hawaiʻi, and (3) ʻukulele by way of those who happen to be visiting or touring Japan. They form a critical part of the circuitry by which ʻukulele moves in and through Japan, helping create what Minako Waseda calls "Japanese Hawaiian Music" (Waseda 2013).

Hawaiʻi-born Nisei (second-generation Japanese American) brothers "Harry" Yukihiko Haida (nee Haruhiko; 1909–1986; known as the "Father of Hawaiian Music in Japan") and Katsuhiko Haida brought their knowledge of and enthusiasm for the ʻukulele to Japan in the 1920s when they went initially to repatriate the ashes of their father and stayed to study at university (Yukihiko at Dokkyo Medical School; Katsuhiko at Rikkyo University). Their enthusiasm for Hawaiian music and in-between status with direct access to both Hawaiʻi and Japan helped foster the first ʻukulele boom in Japan. However, they could not have garnered such popularity without the larger context of the craze for ʻukulele in the United States stemming from the 1915 World Exposition in San Francisco. That craze spread across the Pacific to Japan, as part of a wave of enthusiasm for things American. What America wanted, it seems, many parts of the world wanted—and in the 1910s, that was the novelty of the ʻukulele.

Because of overlapping musicians and channels of distribution in Japan, jazz and Hawaiian music—by way of the United States—were intertwined. Both genres shared historical consumption patterns of high social status, the music and their instruments associated not only with the professional stage but also with amateur organizations in upper-middle-class settings of universities and prestigious high schools. By 1927, Ernest Kaai Sr. had published the first instructional book on ʻukulele in Japan, and in 1929 major record labels in Japan sold Hawaiian recordings. In that same year, the Haida brothers formed the highly successful Moana Glee Club of singers and musicians, and performed throughout Japan. The Haida brothers' importance lay not only in performance but also in teaching Hawaiian music, composing Hawaiian songs in Japan, recording Hawaiian music on Nippon Victor, and exposing many Japanese to live performances of Hawaiian music. Unlike visiting musicians, the Haida brothers stayed and lived in Japan as a permanent fixture of the entertainment scene, which included Hawaiian music, retaining their associations with Hawai'i, especially through long-standing Japanese American networks.

Another Japanese American who helped promote Hawaiian music was Tsutomu "Buckie" Shirakata (1912–1994), a Nisei born in Hawai'i and encouraged by Yukihiko Haida to make a career in Japan. A University of Hawai'i graduate, Shirakata traveled to Japan in 1933 as a member of the Aloha Hawaiian Trio composed of two other Nisei, Satoru Moriwaki and Charles Nosaka. The trio had won an audition offered by a Honolulu radio station, which included the trip to Japan, where they performed and recorded for Nippon Columbia. Shirakata went back to Hawai'i to complete his university studies, but returned to Japan upon graduation and joined jazz and Hawaiian music groups, eventually forming his own, Aloha Hawaiians, in 1940 and opening a Hawaiian music teaching studio in that same year. Known primarily for his steel guitar playing, he also performed on the 'ukulele. He published an instruction book for 'ukulele and made many recordings of Hawaiian music on Nippon Columbia under "Ray King and His Orchestra," a group comprising Japanese and Japanese Americans.

The musical expression with which 'ukulele was most commonly—though not exclusively—linked was that of Hawai'i. Any discussion of 'ukulele in Japan must therefore consider the state of Hawaiian music in general (i.e., a music genre focused on Hawai'i) in Japan, as well as music (typically Western popular songs) performed on the 'ukulele. Both Hawaiian music and 'ukulele music in Japan affirmed their prewar high status not only through the class position of the Japanese Americans who performed (mostly university graduates), but also through some of its most public Japanese practitioners. For example, Asabuki Eiichi (1909–1993), primarily a xylophonist and vibraphonist, and a pupil of Haida Yukihiko's, formed his own music group, the Kalua Kamaainas, in 1940, which performed in Tokyo until the war disrupted their livelihood. Asabuki was the son of the president of Mitsukoshi Department Store. Another steel guitar student of Haida's was Homma Toshiaki, who became president of Mikimoto Pearls. And another Hawaiian music enthusiast was Inumaru Tetsuzō, who became president of the Imperial Hotel chain in Japan. Although these men may not have been 'ukulele specialists, their performances of Hawaiian music likely included 'ukulele.

What is important to note in this very brief historiography of Hawaiian music in Japan is the relatively low-key role that the ʻukulele and its players had, apart from the Haida brothers. Although the ʻukulele was part of the characteristic sound of music associated with Hawaiʻi in Japan and elsewhere, perhaps because of its relative small size—both physically and sonically—it did not command the center stage. Instead, the ʻukulele tended to play background to other instruments such as steel guitar, which seemed to carry the weight of Hawaiian music performance in Japan.

The late 1930s and 1940s represented both a heyday for Hawaiian music performance in Japan with numerous recordings released, as well as a low point with the ban placed upon "enemy musics," which included Hawaiian songs, in 1943. While the ban forced professional musicians—including ʻukulele players—to retire or perform other kinds of musics, amateur fans and musicians went underground or found other covert means to retain their interest in the ʻukulele. Some listened to their Hawaiian music records at home with the volume turned low; others played their instruments secretly. In fact, according to one report, Terabe Yoriyuki, a pilot for the Imperial Japanese Navy, claimed to take his ʻukulele on board and played while flying (Berger 2012, 379).

Soon after the war's end in 1945, the ʻukulele returned to the public music scene, forming part of the second ʻukulele boom of popularity in Japan. Hawaiian music groups quickly formed primarily from prewar bands, performing at U.S. military camps, and eventually before general Japanese audiences. Postwar Japan experienced a tremendous Hawaiian music boom, with some three to four thousand student Hawaiian music bands. The postwar Hawaiʻi boom built upon various media images that perceived Hawaiʻi as "Yume no Shima"—the islands of one's dreams. In 1952 the Far Eastern Network began broadcasts of the tremendously popular radio show *Hawaii Calls* directly from Hawaiʻi. Sales of *Hawaii Calls* record albums were bestsellers. In 1955, in response to the popularity of the ʻukulele, string instrument dealer Kiwaya Musical Instruments Co., Ltd. decided to make the ʻukulele its main featured instrument and focus its marketing and promotion of it. One pattern of Hawaiian record sales established during the postwar period was the association of Hawaiian music with summertime. Therefore, ʻukulele became associated with "summer music": ʻukulele recordings were sold primarily during summer months, linked with beer gardens as part of seasonal trade (Berger 2012, 381).

In 1959 Haida Yukihiko organized the Nihon Ukulele Association (NUA), which continues through the 2000s as the main institutional structure of ʻukulele players in Japan. Haida formed the organization with the goal of "promoting the ukulele ... as one of the easiest musical instruments for the amateurs to play" (Nihon Ukulele Association). His inspiration for organizing amateur musicians was meeting with Japanese American master ʻukulele musician Herb

Ohta (b. 1934; aka Ohta-san), then stationed as a Marine in Japan. Ohta's contribution to ʻukulele performance in Hawaiʻi and Japan was as a solo artist not confined to Hawaiian music. A protégé of Hawaiian musician Eddie Kamae (1927–2017), who played both jazz and Hawaiian music, Ohta followed his teacher's lead. Rather than approaching ʻukulele as a strumming chordal accompaniment, Ohta emphasized the expressivity of plucked jazz solos and contemporary songs on ʻukulele. Ohta remains an Honorary Member of NUA, along with other musicians primarily based in Hawaiʻi. He represents the Japanese American face of ʻukulele solo artistry in Japan that has only recently been supplanted by a younger generation. In spite of younger and flashier ʻukulele musicians from Hawaiʻi, Ohta retains a faithful following in Japan as the template of musicianship. For many, he remains the quiet but solid apex of ʻukulele artistry.

In contemporary Japan, ʻukulele joins other forms of associated Hawaiiana, from hula, steel guitar, and slack key guitar to surfing, clothing, and food, in a continuing "Hawaii boom"—and third ʻukulele boom—that began in the 1990s. This "Hawaii/ʻukulele boom" mixes genders and generations in its bid for paradise. In particular, the ʻukulele has been linked to happiness and well-being through the notion of *iyashi* (healing). Here is a soothing paradise that attends to what is perceived as the organic shape of the instrument, as well as the soft sound of its strummed and plucked strings. Even when the music is not Hawaiian, the ʻukulele retains associations with the islands.

In the late 1990s, the ʻukulele took on another level of appeal by becoming a fashion icon with its adoption by young women who carried it around, sometimes color-coordinated with their outfits, because it "looks cute" (Japan Echo 1999). ʻUkulele shops in Japan reflect this visual aspect, offering many consumer options in the instrument (styles, shapes, colors, decorations), and perhaps more importantly, the carrying case. ʻUkulele as fashion suggests multiple purchases by female fans, to coordinate with one's outfit if not also one's general public image. One evidence of the fashionable, visual-oriented attitude toward ʻukulele in contemporary Japan is the placement of a full-length mirror in many showrooms. Another evidence of ʻukulele as fashion can be found in the ʻukulele magazines published in Japan that feature the latest trends in goods, displaying different colorful bags and cases, picks, pegs, and stands (Konno 2013, 22–23).

For many readers of those magazines and customers in that showroom, the contemporary Japanese American face of virtuosic ʻukulele performance and part of the reason for the ʻukulele boom that continues is fifth-generation Japanese-Okinawan American Jake Shimabukuro. Shimabukuro's wildly enthusiastic fan club in Japan, populated primarily by young women who treat him like a rock star, presents a younger face of ʻukulele consumption and fandom. Shimabukuro performs regularly in Japan on tour to sold-out crowds. Recognizing the paradisical potential of the ʻukulele virtuoso, in 2004 the Hawaiʻi Tourism Authority hired Shimabukuro as spokesperson promoting tourism in Japan. He also performs as a Japanese American with ancestral ties to Japan (Okinawa): although he does not speak Japanese, he contributes to ongoing Japan–U.S. relations through humanitarian efforts, such as recording a song—"The *Ehime Maru* (In Memory of)"—in commemoration of the *Ehime Maru* incident in which nine members aboard a Japanese training ship were accidentally killed by a U.S. Navy submarine off the coast of Oʻahu in 2001 (Shimabukuro 2001; Uketoday 2010) as well as visiting and performing at shelters for victims of the Tōhoku triple disaster in 2011, filmed by Nihon Hōsō Kyokai (NHK) in a 2012 documentary (Nihon Hōsō Kyokai 2012). Shimabukuro clearly uses ʻukulele to extend humanitarian efforts to build bridges enabled by a particularistic Japanese American–Japan/Hawaiʻi positioning. In the hands of a younger generation such as this, ʻukulele may enable new paradisical positionings that move Japanese *iyashi* toward more than feeling good.

Toward a Political Economy of Paradise

What do we make of this brief history of ʻukulele in Japan—from the first boom in the 1920s and 1930s to the second boom in 1950s to the third boom in 1990s on? What insights upon the contemporary scene can we draw? On the Poepoe Hawaiian Culture Center website, Sekiguchi waxes philosophical: "The world is trying to change its way of thinking from material to the importance of the 'heart.' The way of thinking 'Happiness lies in the mind/heart' was the basic philosophy in a culture that values nature, including Hawaii . . . Hawaiian culture has been widely accepted by different people in the world, and is nothing more than an indication of what people really need the most by living in this modern society" (Poepoe Hawaiian Culture Center). In short, what Sekiguchi proclaims is a universal need for "healing" and "heart" to be found as a nature-based source of happiness qua paradise in something like the ʻukulele. Whereas Sekiguchi indicates that "Happiness lies in the heart" (*shiawase wa kokoro no naka ni aru*), I extend this to suggest that Sekiguchi's philosophy may be paraphrased as "Paradise lies in the heart and ʻukulele is its sound."

Situating paradise in one's heart theoretically takes the concept out of time, space, and specific events. And yet, that heart is hardly insulated from the realities of histories, nations, globalism, and consumer markets. Indeed, Sekiguchi himself frames the "need" for the "healing" and "heart" of nature-based paradise in modernity. ʻUkulele thus becomes a nostalgic rejoinder, a turn back to nature, an intimate yearning for the distant. Moreover, according to Sekiguchi, this yearning is shared by others living in an industrialized, modern world. In short, modernity brings both the yearning for paradise and access to its object of desire, found sonically and materially here in the ʻukulele.

Let us thus return to the notion of a political economy of paradise, framing this construction of paradise in nostalgia as the past and distant, and, more importantly, situating Hawaiʻi (through the ʻukulele) as the past and distant made portable and accessible in the very sonic materiality of the four-stringed instrument. One may interpret the ʻukulele as a metaphor for paradise tamed, miniaturized, and aestheticized. Indeed, these actions upon paradise (or a place identified as paradisical, such as Hawaiʻi) have grave political implications, pointing toward colonialist attitudes of appropriation, turning a back upon the very real sociopolitical problems in the place of origin (Yaguchi 2011).

These implications intertwine with issues of simplicity, flexibility, and mobility surrounding the instrument. The appeal of the ʻukulele lies in the *simplicity* of the playing (available to children and adults; learned through three chords; ushered in by a plethora of teaching in books and on the internet) that makes this paradise available as one's own. The infrastructure of appeal builds upon the *flexibility* of the instrument (a toy or a "real" instrument or both; an accompaniment to singing or a solo instrument; a three-chord simple strum or a virtuosic fingering; a wide range of prices so that one may gradually escalate one's commitment and relationships to the ʻukulele through successive purchases to more expensive instruments, differently sized instruments, multiple instruments in different styles and for different purposes) that makes this a widely distributed and consumed form of paradise. The practices of paradise lie in the *mobility* of the instrument (often purchased as a souvenir of Hawaiʻi or as a gift for a child; small enough in size to be able to accompany a person in daily life on trips; low enough in price to suggest a low-risk investment), encompassing a broad range of contexts for this form of paradise.

Many of these aspects can be said equally about the ʻukulele in various of its global markets of popularity, from Canada to Britain to Thailand (Coleman and Meagher 2009). However, what gives consumption in Japan particular resonance is its historical relationship with Hawaiʻi. This includes the relative geographical proximity, the presence of Japanese Americans through immigration that began in the late nineteenth century, and the many images and iterations of Hawaiʻi in Japanese media, particularly from the postwar period onward. An important access point for ʻukulele in Japan has been Japanese Americans of different generations and historical time periods. The presence of Japanese Americans from Hawaiʻi in the Japanese popular music scene has constituted what is perceived as a racialized link to American popular music—including ʻukulele—not afforded by white, African American, Latin American, or other musicians. Although some older Japanese ʻukulele fans point to the Japanese language facility of the earlier generations of Japanese Americans who helped popularize ʻukulele in Japan, this argument overlooks the tremendous popularity of Jake Shimabukuro, who at least initially spoke no Japanese when he began touring Japan and freely admits his lack of Japanese language facility.

What these elements point to is a paradise that is attainable within limits. Those limits include the ambiguity of Japanese Americans. Racialized as Japanese, nationalized as an intermediary bridge, culturalized as still representative of Hawaiʻi, the familiar-and-foreign Japanese Americans have formed a crucial component of this paradise found. They provide Japan with a unique conduit to the ʻukulele that is direct and long-lasting. Japanese Americans resolve the issue of authenticity that often plagues the Japanese performance of foreign musics. In contrast with issues of authenticity arising from Japanese musicians of jazz, hip-hop, or reggae (Atkins 2001; Condry 2006; Sterling 2010), the authenticity of Japanese Americans in Japan performing ʻukulele lies simultaneously in their birthplace of Hawaiʻi, as well as their Japanese blood and, in earlier generations, adopted residence. To the question "Are they Hawaiian enough?" Japanese Americans need only look to the legitimacy of their ʻukulele performance in the place of their birth and upbringing. With Japanese Americans performing ʻukulele, Japanese nationals can have their cake (i.e., an authentic performer of ʻukulele from Hawaiʻi) and eat it, too (i.e., that performer is one of us, or nearly so).

Those limits may also be found in temporality. The seasonality of the ʻukulele's promotion as "summer music" suggests a paradise that can be visited and revisited on a regular basis. In short, as each season is made sense of and by other seasons, so, too, is this paradise defined by the wintering of its presence. Currently associated with *iyashi* (healing), the sound of the ʻukulele serves as respite amid the clamor of everyday life. In the hands of a new breed of Japanese American ʻukulele musicians, paradisical *iyashi* may minister to not only personal healing but also international humanitarianism.

A political economy of paradise recognizes ʻukulele in Japan as this—cultural appropriation of a tropical salve to modern wounds—but it also recognizes the very real potential for that salve to accommodate wounds on more than an individual scale. Japanese are not alone in this yearning, of course, but the fervor and patternings, the *kata* (form) of the run to pluck this paradise, sometimes en masse, suggest a political economy framed within precarities (Allison 2013). As the recent physical and socioeconomic disasters have precipitated a sense of crisis in Japan, the simplicity of the plucked paradise comes at its own cost of bread-and-circus escapism. Here is paradise, at once found and fraught. Nevertheless, the problems surrounding such a paradise are of little concern to the many fans of ʻukulele in Japan. I return to Sekiguchi's statement: "When I play the ʻukulele I never feel depressed." Or take the slogan of Kiwaya Musical Instruments, Co., Ltd., found on the company's website in English, and quoted earlier: "Offering happiness through the ukulele." These statements may speak at the level of individual affect, but the lessons of paradise in Japan apply in a broader sense. In the hands of musicians, entrepreneurs, and instrument purveyors alike, the 'ukulele performs as the simple sound of possibility. Herein lies the possibilities of healing—large and small—through active engagement within a plucked paradise. That plucked paradise constitutes the rebounded musical wave, shaped over time and place, lapping at the shores of Japan from Hawai'i and back again.

References

Allison, Anne. 2013. *Precarious Japan*. Durham, NC: Duke University Press.

Atkins, E. Taylor. 2001. *Blue Nippon: Authenticating Jazz in Japan*. Durham, NC: Duke University Press.

Berger, John. 2012. "'Ukulele," in G. Kanahele and J. Berger, eds., *Hawaiian Music and Musicians: An Encyclopedic History*, 830–857. Honolulu: Mutual Publishing.

Boehm, Deborah. 2011. "Let's Make Happy Aloha Music Time!" *Hana Hou: The Magazine of Hawaiian Airlines* 14, no. 2. http://hanahou.com/pages/Magazine.asp?Action=DrawArticle&ArticleID=955&MagazineID=61. Accessed July 28, 2014.

Coleman, Tony, and Margaret Meagher. 2009. *Mighty Uke: The Amazing Comeback of a Musical Underdog*. Video recording. Toronto: Tiny Goat Films, Ltd.

Condry, Ian. 2006. *Hip-Hop Japan: Rap and the Paths of Cultural Globalization*. Durham, NC: Duke University Press.

Hosokawa Shuhei. 1994. "East of Honolulu; Hawaiian Music in Japan from the 1920s to the 1940s," *Perfect Beat* 2, no. 1: 51–67.

Japan Echo. 1999. "Ukulele Craze Again: Hawaiian Instrument Strikes a Chord with Japanese Hearts," *Trends in Japan*, September 7. http://web-japan.org/trends00/honbon/tj990908.html. Accessed October 27, 2013.

Kiwaya Musical Instruments Co., Ltd. http://www.kiwaya.com/english. Accessed August 18, 2014.

Kobayashi Masayoshi. n.d., *Ukurere Kaidokubon* (Pleasant Ukulele Book). Tokyo: Heironsha.

Konno Seyzi. 2013. "Uke Guzzu no Torendo Tambō" (Hunting for Trends in Ukulele Goods). *Ukulele Alamode*, August 29, 22–23.

Mark, Steven. 2011. "Ukulele Week Features Kazuyuki Sekiguchi and Hawaii Master Herb Ohta," *Star-Advertiser*, February 11. http://www.honolulupulse.com/2011/02/ukulele-week-features-kazuyuki-sekiguchi-and-hawaii-master-herb-ohta. Accessed September 14, 2013.

Nihon Hōsō Kyokai. 2012. "Tomorrow beyond 3.11. My Fukushima Home," November 19.

Nihon Ukulele Association. http://e-nua.com/index.html. http://e-nua.com/history/history-e.html. Accessed August 8, 2014.

Novak, David. 2013. *Japanoise: Music at the Edge of Circulation*. Durham, NC: Duke University Press.

Poepoe Hawaiian Culture Center. http://www.poepoehcc.com/en/about. Accessed October 30, 2013.

Savigliano, Marta. 1995. *Tango and the Political Economy of Passion*. Boulder, CO: Westview Press.

Shimabukuro, Jake. 2001. "The *Ehime Maru* (In Memory Of)." Charlotte, NC: Surfside Records.

Sterling, Marvin D. 2010. *Babylon East: Performing Dancehall, Roots Reggae and Rastafari in Japan*. Durham, NC: Duke University Press.

Takumi Ukulele Company. http://takumiukulele.com/kiwayaukuleles.html. Accessed August 5, 2014.

Tranquada, Jim, and John King. 2012. *The ʻUkulele: A History*. Honolulu: University of Hawaiʻi Press.

Uketoday. 2010. "Jake Shimabukuro Talks about the Ehime Maru.m4v." https://www.youtube.com/watch?v=oNUnn7aG-sM. Accessed August 9, 2014.

Ukulele Foundation of Hawaiʻi. n.d. http://ukulelefoundation.org. Accessed August 9, 2014.

Ukulele Picnic in Hawaii. n.d. http://www.ukulelepicnicinhawaii.org/en/about_foundation.html. Accessed August 9, 2014.

Waseda Minako. 2013. "Japanese-American Musicians as Pioneers of 'Japanese' Hawaiian Music." Unpublished paper presented at meeting of International Council on Traditional Music. Shanghai.

Yaguchi Yujin. 2011. *Akogare no Hawaiʻi* (Longing for Hawaiʻi). Tokyo: Chūōkoron Shinsha.

CHAPTER 9

Hawaiian and American Pasts Confronting a Native Hawaiian and a Globalized Present

REWORKING HAROLD ARLEN'S "OVER THE RAINBOW" BY ISRAEL KAMAKAWIWO'OLE

Ricardo D. Trimillos

THIS chapter is part of a larger ongoing study on localization and meaning making against a global matrix, which is not synonymous with glocalization (Robertson 1995). In keeping with the theme of "making waves"—actual, virtual, and metaphorical—I consider as excellent example the 1990 cover[1] of "Over the Rainbow"[2] (hereafter OTR) by the late Israel Kamakawiwoʻole (1959–1997), a Native Hawaiian.[3] His reworking is a local Island product (Kamakawiwoʻole 2001, 10) that decentered and—as we shall see—in part replaced the original OTR composed by Harold Arlen (1905–1986) in 1938 for the 1939 film *The Wizard of Oz* starring ingenue Judy Garland (1922–1969). The cover of OTR narrates a multivalent process that alternatively engages localization and globalization, in which local and subject agency constitutes a repository for empowerment that propels a localized reworking of an American and hegemonic cultural icon back into a globalized and commercialized space.

The Kamakawiwoʻole version of OTR constitutes a significant link in a chain of events for this musical artist who emerged from the second Hawaiian Renaissance[4] (G. Kanahele 1979b), a reclamation of Hawaiian language and culture, and forged a trajectory leading to concerns for Hawaiian Sovereignty, the demand for political and economic self-determination by Native Hawaiians (Goodyear-Kaʻōpua, Hussey, and Wright 2014). The second Hawaiian Renaissance was a remarkable movement to rediscover and regain Hawaiian identity through language and performance begun in the 1970s, informed by the rhetoric of diversity and the dynamics of social activism arising from issues of civil rights, land rights, and an unsatisfactory conclusion to an unpopular Vietnam war.[5] The burgeoning tourist industry had essentialized Hawai'i as a paradise of surf, palm trees, and pristine, unpopulated white sand beaches. In 1961 Elvis Presley had already reglobalized "Blue Hawaii." Gidget and the Brady Bunch had constructed Hawai'i as a place to resolve white middle-class adolescent angst against a background of brown-skinned natives.[6] Faced with this corporate and commoditized image Native Hawaiians and other Hawai'i-born Locals began to question the American Dream as neither totally satisfying nor completely attainable. They noted the emergence of voices from other parts of minority America, and began to add their voices—and music—to issues of cultural diversity within an increasingly socially charged soundscape. The Hawaiian Renaissance was named and brought to greater awareness by George Kanahele (1930–2000), a thoughtful indigenous spokesperson (G. Kanahele 1971). He initiated and edited the landmark *Hawaiian Music and Musicians: An Illustrated History* (1979a), the first major reference work on Hawaiian music by a Native Hawaiian. It is in the milieu of this Hawaiian Renaissance that Iz and his reworking of OTR might be understood.

This discussion brings into play a number of dialogic processes related to signification, identity, hybridity, entextualization, and intertextuality. These processes inform both the performance of the song and its performer, Israel Kamakawiwo'ole, who for purposes of brevity and authorial distance is referred to hereafter by his nickname, Iz.[7] While the Hawaiianness of the Iz version is putatively tied to the persona of the performer and reinforced by the signifying sound of 'ukulele, often overlooked are the ways in which Hawaiian musical features—both pre-Contact and post-Contact—inform its sonic gestalt. I consider sonic dimensions of performance, contrasting the Iz version with the Arlen[8] 1938 original as urtext. I argue for the sonic as basis for an alternative and productive approach to understanding expressive culture as history and as performed identity.

The properties of signification are multivariate and include items as specific as the performance of a named piece of music during a particular event and as general as a vocal melodic gesture. In the Hawaiian realm, an example of a high degree of specificity concerns the 1986 Merrie Monarch *hula kahiko* (ancient style dance) competition in Hilo town on the Big Island. For that competition a chant about the three destructive winds of the deity Hina from the island of Moloka'i was about to be performed. A freak and unexplainable storm caused a complete power failure disrupting the festival for more than an hour, after which the decision was made not to perform the chant (Skillman 2012). Some explained the blackout as an expression of displeasure by Pele, Big Island goddess of fire, because to perform a chant honoring Hina on the Big Island was disrespectful to Pele, its resident diety. In contrast to the specificity of a single performance event of a named chant, sonic signification can also be general, for example, drawing upon a repertory of melodic or rhythmic gestures generally known and widely shared among practitioners of a genre. As a Hawaiian example, a traditional chanting technique called *ʻiʻi* can be interpolated during performance by a chanter. It results in the prolongation of the vowel of a single syllable in the the delivery of a logogenic *oli* or chant (Tatar 1982). The discussion of vocal treatment will consider aspects of *ʻiʻi* encountered in the Iz version of OTR.

The role of music in identity construction has been a central focus of ethnomusicology as well as related fields, including performance studies, area studies, popular culture, and anthropology. While of late identity has been tied principally to concerns—if not anxieties—about belonging or owning in respect to nationality and ethnicity, other forms of identity have emerged through mediatization and diaspora, for example, taste cultures (Gans 1974). Another aspect is the performance of identity, either quotidian or staged. In this regard Mark Slobin's relational categories of the subcultural, intercultural, and supercultural from his signal study on minority music, *Subcultural Sounds: Micromusics of the West* (1993), are useful.

The emergence and attention to hybrid or fusion forms, particularly with genres that are commoditized and mediatized as "popular music," are also informative for identity formation and concerns for "who owns what." In this regard the issues Sutton raises in his essay on fusion genres in Korean pop music (2011) have promise for examining Iz's OTR as a composition from the pre–Pacific War genre of the film musical that is reinterpreted through a native and minority performer, intended for a commercial recording industry clearly identified as Hawaiian. Hawaiian music itself encompasses a range of repertory and differentiated musical styles, many of which are themselves products of fusion between Hawaiian elements—both pre-Contact and post-Contact—and introduced features including triadic harmony, tempered tuning, gendered vocal range, plucked string instruments, and lyrics using the English language. Sutton's discourses of nationalism, globalism, modernity, and commercialism (ibid., 16) can readily transfer to the consideration of Iz's cover of OTR.

I also engage a brief discussion of entextualization, a theory that has historical implications (Urban 1996). Drawing upon the work of Ochoa Gautier (2012) and Mosley (2013), I use entextualization to denote the act of removing a music from its context of origin initiated by a single individual that then presents the possibility of alternative or variant meanings, which are local or agenda-specific. The act of removal is key for entextualization and differentiates it from the process of recontextualization, a distinction also made by Ochoa Gautier (2012, 392). I consider entextualization itself to be a moment of empowerment and of taking power (Bauman and Briggs 1990). In the case of Iz these moments have significance for his positionality as a subaltern figure and an aboriginal minority who appropriates and re-forms a composition from musical theater, a genre that signals mainstream and capitalist American elitist privilege. The OTR cover by Iz includes acts of entextualization that engage lyrics, features of sound, and formal musical and literary structures.

I begin by making some structural comparisons between the two versions. I then discuss the lyrics as sounded word and then interrogate three aspects of the "musical-technical"—melody, harmony, and vocal treatment, suggesting how Iz "Hawaiianized" this Broadway-style tune.[9] I conclude with tentative observations about entextualization and intertextuality.

Formal Structure: Thirty-Two-Bar Ballad

The formal structure of the Arlen original (Arlen and Harburg [1938] 1985) is the thirty-two-bar ballad, a standard form for Tin Pan Alley pop songs. As a template, the thirty-two-bar ballad was the basis for hundreds of popular songs during pre–Pacific War decades, providing a familiar and convenient structure for the pop music industry, and ready material for exploitation by jazz improvisation, itself an interesting case of black appropriation of a white creative expression (or in terms of class, a downtown appropriation of an uptown genre).

Structurally the ballad form consists of chorus A, chorus B, the bridge, and chorus C, each eight bars in length. Although there are a few variants of this two chorus-bridge-chorus schema, this is the form most commonly encountered. The eight-bar duration for each section is standard and generally remains unchanged.

The overall structure of the original Arlen OTR is summarized in the right-hand column of table 9.1, a comparative schematic of structures of the two versions. It begins with an instrumental introduction of eight bars and continues

Table 9.1 Comparison of Form of "Over the Rainbow"

Israel Kamakawiwo'ole	*Edgar Harburg/Harold Arlen urtext*
Intro 8 bars (vocalise)	Intro 8 bars (instrumental)
Chorus A 8 bars (somewhere . . . high)	Chorus A 8 bars (somewhere . . . high)
Chorus B 8 bars (somewhere . . . fly)	Chorus B 8 bars (somewhere . . . skies)
Bridge 8 bars (someday I'll)	Bridge 8 bars (someday I'll . . .)
Chorus C 8 bars (somewhere . . . fly)	Chorus C 8 bars (somewhere . . . fly)
Chorus A 8 bars RPT	
Chorus B 8 bars RPT	
Bridge 8 bars RPT (someday I'll . . .)	Bridge 8 bars RPT
Chorus C 8 bars RPT (. . . high)	Chorus C 8 bars RPT
Outro 8 bars (vocalise)	Coda (4 instrumental + 4 vocal)

on to the first statement of the main content of thirty-two bars. The thematic material of the thirty-two bars can be diagrammed as A1, A2, B1 (bridge), A3. Arlen specifies that the ballad proper is to be repeated in its entirety, forming a second complete statement. Arlen concludes with a coda of eight bars, consisting of four bars of instrumental interlude followed by four bars with vocals.

Iz's performance[10] is presented in greater detail in figure 9.1. He begins with five bars of reggae riff for solo 'ukulele followed by the often-quoted introduction of vocalise and 'ukulele.[11] He then presents the first statement of the ballad content, structurally duplicating the Arlen melodic material—A1, A2, B1 (bridge), A3. However he shortens the second statement by repeating only the bridge section and the final chorus C, a commercial performance practice known as "back to the bridge." This performance sequence results in a different sequencing of the musical content of the ballad material and its concomitant sonic effect: A1, A2, B1 (bridge), A3 + B2 (bridge), A4. By restating the opening vocalise at the end of the piece, Iz creates a closed form that draws a clear parallel to the *kāhea* (call) feature that opens and closes a traditional *mele hula* (danced piece). The *kāhea* of *mele hula* and the introductory vocalise in Iz's OTR suggest another parallel—both are vocalized elements external to the principal musical and textual content.

The Sounded Word: Text

I now turn to the text (lyrics) as the sounded word. Its importance in Hawaiian culture is expressed by the often-invoked saying, "*I ka 'ōlelo no ke ola, i ka 'ōlelo nō ke make*" (In the word is life, in the word is death). Upon first encounter with

A1 TEXT 1

	some-	where	over the	rainbow		way up	high	
IZ	D		f#		G		D	
ARLEN	d	b	f#	----A7	G		D	D7
				rain----				
	some-	where	over the	bow	way	up	high	

		dreams that							(extension)	
and	the	you	dream of	once in a	lulla-	bye				
G		D		A7		b			b	G
G	g	D	B7	E7	A7	D	e	A7	/	/
there's	a	land that I	heard of	once in a	lull-a	bye				

Figure 9.1 Comparison of chord structures.

the Iz text, one might think he fails to remember the lyrics accurately or at least "the lyrics were slightly wrong" (Lynskey 2010). The Arlen original[12] is shown in the right column in table 9.2, and the Iz version with departures from the Arlen in bold on the left. Each text line is assigned a letter-number code to facilitate comparison.

Did Iz remember the lyrics incorrectly? This is not likely. First, Iz—like most Hawaiian artists—had an incredible memory for a vast repertory of Hawaiian *mele* (song) in two languages, Hawaiian and English. Second, the Hawaiian tradition of *mele* respects the integrity of the sounded word as prescribed, a value continually emphasized in *hālau* (traditional school of learning) and central to the transmission of Hawaiian language–based performance, including genealogies, sayings, and storytelling, as well as hula and *oli* (chant). Iz was part of that tradition and knew Renaissance *kumu hula* (hula masters) Darrell Lupenui, Thaddius Wilson, and O'Brian Eselu active on the Wai'anae Coast. Third, there is strong internal evidence that departures from the Arlen text are not accidental: he performs the text of the companion song in the recorded medley "Over the Rainbow"/"What a Wonderful World" (Weiss and Thiele 1967) without any structural changes.[13] Therefore, I argue that text changes by Iz to the Arlen original are deliberate and internally logical, a claim I return to in the discussion of entextualization.

The Music-Technical

The next three sections rely upon music-technical analyses, through which I intend to show that musical sounds do carry social, cultural, and political implications, both explicit and implicit.

Melody

Melody in Hawaiian genres are often categorized as either pre-Contact (*kahiko*) or post-Contact (*'auana*) with the latter influenced by Protestant hymnody, although recent research suggests that the sea chantey and other maritime musics also constitute important sources of "Western" melodic ideas (Carr 2014). One aspect of melody is ambitus or range, that is, the relative distance between the lowest and the highest pitch of a melody expressed as "intervals" of different sizes based on the twelve-tone chromatic scale currently in widespread use. A narrow range (a major third or less) is recognized for Hawaiian melody in general (G. Kanahele 1997a, 58) and is a major style characteristic of nineteenth century Hawaiian chant (Tatar 1982). A narrow ambitus continues to be characteristic of post-*'auana* melody, for example, the terraced descending melody

Table 9.2 Comparison of Text of "Over the Rainbow"

Israel Kamakawiwo'ole version (CD Alone in IZ World BBCD5907, 2001)	*Edgar Harburg/Harold Arlen urtext*
Oo—	
A1.1. somewhere over the rainbow	A1.1 somewhere over the rainbow
A1.2 way up high	A1.2 way up high
B2.3 **and the dreams that [you dream of]**	A1.3 there's a land that I heard of
A1.4 once in a lullabye [—ye—o—]	A1.4 once in a lullaby
B2.1 somewhere over the rainbow	B2.1 somewhere over the rainbow
D4.2 **bluebirds fly**	B2.2 skies are blue
B2.3 **and the dream that [you dream of]**	B2.3 and the dreams that you dare to
B2.4 dream[s] really do come true—oo	B2.4 dream really do come true
C3.1 someday **I** wish upon a star	C3.1 someday I'll wish upon a star
C3.2 wake up where the clouds are far behind me	C3.2 and wake up where the clouds are far behind me
C3.3 where trouble melts like lemon drops	C3.3 where trouble melts like lemon drops
C3.4 **high** above the chim[i]ney top	C3.4 a way above the chimney tops
C3.5 that's where you'll find me oo	C3.5 that's where you'll find me
D1.1 somewhere over the rainbow	D4.1 somewhere over the rainbow
D4.2 bluebirds fly	D4.2 bluebirds fly
B2.3 **and the dreams that you dare to**...	D4.3 birds fly over the rainbow
X5.3 **oh why oh why can't I - I oh**	D4.4 why then oh why can't I?
C3.1 someday **I** wish upon a star	C3.1 someday I'll wish upon a star
C3.2 wake up where the clouds are far behind me	C3.2 and wake up where the clouds are far behind me
C3.3 where trouble melts like lemon drops	C3.3 where trouble melts like lemon drops
C3.4 **high** above the chim[i]ney top	C3.4 a way above the chimney tops
C3.5 that's where you'll find me oo	C3.5 that's where you'll find me
A1.1 **somewhere over the rainbow**	X5.1 if happy little bluebirds fly
A1.2 **way up high**	X5.2 beyond the rainbow
B2.3 **and the dream that you dare to**	
X5.3 why oh why can't I - I	X5.3 why oh why can't I?
oo oo uh eh eh eh...	

of “Nā Ali‘i,”[14] composed by Samuel Kuahiwi ca. 1930 (King [1943] 1948, 86–87). In addition melodic leaps appear as an additional characteristic for post-Contact twentieth century genres (G. Kanahele 1979a, xxvii; Smith 1959, 52).

As evident in the comparative transcription (see fig. 9.2), Iz avoids the octave leap of the Arlen original[15] by substituting an iteration at the unison (measure 1). This iteration recalls similar iteration patterns typical of *mele oli* and present in Hawaiian song, for example, in “Nā Ali‘i” cited earlier. The next motif (m. 2) encompasses the range of a third. After the mid-phrase caesura the leap of a minor 6th duplicates the Arlen original (m. 3). Thus the opening phrase mm. 1–4 (“somewhere / over the rainbow / way up high”) presents a quasi-musical parallel to the history of melodic formation in Hawaiian music: it begins chant-like, opens up to intervals of a third typical of *hula ku‘i* (harmonically based song or chant), and cadences with large leaps found in mid-twentieth-century Hawaiian song.

Harmony

However it is in the harmonic organization that Iz makes his mark, namely in harmonic progression and in harmonic rhythm. These changes, together with the sound of ‘ukulele, underscore the Hawaiianness of the Iz version.

Harmonic Progression denotes the sequence of chords throughout a piece, which is expected to follow an established “grammar.” As a major change from the Arlen original, Iz uses a deceptive cadence at the end of each chorus, sounding the vi chord, a minor chord, instead of Arlen’s tonic I major chord. Avoiding a cadence on the tonic defeats any feeling of finality or rest, as seen in fig. 9.2.

Iz cadences either on G major, the subdominant IV chord, or b minor, the distinctive submediant vi chord already cited. In contrast, Arlen cadences consistently on the tonic chord, providing many points of rest for the melody. By avoiding a clear-cut ending (the final vocalise fades out),[16] Iz sonically creates a kind of *ha‘ina* or formulaic final strophe[17] typical of many *mele ku‘i*.

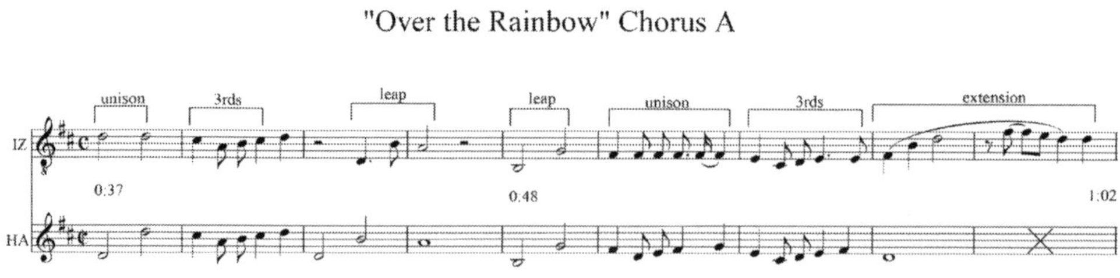

Figure 9.2 Comparison in transcription of melody in chorus A.

Harmonic rhythm denotes the pattern of durations formed by the number of beats between chord changes. If the chord changes are frequent, for example, every beat or every two beats, the harmonic rhythm is described as fast and creates a dense chordal sequence or string. However when there are few chord changes, for example, every four beats or every eight beats, the harmonic rhythm is described as slow and provides an economical chordal understructure that does not detract from the more frequent changes of information in the text and the melody.

Figure 9.1 presents a comparison of harmonic rhythm of the two versions for the first phrase of eight bars. Iz chord changes appear on the upper chord line labeled *IZ;* the Arlen version as comparison appears immediately below and labeled *ARLEN*. As this figure illustrates, Arlen changes chords every two beats. Therefore, the Arlen exhibits a fairly fast harmonic rhythm, which is further reinforced by comparing the low ratio of melodic and text changes to chord change. An examination of the complete score reveals that Arlen's harmonic rhythm is asymmetrical, using four values of duration—one beat, two beats, three beats, and four beats—as building blocks for his harmonic rhythm. As illustrated in the first four measures of the first Chorus, shown in figure 9.1, the durations for each chord exhibit uneven lengths:

// 2 beats + 2 beats + 3 beats + 1 beat / 4 beats + 2 beats + 2 beats //

In contrast the Iz version shows a slower and consistent regular harmonic rhythm. It changes chords every four beats, that is, on every measure as seen in figure 9.1, thereby establishing a pattern of chord changes regularized by a four-beat unit. Pointing up another correspondence with Hawaiian music, the four-beat unit is also the basis for rhythmic patterns in *hula pā ipu* and *hula pahu*.[18] For example, the well-known rhythmic pattern *kahela* (also known as *kāholo*) for the *ipu* (struck gourd idiophone) consists of a four-beat motif, each beat marked by the *ipu* sounded on its base (notated as a quarter note) as shown in figure 9.3. The chord changes in the Iz version, using a harmonic rhythm organized by four beat units, clearly references a preexisting Hawaiian organization of musical time. Vocal treatments that relate to established Hawaiian practices are not always so clear.

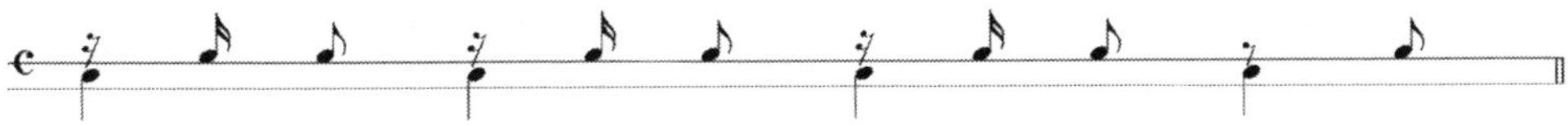

Figure 9.3 *Kahela pattern.*

Vocal Treatment

A number of distinct vocal treatments contribute to what listeners refer to as "a Hawaiian sound" or "Hawaiian style." These include falsetto, distinctive breaks in the voice, and the liberal use of portamento transitions ("sliding") between pitches (Smith 1959). However not all Hawaiian features are so evident: two vocal treatments—*'i'i* and *aheahe*—encountered in the Iz version emerge only after close analysis of the music; they have implications for political and cultural meaning making. Both reference techniques employed in *kahiko* (pre-Contact) chant: *'i'i* is the prolongation of a text syllable, and *aheahe* is a reduction in volume on a syllable, making it softer.

The *'i'i* technique in chant is one of a limited number of ways for the chanter to personalize a *mele*. The textual material for a composed *mele* is set and must be replicated exactly, reflecting respect for the integrity of the word. The traditional narrow ambitus for chant melody is also a stylistic given, which does not provide for any aesthetic climax through melody, for example, ending on an optional high note as a vocalist might do for monarchy style songs such as "Kamehameha Waltz" or "Paokalani." The *'i'i* lengthening a single syllable is one such means for personal expression open to the chanter. If the performance is for a favorite personage, for example, an important guest present at a gathering or for a performance that takes place in a special location, such as the site of a historic *heiau* (temple complex), the chanter may be moved or inspired by the specific occasion. In such a case, a chant that ordinarily can be completed in ninety seconds, for example, "Oli Aloha," might be extended through multiple extensions of *'i'i* on significant syllables and at the end of text lines to a duration double or triple the usual time length. By interpolating multiple *'i'i* extensions the chanter personalizes the delivery, often conveying a heightened sense of aloha for the relevant person or place. Not surprisingly the chanting style to express romantic love (*mele ho'oipo*) is one that encourages melodic extensions.

Iz employs such melodic extensions in his treatment of OTR. Although Iz follows the general structure of the thirty-two-bar form, he extends each of the chorus sections by four additional beats of vocables, usually on "o" or "oo," which clearly references the practice of *'i'i* in *mele oli* chanting. By so doing each chorus section becomes nine bars long rather than the standard eight, resulting in a "ballad form" that is thirty-five bars rather than thirty-two bars long: chorus A of nine bars; chorus B of nine bars, bridge of eight bars, and chorus C of nine bars. It is clear the extensions are preplanned and intentional; the introductory vocalise is also nine bars long, although there are no relevant text syllables upon which to base an extension.

Why might he have done this? Given his activist stance concerning Hawaiian cultural and political sovereignty, this alteration suggests a sonic gesture of resistance against the containment of the thirty-two-bar form, which functions as a template in the production of American popular music. The appearance of the thirty-two-bar ballad as a "tool" for commercial music production is historically contemporaneous with the onset of the assembly line in the first decades of the twentieth century using standardized forms and procedures for the production of appliances, cars, and other commodities. A similar commodification and standardization of music was enabled by technologies of recording and the advent of mass media. Popular music and the thirty-two-bar ballad supported, reified, and resonated with the zeitgeist of a Fordist America. Tin Pan Alley and the thirty-two-bar ballad were the musical counterparts to the assembly line and its tools.

If Iz's thirty-five-bar ballad can represent a gesture of resistance against the limitations of the thirty-two-bar ballad template, then the subtext of resistance receives reinforcement and another layer of meaning by his decision to use the reggae strum as ʻukulele accompaniment. The sounds, particularly the rhythms, of reggae signify a status of the subaltern and a mode of minority resistance originating in Jamaica and presently globalized through commodification and mass distribution (Middleton 2015). Notable in the selection of signifiers from reggae, Iz selects instrumental features and not vocal ones, which reinforces the primacy of the *leo* (voice) for a Hawaiian identity and a Hawaiian music.

The second instance of the voice and its Hawaiian treatment is so subtle and infrequent that it might escape general notice. At one point in the repetition of the closing chorus Iz employs the chant technique *aheahe* (softened timbre). It occurs on the word *and* at elapsed time marker 2:49 ("somewhere over the rainbow way up high *and* the dream that you dare to—why oh why can't I?") The usual execution of *aheahe* is to produce the sound with an inhaled breath rather than with an exhaled breath (P. Kanahele 1986), which Iz appears to do in this performance. To the casual listener Iz may appear to have not articulated the word *and* at all; however in terms of kinetic (rather than sounded) performance the entire text is complete—the integrity of the word is maintained. A general listener not aware of this technique might simply consider the inhalation of the word or its apparent absence as symptomatic of the well-known respiratory difficulties Iz had, which were exacerbated by morbid obesity and an ongoing problem with substance abuse. In many tracks the heavy breathing caught on the raw recordings was edited out in post-production. Regarding *aheahe*, it is possible that Iz himself was not aware of it as a named technique of the Hawaiian *leo*. Even if he did not, it is highly probable that *aheahe* was part of an internalized soundscape, given his position at the onset of the Hawaiian Renaissance and his association with its *kumu hula* and *mele Hawaiʻi* practitioners.

Entextualization

In the course of this chapter I have referenced some of the theoretical issues touched upon at the outset, pointing out how they apply or were apparent within the narrative of OTR. However, entextualization is particularly germane to the thrust of this study and merits further discussion here. Entextualization, specifically as an act of removal from an original context, is significant and multilevel in the case of the Iz version of OTR. One level is semantic text and another concerns the musicking[19] body.

The Semantic Text

The text as re-formed by Iz has literary and political significance. His rearrangement of Arlen's original text lines (indicated by the letter-number codes) is not random but deliberate. While the rearrangement changes the sense of the semantic text, as I point out below, Iz still retains the Arlen words as form, reflecting the Hawaiian value of respect for *'ōlelo*, the word as life and death. Other reworkings of preexisting compositions show less respect for the word as semantic carrier, for example, the reportage of a Finnish rap entextualization of the Spanish-Portugese reggae song "Danza Kuduro" shows a disregard for the intent, sense, and word meanings of the Latin original (Lepänen et al. 2013).

As semantic text, the Iz version gives greater agency to the singer, who takes the moment of empowerment to recenter and refocus the affect of Arlen's words. For example, he changes line B2.3 from Arlen's tentative "and the dreams that you **dare to dream**" to the more proactive "and the dreams that you **dream of**" (author's emphasis). Similarly, in line C3.1 he changes the conditional "I'll wish" to the declarative "I wish."[20]

In the Arlen original Dorothy's regret is she cannot fly like the bluebirds beyond the rainbow, presumably back to Kansas ("If happy little bluebirds fly beyond the rainbow, why oh why can't I?"). Iz subverts this ego-centered sentimentality by reordering lines B2.3 and X5.3. So reordered, his inability is not to fly beyond, that is, an act of escape. Implied by the dramatic ellipsis, his frustration appears to be for an inability to "dare to dream" in the context of community—it is the dream that others already possess ("And the dream that **you** dare to—why oh why can't I?"; author's emphasis). That vision could very well be sovereignty.

Iz was one of the first Hawaiian performers to advocate for Hawaiian cultural and political sovereignty and to project musically a late twentieth-century space for *ka lāhui*, the Hawaiian nation. The chronology of his song releases related to sovereignty traces a shift in his public political stance and in the conceptual use of power. The early 1978 classic "Hawai'i 78" is a poignant but nonconfrontational critique lamenting the loss of Hawaiian culture and the encroachment of materialistic modernity on the Islands; he invokes the authority of bygone monarchs and calls up images of a desecrated land. The single reference to empowerment in "Hawai'i 78" is coded and effectively hidden in the famous utterance by King Kamehameha III, *"Ua Mau ke Ea o ka Āina i ka Pono."*[21] Throughout the course of this song primarily in English the declaration that power resides with the Hawaiian people remains in *'ōlelo Hawai'i*—untranslated into English. In this format the sentiment of empowerment cannot be fully apprehended by a largely Anglophone listenership. The quotation itself is an object of entextualization and recontextualization: in 1959 it was adopted as the motto of the State of Hawai'i, and it is in this subcultural context that most local listeners perceive it. Its significance is largely as symbol of a modern political entity, the State of Hawai'i, rather than as a declaration of populist power proclaimed in the semantic message of the text.

The shift in political stance is clear by 1995 with the release of the track "E Ala Ē" on the album of the same name. This song evidences a change in rhetoric from reflection on what has been lost to an exhortation to proactive resistance. "E Ala Ē" is unequivocally confrontational, calling on Native Hawaiians to arise (*e ala ē*), projecting the image of Hawaiians as warriors ("we the warriors born to live on what the land and sea can give") and expressing his vision for a future ("give our children liberty"). Even the whimsical "Maui Hawaiian Sup'pa Man" (1994?) justifies force when necessary to achieve an important task (in the Iz version, the demigod Māui bringing fire to mortals) ("with no other choice he [Māui] had to get mean"). Given the position of OTR in the sequence of output, recorded in 1988 between Iz's awareness of loss expressed in 1978 and his call for action explicit in 1995, the subtext of "Over the Rainbow" as a dream and vision for the restoration of Hawaiian sovereignty carries a great degree of plausibility. With this reading, the apparent non sequitur of B2.3. followed by X5.3 ("...and the dreams that you dare to...why oh why can't I?") takes on another meaning that not only has its own logic but suggests a *kaona* (hidden meaning) of great poignancy.

The Musicking Hawaiian Body

For entextualization of music, I focus here only on acts of removal from the Iz persona. In many of the post-1990 appropriations of his OTR, only the 'ukulele reggae riffs and vocables of the introduction are heard, for example, the commercial for Toys"R"Us (1997) and the series of commercials for Rice Krispies (2011). In the excerpted vocalise Iz is heard only as another instrument producing an untexted melodic line. His identity as a human person much less *kanaka maoli* (Native Hawaiian) is nonexistent. Only with the onset of the text of OTR does language sonically humanize the singer—in these commercials the texted portion is excised. The vocalise standing alone constitutes a moment of erasure —the melody might well have been produced electronically, similar to the final sustained high E-flat of Sarah Brightman's remarkable performance in the duet "Phantom of the Opera" from Andrew Lloyd Webber's 1986 musical.

The track for the credits crawl of the film *Meet Joe Black* (1998) does include the sung text as does the nondiegetic track in the television series *ER* "On the Beach" (2002) portraying the final days of Dr. Mark Greene; both include the medley of "Over the Rainbow" paired with "What a Wonderful World" (Kamakawiwoʻole 1993, 14). However, in these tracks Iz remains literally disembodied. The listener has no indication that the singer is *kanaka maoli* or that his physical size embodies considerable *mana* (spiritual power)—both of which are meaningful to and celebrated in their original Island context.

To close this exploration of entextualization, I offer a few observations about historicizing intertextuality, an outcome of entextualization. For intertextuality within the domain of musical repertory, the listener must know the previous musical text, in this case the Arlen urtext. However most Local youth are not familiar with the 1939 film *Wizard of Oz* and Arlen's OTR. Perhaps the closest musical theater reference for them would be the 1974 musical *The Wiz* by Charles Smalls made known internationally through its version as a feature film in 1978. However, in this African American retelling of the story, OTR does not appear. Thus for local youth and probably for many of their worldwide counterparts, it is the Iz version that becomes urtext upon which to play out the film and television soundtracks previously cited, as well as the model upon which to base various cover versions recorded by international artists or to appropriate for vocal competitions such as *American Idol*.[22]

To conclude, Iz's OTR was a sensation initially within the community of Hawaiian music consumers—both on-Island and in the diaspora, and only later among globalized networks of mediatized and globalized popular culture (Kamakawiwoʻole 1990). While the two groups of consumers are not completely separate, each traces a different context for transmission and therefore presumably internalizes a different mode of reception. If this is so, then Iz's OTR *as sound* resonates with different social and cultural backgrounds—that is, there is something inherently coherent in its sonic nature that "grabs" a diversity of listeners. Employing music analysis, I have suggested features contributing to that coherence. Taking into account these features, I conclude that music as *sounded performance*—rather than cultural object—does inform diverse histories and their cultural meanings. As a memorable case in point the sounds of the *mele* "Over the Rainbow" delivered by Israel Kaʻanoʻī Kamakawiwo'ole unequivocally do locate "our pasts before us" as they continue to make aesthetic, cultural, and political waves for an ongoing reification of *kanaka maoli* Hawaiianness.

Notes

I thank Dr. Teri Skillman and Aaron Salā for their critical reading and commentary of this chapter, and Froilan Fabro for technical assistance. I am indebted to co-editors Fred Lau and Chris Yano for organizing this anthology on the occasion of my seventy-fifth birthday.

1. The first release is (Kamakawiwo'ole 1990, 7) by Discos Tropical. Most histories erroneously cite as first release *Facing Future* (Kamakawiwo'ole 1993, 14).

2. Track 7 is a medley of "Over the Rainbow" and "What a Wonderful World." Only the first title is discussed in this paper. "What a Wonderful World" was written by Robert Thiele and George Weiss and first recorded by Louis Armstrong (1967).

3. Biographical information on Kamakawiwo'ole can be found in de Mello (n.d.) and Kois (2010).

4. The first Hawaiian Renaissance took place during the reign of HRH David Kalākaua.

5. For one account of the social and historical context of music at the beginning of the Renaissance see Lewis (1991).

6. *Gidget Goes Hawaiian*, starring James Darren and Deborah Walley, was released in 1961. *The Brady Bunch* television series produced the episode "Hawaii Bound" in 1972.

7. A more familiar appellation is Bruddah Iz.

8. Throughout this paper the 1938 original is identified by its composer, Harold Arlen (1905–1986). Edgar Y. Harburg (1896–1981) was the lyricist.

9. Although "Over the Rainbow" was composed for film, *The Wizard of Oz* was essentially a musical theater piece on film, and Arlen was known as a composer for musical theater.

10. The discussion is based on the single cut of OTR from the CD *Alone in IZ World* (Kamakawiwo'ole 2001, 10). There is no full score transcription of this version in print, although there is an edited score for voice, 'ukulele/guitar of the medley "Over the Rainbow/ What a Wonderful World" (Kamakawiwo'ole 2005, 64–67).

11. Eight bars of 'ukulele solo precedes the vocables, often edited out in soundtracks.

12. For clarity and consistency in the comparative discussion the original text is identified by the composer Arlen, although it is the work of lyricist Edgar Y. Harburg.

13. The song was made famous as recorded by Louis Armstrong (1967).

14. In the published manuscript the title appears as "Na 'Lii" (King [1943] 1948, 86–87). For translations and background of Hawaiian songs cited in this chapter, consult the valuable online resource Huapala (www.huapala.org).

15. For purposes of comparison the original (Arlen and Harburg 1938) is transposed to the key of D major; the original key is C major.

16. In his closing vocalise (Kamakawiwo'ole 2001, 10) Iz does not end with a cadence at all: he fades out on the G chord (subdominant).

17. One in general use is "Ha'ina 'ia mai ana kapuana" (give the summary [of the song]).

18. Hula accompanied by the gourd (*ipu*) and the sharkskin drum (*pahu*), respectively.

19. "Musicking" is a useful term to reference collectively all aspects of music performance, as process coined by Christopher Small (1998).

20. The tense change may also be informed by Pidgin English rhetoric.

21. Its best known translation is "The life of the land is perpetuated in righteousness," although alternate translations replace "life" with "sovereignty."

22. See, for example, Jason Castro's cover of the Iz cover performed for the *American Idol* Top 8 broadcast in 2008.

References

Arlen, Harold, and Edgar Y. Harburg. [1938] 1985. "Over the Rainbow." In *The Harold Arlen Songbook*, by Harold Arlen, ed. David Bickman, 112–115. MMS. New York: MPL Communications.

Armstrong, Louis. 1967. *What a Wonderful World*. New York: ABC Records; London: His Master's Voice. LP single.

Bauman, Richard, and Charles L. Briggs. 1990. "Poetics and Performance as Critical Perspectives on Language and Social Life." *Annual Review of Anthropology* 19: 59–88.

Carr, James Revell. 2014. *Hawaiian Music in Motion: Mariners, Missionaries, and Minstrels*. Urbana: University of Illinois Press.

Castro, Jason. 2008. [Performance of] "Over the Rainbow." https://www.youtube.com/watch?v=aVhepGj21Bw.

de Mello, Jon. n.d. IZ biography, http://www.izhawaii.com/biography.

Gans, Herbert J. 1974. *Popular Culture and High Culture: An Analysis and Evaluation of Taste*. New York: Basic Books.

Goodyear-Kaʻōpua, Noelani, Ikaika Hussey, and Erin Kahunawaikaʻala Wright, eds. 2014. *A Nation Rising: Hawaiian Movements for Life, Land, and Sovereignty*. Durham, NC: Duke University Press.

Kamakawiwoʻole, Israel. 1990. *Ka ʻAnoʻi*. CD. Honolulu: Discos Tropical [Tropical Music Inc.].

———. *Facing Future*. 1993. CD. Honolulu: Big Boy Records.

———. *E Ala Ē*. 1995. CD. Honolulu: Big Boy Records.

———. *Alone in IZ World*. 2001. CD. Honolulu: Big Boy Records.

———. "Over the Rainbow/What a Wonderful World." 2005. In *IZ: The Songbook Collection*, transcr. Hemme Luttjeboer, 64–67. MMS. [Van Nuys, CA]: Alfred Music.

Kanahele, George S. 1971. "Hawaiian Music in Death Throes." *Honolulu Advertiser*, June 3: B20.

———, ed. 1979a. *Hawaiian Music and Musicians: An Illustrated History*. Honolulu: University Press of Hawaiʻi.

———. 1979b. "The Hawaiian Renaissance." http://kapalama.ksbe.edu/archives/pvsa/primary%202/79%20kanahele/kanahele%2010.htm.

Kanahele, Pualani Kanakaʻole. 1986. Pers. comm., Washington, DC.

King, Charles E. [1943] 1948. *King's Book of Hawaiian Melodies; Illustrated Souvenir Collection* (The Blue Book). MMS. Miami Beach: Hansen House.

Kois, Daniel. 2010. *Facing Future*. New York: Continuum.

Lepänen, Sirpa, Samu Kytölä, Henna Jousmäki, Saija Peuronen, and Elina Westinen. 2013. *Entextualization and Resemiotization as Resources for (Dis)identification in Social Media*. Tilburg Papers in Culture Studies 57. Tilburg, Netherlands: Tilburg University.

Lewis, George H. 1991. "Storm Blowing from Paradise: Social Protest and Oppositional Ideology in Popular Hawaiian Music." *Popular Music* 10, no. 1: 53–67.

Lynskey, Dorian. 2010. "Somewhere over the Rainbow... Lies a Crock of Gold." *The Guardian*, 5 December. http://www.theguardian.com/theguardian/2010/dec/05/somewhere-over-rainbow-israel-kamakawiwoole.

Middleton, Darren J. N. 2015. *Rastafari and the Arts: An Introduction*. New York: Routledge.

Mosely, Roger. 2013. "Entexualization and the Improved Past." *Music Theory Online* 19, no. 2. http://www.mtosmt.org/issues/mto.13.19.2/mto.13.19.2.moseley.html.

Ochoa Gautier, Ana María. 2012. "Social Transculturation, Epistemologies of Purification and the Aural Public Sphere in Latin America." In *The Sound Studies Reader*, ed. Jonathan Sterne, 388–404. New York: Routledge.

Robertson, Roland. 1995. "Glocalization: Time-Space and Homogeneity-Heterogeneity." In *Global Modernities*, ed. Mike Featherstone, Scott Lash, and Roland Robertson, 25–44. London: Sage.

Skillman, Teri L. 2012. "The Merrie Monarch Festival in Hilo, Hawai'i: Sovereign Spaces Reclaimed and Created through Hula Competition, 1963–2010." Diss., University of Hawai'i at Mānoa.

Slobin, Mark. 1993. *Subcultural Sounds: Micromusics of the West*. Hanover, NH: Wesleyan University Press.

Small, Christopher G. 1998. *Musicking: The Meanings of Performing and Listening*. Middletown, CT: Wesleyan University Press.

Smith, Barbara B. 1959. "Folk Music in Hawaii." *Journal of the International Folk Music Council* 11: 50–55.

Sutton, R. Anderson. 2011. "'Fusion' and Questions of Korean Cultural Identity in Music." *Korean Studies* 36: 4–24.

Tatar, Elizabeth. 1982. *Nineteenth Century Hawaiian Chant*. Pacific Anthropological Records 33. Honolulu: Bernice Pauahi Bishop Museum.

Urban, Greg. 1996. "Entextualization, Replication, and Power." In *Natural Histories of Discourse*, ed. Michael Silverstein and Greg Urban, 21–44. Chicago: University of Chicago Press.

Weiss, George D., and Bob Thiele (aka George Douglas). 1967. *What a Wonderful World*. MMS. Weehawken, NJ: Abilene Music.

CONTRIBUTORS

David Harnish, PhD (UCLA), is a professor and chair of the Music Department at University of San Diego. He has published fifty articles, the book *Bridges to the Ancestors: Music, Myth, and Cultural Politics at an Indonesian Festival,* and two acclaimed volumes of essays. He is a double Fulbright and National Foundation Scholar, co-directs Balinese Gamelan Gunung Mas at University of San Diego, and serves as an academic liaison to the Kyoto Prize Symposium.

Frederick Lau is the chair and professor of ethnomusicology and director of the Center for Chinese Studies at the University of Hawaiʻi at Mānoa. He is the author of *Music in China* (Oxford, 2008) and co-editor of *Vocal Music and Cultural Identity in Contemporary Music: Unlimited Voices in East Asia and the West* (Routledge, 2012), *Locating East Asia in Western Art Music* (Wesleyan, 2004). Lau is the president of the Society for Asian Music and editor of a book series titled Music and Performing Arts of Asia and the Pacific, University of Hawaiʻi Press.

Henry Spiller is an ethnomusicologist whose research focuses on Sundanese music and dance from West Java, Indonesia. He is the author of several award-winning books and many articles on Javanese performing arts. His most recent book, *Javaphilipa: American Love Affairs with Javanese Music and Dance* (2015, University of Hawaiʻi Press), won the 2016 Bruno Nettl Prize award from the Society for Ethnomusicology. Spiller earned his PhD in music from the University of California, Berkeley, and currently is a professor of music at the University of California, Davis.

R. Anderson Sutton taught ethnomusicology at the University of Wisconsin–Madison from 1982 to 2013, also serving three terms as director of UW–Madison's

Center for Southeast Asian Studies. He currently serves as dean of the School of Pacific and Asian Studies and assistant vice chancellor for international and exchange programs at the University of Hawai'i at Mānoa. His four books, two edited volumes, and more than fifty journal articles and book chapters have addressed musical aesthetics, improvisation, cultural politics, media, and hybridity in Indonesia and South Korea.

Kati Szego joined the School of Music at Memorial University of Newfoundland in 1995, establishing its program in ethnomusicology. Ongoing projects on Hawaiian choral music, falsetto, and yodeling address her broader interests in intercultural processes and embodied voices. Kati is in the process of reconstructing an opera libretto written by Queen Lili'uokalani and is examining the roles of women in 'ukulele revivals now sweeping North America and Europe. She is editor of the *Yearbook for Traditional Music.*

Ricardo D. Trimillos is a professor emeritus in Asian studies and ethnomusicology at the University of Hawai'i at Mānoa. He researches on the expressive arts of Hawai'i, the Muslim Philippines, the Lowland Philippines, and Japan. His ethnomusicological foci include ethnic identity, public policy, gender, and pedagogy. He is published in three languages and has been a consultant to various governments. He performs and has taught Japanese *koto* and *gagaku* and Filipino *rondalla* and *kulintangan.*

Andrew N. Weintraub is a professor of music at the University of Pittsburgh, where he teaches graduate and undergraduate courses in ethnomusicology and popular music and directs the University Gamelan program. He is the author of *Power Plays* (2004) and *Dangdut Stories* (2010), editor of *Islam and Popular Culture in Indonesia and Malaysia* (2011), and co-editor of *Music and Cultural Rights* (2008) and *Vamping the Stage* (2017).

Deborah Wong is a professor of Music at the University of California, Riverside. She specializes in the musics of Asian America and Thailand and has written two books. She is a past president of the Society for Ethnomusicology, the chair of the advisory council for the Smithsonian Institution's Center for Folklife and Cultural Heritage, and a series editor for the Music/Culture series published by Wesleyan University Press.

Christine R. Yano is a professor of anthropology at the University of Hawai'i and has conducted research on Japan and Japanese Americans with a focus on popular culture. Her publications include *Tears of Longing: Nostalgia and the*

Nation in Japanese Popular Song (Harvard University Press, 2002), *Crowning the Nice Girl: Gender, Ethnicity, and Culture in Hawai'i's Cherry Blossom Festival* (University of Hawai'i Press, 2006), *Airborne Dreams: "Nisei" Stewardesses and Pan American World Airways* (Duke University Press, 2011), and *Pink Globalization: Hello Kitty and Its Trek across the Pacific* (Duke University Press, 2013).

INDEX

Page numbers in **boldface** type refer to illustrations and tables.